Pedagogies of Quiet

Pedagogies of Quiet

Silence and Social Justice in the Classroom

Monica Edwards

ROWMAN & LITTLEFIELD
Lanham • Boulder • New York • London

Published by Rowman & Littlefield
An imprint of The Rowman & Littlefield Publishing Group, Inc.
4501 Forbes Boulevard, Suite 200, Lanham, Maryland 20706
www.rowman.com

86-90 Paul Street, London EC2A 4NE, United Kingdom

Copyright © 2024 by Monica Edwards

All rights reserved. No part of this book may be reproduced in any form or by any electronic or mechanical means, including information storage and retrieval systems, without written permission from the publisher, except by a reviewer who may quote passages in a review.

British Library Cataloguing in Publication Information Available

Library of Congress Cataloging-in-Publication Data

Names: Edwards, Monica, 1976– author.
Title: Pedagogies of quiet : silence and social justice in the classroom / Monica Edwards.
Description: Lanham, Maryland : Rowman & Littlefield, 2024. | Includes bibliographical references. | Summary: "Pedagogies of Quiet: Silence and Social Justice in the Classroom explores the historical context of silence and silencing in the college classroom and presents, with empirical support, a path toward valuing a quiet ethos into our pedagogical praxis"—Provided by publisher.
Identifiers: LCCN 2023055571 (print) | LCCN 2023055572 (ebook) | ISBN 9781475867800 (cloth) | ISBN 9781475867817 (paperback) | ISBN 9781475867824 (epub)
Subjects: LCSH: College teaching—Social aspects. | Social justice and education. | Classroom environment.
Classification: LCC LB2331 .E384 2024 (print) | LCC LB2331 (ebook) | DDC 378.1/25—dc23/eng/20231212
LC record available at https://lccn.loc.gov/2023055571
LC ebook record available at https://lccn.loc.gov/2023055572

Contents

Acknowledgments	vii
Introduction: Stumbling into Silence	1
Chapter 1: Silence as a Problem	19
Chapter 2: It's Not All Talk: Listening to (Quiet) Students	51
Chapter 3: Silence as a Solution: Social Justice Education and Pedagogies of Quiet	83
Chapter 4: (Quiet) Participation Leaves the Classroom	119
Chapter 5: Quiet Technology in the Classroom	151
Conclusion: Quiet Spaces	181
Appendix A: Overview of Survey Data	201
Appendix B: Participation Journal Template	205
Bibliography	209
About the Author	221

Acknowledgments

One page in a book doesn't match the gratitude I feel for the people in my life who supported me throughout this project. That said, I will try on this page and with these words.

There was one key moment of synergy that happened in the early stages of me grappling with how to respond to such quiet students. My wife and I were sitting side by side reading, as we often do, and she said, "I think you should read this book." It was Susan Cain's book *Quiet: The Power of Introverts in a World That Can't Stop Talking*, and it proved a pivotal catalyst for my teaching and ultimately for the ideas that are developed in this book. That moment is, of course, just one moment among many where Tori listened to me, brainstormed with me, and encouraged me. I couldn't ask for a better partner. Thank you for sharing this book with me and your life with me.

Along the way my parents—Larry and Coreen Edwards—brought me books about writing, reminded me to remove all the unnecessary "thats" in the text, and answered the phone every time I called. Having proud parents cheer me on helped to make the writing process more joyful.

My dearest friend Meghan Burke—herself a sociologist, qualitative researcher, and author of three books—served as my first reader, helping me to craft that first draft into a more meaningful piece of scholarship. Where there are good transitions in these pages, Meghan nudged me there. She is a loyal and compassionate friend who continually reminded me that my ideas were important and worthy of being out there in the world at large.

Importantly, I'd like to thank Dr. Travaris Harris for always bringing me into conversation with colleagues outside of my division and generally cheerleading my work in the classroom across campus. Much appreciation to my colleagues who not only incorporated quiet practices into their classrooms but shared the survey instrument with their students.

And finally, I'd like to thank all my students for engaging in the teaching and learning process alongside me. In particular, I am forever indebted to the students who participated in this study. Your candor, vulnerability, and openness make my pedagogy better and teaching every day worth it.

Introduction
Stumbling into Silence

The first piece of advice I received as a freshly minted instructor was: "Learn how to pause; learn how to let the silence be, rather than filling it up yourself." It went in one ear and out the other. I forgot about it entirely until I began researching for this project and, ultimately, this book. Now I see it for what it is: the truest advice I've ever received and the hardest to implement. And I know I am not alone: Mary Rose O'Reilly wrote, "after twenty-five years of teaching, it takes all the courage I have to keep silence for a minute and a half after reading a poem aloud, or asking a question that heads us all for the depths of experience."[1] Now I am coming to you, my fellow teachers of all students—including those often left out of the conversation, in particular, community college students—and articulating a teaching philosophy titled "pedagogies of quiet," urging us all not to fear but to cultivate (more) quiet and silence in our classrooms.

In the ensuing years between receiving that sage advice in 2004 and 2017, I had plenty of difficult students, quiet students, and overtalkative students. I've had that overall feeling in the classroom that everyone wants a nap. I've had moments of triumph and moments of struggle. I've had doubts but just as many moments filled with my overflowing ego. Upon the stage—literally, in the context of a large lecture hall—I've lived in and enjoyed the state of flow.[2] But in the fall of 2017, I had *the* class. The one that changed me. They were so very and painfully quiet, and it tripped me up completely. And to throw salt in the wound, I noticed a racialized pattern in their final grades that was hard to face, adding to the sirens that were blaring at me to change something about my teaching praxis. Those failed and foiled attempts have since shaped the pedagogy that my own and others' research suggests has the power to alter both students' lives and our own: they said nothing, and they changed me profoundly, and I have learned (and am still learning) how to pause and to relish in the quiet and cultivate productive silences.

Most of the students surveyed for this project say they often don't feel comfortable talking in class. As my data highlights, there are many reasons for this, ranging from fear of judgment to a lack of clarity around the content to the timidity of some English language learners (see chapter 2 for a detailed exploration of this data). But their uncertainty around speaking wasn't outright unwillingness. When asked in a survey question regarding whether they are willing to speak in class, they were given answer options for "yes," "no," or "sometimes/depends." Most of the students responded with the latter two options.

This data led me to an exploration of practices—such as reflective journaling, moments of silence, and classroom technologies—that cultivate quiet and silence, in part to be able to engage those "no" students, whom Susan Cain argues struggle to find value in society—and classrooms—that prefer extroversion.[3] But the bigger lesson, of course, is that these practices benefit everyone. And while it's true that we can use silence as a praxis that primarily functions to enhance dialogue, I will caution against using quiet pedagogical strategies in such a way that continues to prop up dialogue as the ideal. Instead, I hope we will all come to see the value of silence and quiet on their own as a necessary space for students to reflect and learn about themselves and their learning needs. The goal is to find a way, while allowing silence, to engage students deeply with the content that we are teaching and, thus, with themselves and the world.

KIDS THESE DAYS: PROFESSORIAL HEGEMONY

I have a very clear memory from my early days as a tenure-track professor: one day, I stood outside a colleague's office door, talking with members of my division. I felt excited to be included in such a discussion; after years of graduate school and part-time teaching, I felt that inclusion in such a "water cooler" circle meant I'd "made it." There were five of us, three men and two women, all white people with PhDs. The conversation centered on faculty perceptions of students' failures: their boredom, poor writing skills, and lack of curiosity. One colleague spoke with a particularly pejorative tone, and his voice sticks in my memory most. Bryan Dewsbury writes that in the process of reimagining his pedagogy, he needed to "reflect on the role that [his] own historical biases and privilege potentially played on the expectations that [he] had for [his] students,[4]" and it is clear to me now that in the moment of my water cooler conversation, none of us were engaged in such reflection. Yet now I can see that it was clearly needed.

Nicholas and Baroud write about this, arguing that the "dominant narrative of 'students these days' circulates unofficially in conversations on and off-campus. This narrative laments students' lack of interest, their inability to work and to meet faculty expectations, and their sense of entitlement and privilege."[5] Dewsbury reports a similar experience: "Faculty discussions of student performance focused heavily on student deficits and the many ways in which students seemed incapable of meeting the instructor's definition of quality work."[6] He goes on to highlight how the faculty engaged in these conversations do not explore any social considerations for these dynamics; rather, they are grounded in an individualized and meritocratic understanding of student motivation and learning. Such narratives never seem to hold faculty accountable to or for their praxis.

These "kids these days" tropes are here referred to as faculty "moves to innocence."[7] In the context of settler colonialism, Tuck and Yang explore "settler moves to innocence" as "evasions . . . that problematically attempt to reconcile settler guilt and complicity, and rescue settler futurity."[8] In the context of teaching, I will theorize that faculty engage in such strategic maneuvers—*faculty moves to innocence*—to avoid self-reflection and pedagogical change by blaming students for any issues that emerge in the classroom experience. Like the settlers Tuck and Yang speak of, these maneuvers allow faculty to ignore their complicity in classroom problems (for example, lack of student engagement) and maintain their "rightful" position of control in the classroom space.

The power dynamics between faculty and students are often cited as impediments to an "emancipatory education."[9] And yet even those of us whose very object of study is power and inequality fail to recognize our positionality and complicity in our roles as professors. As Michael Armato writes, spaces such as conferences and classrooms allow "academics [space] to offer criticism of the world while failing to acknowledge our location and complicity in the reproduction of that world. This produces an academic fallacy: because we intellectually know, research, or teach critically about something, we are thereby not complicit in reproducing that which we criticize."[10] One reason for this failure to see on our part is because scholarly work on pedagogy and complicity tends to focus on *what* we teach students and how we interact with students when *they* engage in complicity practices or frames pedagogy through the lens of the teacher. All the while, we continue with our own complicit pedagogies that reproduce inequalities, even as some of us teach content that aims to dismantle them. As a result, I will be arguing in this book that we need to turn the lens on ourselves, on our own practices, and on the ways in which our classroom pedagogy—including our behaviors, such as how we use our bodies, our tone of voice, our assessment practices, and our attendance and participation policies—is complicit in maintaining the very inequalities that many of us profess to challenge.

And yet as bell hooks argues, teachers need to be at the center of change, not outside of it. In *Teaching to Transgress*, hooks writes, "if the effort to respect and honor the social reality and experiences of groups in this society who are nonwhite is to be reflected in a pedagogical process, then as teachers . . . we must acknowledge that our styles of teaching may need to change."[11] As part of this justice-oriented change, arguments abound for decentering the "expert-in-the-front-of-the-room" pedagogical approach. Theoretical work on social justice pedagogy—including such frameworks as critical pedagogy, feminist pedagogy, and contemplative pedagogy, among others—argues that we need to think more complexly about the student experience and more creatively about students' relationship to the learning process. As hooks put it: "I share with the class my conviction that my experience is limited, and if someone else brings a combination of facts and experience, then I humble myself and respectfully learn from those who bring this great gift."[12] As a result of this humbling, as AnaLouise Keating argues, "intellectual humility"[13] then is a central component of social justice education and a key route away from complicit pedagogies. Silencing is certainly a strategy of oppressive systems, but silence, when shared and held with care, can also be emancipatory.

In order to pursue pedagogical emancipation, we must recognize that our institutions are as diverse as our students when it comes to the contexts in which we teach: some of us are in the social sciences, and some of us in the STEM fields; some of us are teaching at (elite) liberal arts colleges, while many more of us are teaching at large (sub)urban community colleges. Thus, we also need to think more complexly and creatively about how the institutional context of our teaching shapes the kinds of pedagogies that are most useful for our students. As Nicholas and Baroud write, "our concern is that this seemingly neutral descriptor of students in the twenty-first century may flatten differences in historical access to education and its legacies as well as erase ongoing issues related to class, race, and gender."[14] Indeed, much of the critical pedagogical literature seems to center on the experiences of students in elite educational contexts. But we must ask: Do the social justice strategies that work in that institutional context fit the needs of the students in less privileged institutions, such as community colleges? Or can we broaden our understanding of social justice pedagogy and its outcomes to serve students across these diverse institutional contexts? This book aims to explore these dynamics and attempts to answer these questions. This book participates in this conversation in two primary ways:

1. Rethinking classroom participation: shifting away from only or overvaluing dialogue and talk and moving toward a shared value of silence as a strategy for pedagogies of quiet. The qualitative data collected for this project highlight that this is a social justice pedagogy, given the patterns that emerge in students' articulations of why they are often uncomfortable talking in class. As will be made clear throughout the chapters of this book, however, this cultivated classroom silence

enhances student participation in complex ways, allowing everyone (students and teachers) increased access to more student voices and deepening engagement.
2. Broadening our understanding of the outcomes of social justice pedagogies to include not just the liberatory ideals often espoused in the pedagogical literature but also the more mundane but necessary skills such as time management, meta-cognition, and student-teacher communication. These outcomes, as is made clear in the data that grounds this book, emerge from the quiet pedagogies articulated in the first point.

Silence Leading to Quiet

Throughout this book, I will be using both silence and quiet in reference to my pedagogical strategy. However, I rely on the term "pedagogies of quiet" to refer to the overarching approach. As a result, it's important to delineate what I mean when I say "silence" and "quiet." While both have similar dictionary definitions—silence refers to the "absence of sound" and quiet is "free from noise" or "tending to speak very little"—I will establish relational, pedagogical definitions that are grounded in dynamics of power.[15]

I will start here with my articulation of quiet and what I mean by "pedagogies of quiet" (more detailed explanations will be woven throughout the book). As conceptualized for this project, quiet refers to the agentic experience of the individual in the classroom. In this regard, quiet is an active experience of the individual, understood as a form of engaged participation. In the United States, classrooms are shaped by the "extrovert ideal,"[16] and as such, classroom participation is equated with verbalization. As Ros Ollin writes, "the value and underlying purposes of the dominance of talk within Western formal learning settings represents a particular cultural construct, which gives primacy to the role of vocal communication in the teaching and learning process and exists relatively unchallenged."[17] In the face of this social construct, this book argues that quiet is an equally engaged form of participation rendered invisible by the overvaluation of dialogue and extroversion.[18]

Susan Cain wrote that "some of our greatest ideas, art, and inventions—from the theory of evolution to van Gogh's sunflowers to the personal computer—came from quiet and cerebral people who knew how to tune in to their inner worlds and the treasures to be found there."[19] It is in this articulation of quiet that pedagogies of quiet take their meaning: quiet refers to the active inner world of our students, a world that is always there and full of "treasures," whether we as teachers are tuned in to it or not. This challenges the common notion of the talkative student as active and the quiet student as passive or disengaged. With pedagogies of quiet, the goal is to cultivate the space for the quiet inner world of *all* students to become a valued component of the learning process.

Silence is a central strategy for cultivating the space(s) necessary for pedagogies of quiet. We use silence(s) to create the space for students to discover and explore the ideas and daydreams evoked through the course content. We use silence—the collective absence of sound in the classroom, particularly the absence of talking—to allow students to find their inner quiet. In this way, "quiet is not a performance or a withholding; instead, it is an expressiveness that is not necessarily legible, at least not in a world that privileges public expressiveness."[20] As Kevin Quashie notes, often silence and quiet are seen as "withholding." This is often seen in teachers' understanding of students who are not talking; we tend to think that one of our primary roles is getting students to talk. But as Quashie writes—and as this book proposes—there's an "expressiveness" to be found in quiet, in students' inner lives, and creating space for silence is a methodological approach for engaging with this quiet world.

Silence Disrupting Power

Many of us have an idealized picture of the classroom as a higher learning space involving deep dialogue. As stated, many scholars of social justice pedagogy write about disrupting hierarchical power dynamics that center the professor and instead argue for the students to take a more central role as knowledge producers. For example, DeSantis and Serafina "propose a structure . . . that invites students to value the learning that occurs through and from one another, rather than solely from us as instructors."[21] For them, this is a central feature of a feminist pedagogy centered on social justice, and this engaged classroom discussion has loomed large in my own imagination as well.

In graduate school and my early years as a tenure track professor, I was socialized in such a way that led me to believe my classes should be hard and that my students should be talkative. I had internalized this belief and stood in the front of many classrooms on the first day, semester after semester, and felt tension around this need to make sure the class came off as hard while also creating an inviting space for my students to be talkative and to become leaders. I've since come to question these expectations and to see them through a gendered lens as contradictory: as attempts to create a hard, leadership-oriented male-dominant environment while also trying to construct a socially just, nurturing environment. As I interrogate this inheritance of mine, I wonder: What exactly does it mean for a class to be "hard," and whom does that serve? Why must the "best" students always be so talkative? Why do we value speaking as a leadership quality at the expense of other qualities? To answer these questions and the others that have emerged, I've had to practice reflexivity to explore my role in perpetuating what I had hoped to dismantle through my course objectives and curriculums.

For over a decade, my primary goal in the classroom, beyond teaching my discipline, was to get my students to talk. I was so focused on them—on what they were doing (or weren't doing)—I failed to apply what I knew about patriarchal white supremacy to my own classroom. In the midst of teaching sociology to a remarkably quiet class, I was blind to the "chilly climate" as a factor in my own classroom space. While "feminist analyses of the 'chilly climate' have documented the ways in which women have been and continue to be marginalized within institutions of higher education,"[22] it seems clear that all historically marginalized groups have experienced times of being silenced in the classroom.

One explanation for this "chilly climate": students whose talking effectively silences other students. For example, Lee and McCabe argue that "another possible explanation [for the chilly climate] is the persistence [of dominance] in classroom 'sonic space,' which refers to the sound or vocal space people occupy."[23] One aspect of our careers as teachers managing class discussions has long been managing those students who dominate the conversation. We encourage speaking, and yet, especially in larger classes, we hear—often too much—from only a select few. Thus, Lee and McCabe are exploring what most of us have experienced in our classrooms: how men dominate classroom participation through their voices, through the very means of participation that is most valued.

Through an intersectional lens, we'd see how these dominant participants are often white, straight, cisgendered, and hearing (the list goes on). Male privilege shapes the chilly classroom, and so too does white privilege. Kohli quotes a student who expresses this:

> I always felt that if I raised my hand to voice my opinion about something, or even responded to a question about the material I would say something wrong, and the White students would say "Oh, it's the Mexican girl." Although I was aware that I was in an honors course because I was academically advanced, I still assumed that just because I was Mexican and lived on the poor side of town I was not as smart as them. . . . There was always a feeling of inferiority when I was around White students during my schooling experience.[24]

In this way, it is gendered racism that produces the chilly climate for this student. This aspect of the chilly climate provides us another entrance point to question our hypervaluation of participation-as-talk and creates an opening to argue for collective silence as a way to engage more students through pedagogies of quiet, particularly our historically marginalized students.

Neoliberal Institutions

We are occupying a historical moment that is looking deeply into itself, attempting to come to a greater understanding of how oppression shapes daily life, including in teaching and learning practices. We have lived through a decade of conversations about "fake news" and debating what is in fact "truth," we have witnessed and protested police violence against Black bodies and everyday violence against Asian American women, to the "Big Lie" of the 2020 election, and the political punditry about critical race theory and its role in our classrooms. We have lived (are living) through a global pandemic and the ensuing shutdowns, isolation, fears, and grief. As educators emerging from this pandemic, we are now engaged with the inevitable reckoning—including in the chapters of this book—over (the merits of) online learning and inequities in the educational system.

The twenty-first century has also seen extensive research on higher education and the impact of the neoliberal context on academia. The neoliberal university has, among other things, been exclusive,[25] has focused on employment more so than democracy, has relied upon the "banking model,"[26] and has reshaped time in the classroom.[27] Shahjahan, referencing Judith Walker, calls this "academic capitalism" and explores how capitalist notions of productivity and efficiency have become embedded in higher education institutions, shaping pedagogies, assessment practices, and outcomes.[28] As scholars have worked to explore and make these realities visible, we must do the same deep dive into the ways in which our own teaching practices reify these institutional norms.

In addition to furthering our understanding of the neoliberal shift, scholars have also tended to the ways in which institutions of higher education in general, and classrooms in particular, have functioned to reinscribe inequities around race, class, gender, sexuality, and ability. Garcia Lopez wrote that "curriculum and pedagogy have been employed as an instrument to colonize individuals into Eurocentric American hierarchical practices that include culture, values, and understanding."[29] While I know this to be true on an intellectual level, I am still engaged in an ongoing process of realizing the truth of this colonization in my own practices. I was seventeen years into my career as a sociologist and seven years into my full-time teaching career before I truly saw the ways in which patriarchal white supremacy and Western Enlightenment worldviews were embedded into my praxis. The backdrop of this book is this historical moment, the neoliberal university, and Western patriarchal white supremacy. This book, part sociology and pedagogic philosophy, also explores students in introductory courses at a midwestern community college through empirical data collected across multiple semesters and fieldnotes from my pedagogical transformations as an educator.

The Professorial Ego

One semester, in particular, sparked all the ideas that have become this book. I was teaching a painfully quiet class, and they frustrated me regularly. Mostly, I blamed them. After days, weeks, and now years of intellectual and emotional interrogation, however, I understand my experience through the lens of patriarchal white supremacy and the ego that emerges from that context. Subtly, but certainly, I learned in graduate school and during my early years as a tenure track professor to develop a healthy sense of my own professorial ego. After all, I am an expert in my field! And yet, during this quiet and difficult class, this ego was a central part of the problem.

Since that classroom experience in 2017, I often wonder how I came to expect students to be able to engage in active and participatory discussions about content that I had just introduced to them. It took me many years to learn the material I just presented; years' worth of knowledge condensed into a thirty-minute lecture. And then, I ask my students a question or two following the lecture, and I expect them to push their hands up into the air and discuss ideas with each other with sincere animation. When I get silence instead of this animated discussion, I think they aren't listening or prepared, they are bored, they don't understand the importance of learning, and/or they aren't motivated. I would think of various iterations of "kids these days, and their social media, blah blah." Now, however, I think: How can they engage in such a discussion when they have just heard these ideas for the first time? If it took me years of graduate school and teaching to solidify my understanding, why do I expect them to "get it" right away and in a way that leads to deep dialogue? What if I gave them some silent time to process before asking them to engage in verbal participation instead?

As I interrogated this experience, I also wondered whether expecting immediate verbal participation was a student-centered or a professorial ego-centered practice. I've come to the conclusion that it's more the latter: we get to feel validated when our lectures are "returned" to us through our students' verbal participation. Yes, we ask questions so that we can assess whether they've comprehended the material, but this moment also operates very strongly as a reward system for the professorial ego, and there are plenty of other ways to assess learning. It functions as a mirror of our work as much as their understanding; I cannot deny my impulse to be liked or to be seen as an inspiration.

I will argue throughout this book that there are other, often more meaningful, ways of assessing our students' learning without putting them on the spot for immediate verbal engagement. As Kaufman and Schipper write, "teaching with compassion means finding a way to teach from a place of humility and at times, vulnerability. It means considering the 'big picture' needs of students and prioritizing their growth, development, and well-being over our own needs for validation and approval."[30] In order to do this, however, we must first acknowledge that we have these needs for validation and approval. While we might be aware of these needs while reading student evaluations when we become hyperfocused on the one bad evaluation while ignoring all the good ones, we need to expand this awareness into our everyday teaching activities and into our pedagogy. This is the first step toward professorial vulnerability, what AnaLouise Keating refers to as "intellectual humility,"[31] and away from professorial ego.

This book is an exploration of teaching practices that I refer to as quiet pedagogies, grounded in data that emerged from surveys of over seven hundred community college students. In addition, I incorporate some student assessment examples and field notes from my pedagogical (un)learning and my (re)emergence with a new praxis grounded in social justice and geared toward all teaching contexts. Throughout, I will maintain a particular focus on introductory courses (at all institutions) and the open-access community college level. This book also attempts to connect conversations about pedagogy, assessment, and content rather than address them in isolation, as if they are separate phenomena. Thus, you will find these pages to commingle sociological context, empirical data, pedagogical theories, and teaching anecdotes from the field.

Support for silence and quiet in the classroom is well grounded across multiple theoretical contexts. Those who argue for slow scholarship contend that we should rethink our relationship to time in the classroom while arguing that the "conventional values of 'rigor' deserve some scrutiny."[32] Pedagogies grounded in feminist praxis concur, and advocate for a culture of care,[33] for a restorative approach to teaching that acknowledges "that non-verbal communication modes may be used in the classroom as well."[34] Silence can be seen as a sign of oppression—social science data on the chilly climate make this clear—but it can also be a strategy for engagement.

Critical pedagogical theorists Greene and Macarine wrote that "teachers may well be among the few in a position to kindle the light that might illuminate the spaces of discourse and events in which young newcomers have someday to find their ways."[35] The stated approach in Greene and Macarine's essay is to use classroom dialogue to engage with and challenge hegemonic ideologies and to transform socially constructed power dynamics. And yet the pedagogical practices these authors put forth center (1) the teacher, (2) talking, and (3) the mind. Throughout the pages of this book, I will argue that when we center the teacher, talking, and the mind, these practices reinforce patriarchal white supremacy. As Llewellyn and Llewellyn write, critical pedagogy inflates the "knowledge-bearing, rational, autonomous subject" and "ignores the contextual relations that position women and marginalized 'others' within an abstract, illegitimate place from which to speak."[36]

Peter McClaren, a prominent author of critical pedagogy, wonders: How do we teach to "become more fully human?"[37] Kevin Quashie sees the vibrancy of the quiet, inner world—his work focuses on the richness of Black lives, all while quiet is often denied to Black people in the context of a hegemonic cultural framework—as the most human of spaces.[38] The pedagogical question, in my mind, is most effectively explored in feminist, antiracist, and contemplative pedagogical literature.

bell hooks wrote in *Teaching to Transgress* that we need to interrogate the ways the mind/body split has become embedded into our classrooms. The mind/body split—the Western ideology that functions to maintain human, male, and white superiority—has been institutionalized into the education system, leading to the belief that educational spaces are about encouraging the flourishing of the mind at the expense of our bodies and emotions. And yet, as Laura Rendón points out, "neuroscientific research findings [show] that reason and emotion are not separate and irreconcilable."[39] Feminist and contemplative scholars (among others) have been arguing that we must center the body and emotions in the classroom. I will build on this argument through my promotion of silence as a necessary classroom teaching tool.

My hope here is to bridge all these conversations and create new commonalities, all while focusing on two educational contexts that in my read are often left out: introductory-level courses and the open-access community college. Much pedagogical scholarship is written by faculty teaching undergraduate majors and graduate students, and in fact, a lot of the (anecdotal) evidence comes from the relationships that faculty develop through mentoring these students. This leaves me wondering: Do these teaching practices apply to those without majors, graduate students, and mentees? Thus, my explicit goal in this book is to bring the introductory level classroom and the community college context more clearly into the pedagogical narrative.

Silent Participation: Outline of the Book

Overarching Framework

Throughout this book, it will be argued that we need to shift our hegemonic understanding of silence in the classroom. While we often see it as something to fear or avoid, we could instead see it as an invitation to delve into the expansive inner worlds of our students. Carl Phillips writes that "silence—as in the absence of sound—is an invention of those who can hear." Referencing Ilya Kaminsky, he goes on to say, "what I mean more and more by silence is the relative absence of distraction, or of the usual distractions."[40] Granting students classroom silence is a route toward connection and clarity and away from distractions, including the distractions that come from the few classmates that tend to dominate conversations.

But silence has a habit of making us uncomfortable. Most teachers grapple with the same or similar dynamics with their students: How do we get them interested, keep them engaged, and help them succeed? We share the experience of teaching specific generations of students (Millennials and Gen Z, for example) and can talk about the larger social context our students have been raised in. We can speak to the impact of digital devices on our students' experiences—as well as our own—in the classroom. No matter the geographic or institutional context, there are patterns that emerge for all of us who teach in higher education. And yet? And yet our local contexts do matter, as do our institutional dynamics. There is nuance to be found among all the larger patterns we share. In seeking out this nuance, this book will explore both macro-level dynamics within higher education and the more contextualized location of the introductory classroom, particularly at the community college level.

We will find students in our classrooms who prefer not to participate in large group contexts. We all know that some students will never raise their hands and will never talk in class (except *maybe* in a pair or a small group). And yet most of us spend significant time attempting to get them to speak. Like much of Western culture, we treat this as a binary. I am to see (or am now trying *not to see*) students who talk as "actively participating" and students who never talk as "not participating." An important question disrupts this pattern: "How can we possibly listen to and understand each other if we are all preoccupied with speaking?"[41] Indeed, participation can come in many forms, including quiet ones.

These pages will engage with my argument for pedagogies of quiet; for utilizing silence as a strategy for cultivating the quiet inner world of students and, thus, deepening student engagement. This will be framed and executed in a way that brings many students from the margins (introverts, English language learners, etc.) into the center. Silence and quiet come in many forms, and I will make a case for validating those multitudes. So, in some instances, a quiet pedagogy might mean asking the students to engage in freewriting practices—in a silent classroom—before any invitations to speak in class. In contrast, in other cases, it means offering students a moment of quiet mindfulness practice to reflect on (challenging) course content. It might also mean finding ways, primarily through technological means, to allow students to share their ideas and remain quiet students (for example, those who don't verbally participate in large group contexts but are actively engaged participants in the classroom space). In other words, silence is both a pedagogical means to an end and an end in itself.

It is important to stress what this book is and what it is not. If the reader hopes for specific how-to practices, those are sprinkled throughout the text. Overall, this book is primarily a sociological, empirical exploration of the contexts and contours of our classrooms. The goal is to make sense of silence from the student's perspective. Further, this book will provide detailed evidence, again through student voices, for why specific practices benefit their classroom experience. These pages will not simply detail the practices that are utilized in pedagogies of quiet; they will also describe how these practices shaped students' experience, learning, and success. I advise the reader to avoid jumping right to the "how-to" strategies, thus bypassing the theoretical and empirical underpinnings of the practice. Challenging hegemonic cultural habits is hard work and requires a deep dive; we need to unlearn our assumptions about classroom participation to fully grab hold of why we should value silence and quiet in our students and our classrooms.

Each chapter is a theoretical and data-driven exploration of the teaching strategies I have incorporated into my classroom; I will outline the central themes of the data to build connections to the pedagogical claims I am making. All of the strategies presented in this book are organized around quiet and silence; in essence, I took what I was most afraid of in the classroom and turned it into my greatest asset. Instead of running away from and attempting to fill all the silences that emerge in a classroom, my data (and that of other scholars) supports cultivating silences and using them as central components of teaching and learning.

Chapter Outline

Chapter 1 presents silence as problematic and explores how patriarchal white supremacy has become embedded into institutions of higher education and, thus, the impact this has on faculty socialization and praxis. The chapter starts with the author's standpoint and research methodology. From there, the chapter will focus on the issues that emerge in the context of the neoliberal university, the banking model of education, and the chilly climate. Punctuated with field notes about my socialization process and supporting research, I explore formal and informal dynamics of faculty socialization. Throughout the chapter, the experiences of teachers and students will be contextualized within the larger milieu of the educational system in the United States, making connections between the body, racial and gender identities, and tactics of blame and shame as practices rooted in the institutionalization of colonization and patriarchal white supremacy.

Chapter 2 shifts from this general historical context into a specific one and addresses the question: Why silence? Why should we incorporate pedagogies of quiet into our classrooms? The chapter will elucidate the themes from open-ended survey questions given to students, where they articulate their feelings around classroom participation. Their reasons for not talking in class are illuminating and are presented as a justification for exploring alternate strategies referred to throughout the book as *pedagogies of quiet*. The appropriate context will be provided throughout the chapter, including community college student demographics and the macro-level context of the neoliberal academy, including the subsequent impact on the pace and spaces of learning.

After delving into how silence can be problematic, chapter 3 explores silence as a solution and an essential component of an intersectional pedagogy. The chapter will explore multiple "genres" of pedagogical literature: contemplative, feminist, critical, multicultural, antiracist, and social justice. We will see how these pedagogical theories point us toward silence and quiet. At the center will be an exploration of universal design, contemplative pedagogy, and the slow professor movement. From there, the chapter will explore various participation practices—classroom exercises alongside an argument for labor-based grading—that make up pedagogies of quiet. All practices are tried in the classroom and coupled with fieldwork data to illuminate their effectiveness and capacity for cultivating a playful, engaged, albeit quiet, classroom.

After exploring many practices that fall under the framework of pedagogies of quiet, chapter 4 will focus on one assessment practice in particular—the participation journal—which will take center stage. This assignment, and the student's feelings and commentary about it, highlight the importance of broadening our understanding of participation and valuing multiple ways of engagement. The five themes that emerge from survey data (content engagement, time management, study skills, processing emotions, and building relationships) surrounding these practices and assessments will be explored in detail to highlight the expansive value of pedagogies of quiet for students, teachers, and classroom culture.

Chapter 5 focuses on technology in the classroom. The chapter opens with an exploration of the current historical moment and how our digital devices and social media apps are shaping our brains, our conversations, and our classroom silences. From there, we will utilize a universal design framework to explore how technology can create shared, productive classroom silences and enhance student engagement. The three themes (anonymity and anxiety, increased engagement, and more voices) that emerge from student survey data will frame a discussion about the benefits of utilizing classroom technology, particularly in a way that expands (quiet) students' voices.

The book's conclusion will focus on the title of the book. Thus, this chapter will explore the social justice component of this pedagogical strategy and historically contextualize the generation of students we teach: students reliant on technology and with higher rates of anxiety and depression, having lived through a pandemic, and transitioning to online learning. We are up against a significant number of hurdles in twenty-first-century education, and the conclusion will frame what was presented throughout the book as a trajectory to connect with students who are "alone together"[42] and solidify the argument that pedagogies of quiet are a path toward "education as the practice of freedom."[43]

NOTES

1. Mary Rose O'Reilley, *Radical Presence: Teaching as Contemplative Practice* (Portsmouth, NH: Heinemann, 1998), 6.

2. Mihaly Csikszentmihalyi, *Flow: The Psychology of Optimal Experience* (New York: Harper Perennial Modern Classics, 2008).

3. Susan Cain, *Quiet: The Power of Introverts in a World That Can't Stop Talking* (New York: Crown Publishing, 2013).

4. Bryan M. Dewsbury, "Deep Teaching in a College STEM Classroom," *Cultural Studies of Science Education* 15, no. 1 (2020): 2.

5. Jane Nicholas and Jamilee Baroud, "Rethinking 'Students These Days': Feminist Pedagogy and the Construction of Students," in *Feminist Pedagogy in Higher Education: Critical Theory and Practice*, ed. Tracy Penny Light, Jane Nicholas, and Renée Bondy (Ontario, Canada: Wilfrid Laurier University Press, 2015), 247.

6. Dewsbury, "Deep Teaching in a College STEM Classroom," 2.

7. Eve Tuck and K. Wayne Yang, "Decolonization Is Not a Metaphor," *Tabula Rasa* 38 (2021): 1.

8. Tuck and Yang, "Decolonization Is Not a Metaphor," 1.

9. bell hooks, *Teaching to Transgress* (Oxfordshire, England: Routledge, 2014).

10. Michael Armato, "Wolves in Sheep's Clothing: Men's Enlightened Sexism & Hegemonic Masculinity in Academia," *Women's Studies* 42, no. 5 (2013): 589.

11. hooks, *Teaching to Transgress*, 35.

12. hooks, *Teaching to Transgress*, 89.

13. AnaLouise Keating, *Transformation Now!: Toward a Post-Oppositional Politics of Change* (University of Illinois Press, 2012).

14. Nicholas and Baroud, "Rethinking 'Students These Days,'" 250.

15. "Silence Definition & Meaning," *Merriam-Webster*, accessed March 16, 2022, http://www.merriam-webster.com/dictionary/silence; "Quiet Definition & Meaning," *Merriam-Webster*, accessed March 16, 2022, HYPERLINK "http://www.merriam-webster.com/dictionary/silence"http://www.merriam-webster.com/dictionary/quiet.

16. Cain, *Quiet*.

17. Ros Ollin, "Silent Pedagogy and Rethinking Classroom Practice: Structuring Teaching Through Silence Rather than Talk," *Cambridge Journal of Education* 38, no. 2 (2008): 266.

18. Cain, *Quiet*.

19. Cain, *Quiet*, 5.

20. Kevin Quashie, *The Sovereignty of Quiet* (New Jersey: Rutgers University Press, 2012), 45.

21. Carm DeSantis and Toni Serafina, "Classroom to Community: Reflections on Experiential Learning and Socially Just Citizenship," in *Feminist Pedagogy in Higher Education: Critical Theory and Practice*, ed. Tracy Penny Light, Jane Nicholas, and Renée Bondy (Ontario, Canada: Wilfrid Laurier University Press, 2015), 96.

22. Jillian M. Duquaine-Watson, "'Pretty Darned Cold': Single Mother Students and the Community College Climate in Post-Welfare Reform America," *Equity & Excellence in Education* 40, no. 3 (2007): 229.

23. Jennifer J. Lee and Janice M. Mccabe, "Who Speaks and Who Listens: Revisiting the Chilly Climate in College Classrooms," *Gender & Society* 35, no. 1 (2021): 33.

24. Rita Kohli, "Breaking the Cycle of Racism in the Classroom: Critical Race Reflections from Future Teachers of Color," *Teacher Education Quarterly* 35, no. 4 (2008): 185.

25. Alison Mountz, Anne Bonds, Becky Mansfield, Jenna Loyd, Jennifer Hyndman, Margaret Walton-Roberts, and Ranu Basu, "For Slow Scholarship: A Feminist Politics of Resistance Through Collective Action in the Neoliberal University," *ACME: An International Journal for Critical Geographies* 14, no. 4 (2015).

26. Paulo Freire, *Pedagogy of the Oppressed* (New York: Continuum, 2000).

27. Maggie Berg and Barbara K. Seeber, *The Slow Professor* (University of Toronto Press, 2018).

28. Riyad A. Shahjahan, "Being 'Lazy'and Slowing Down: Toward Decolonizing Time, Our Body, and Pedagogy," *Educational Philosophy and Theory* 47, no. 5 (2015).

29. Vivian García López, and Vivian Gareía López, "The Struggles to Eliminate the Tenacious Four-Letter 'F' Word in Education," *Counterpoints* 422 (2012): 315.

30. Peter Kaufman and Janine Schipper, *Teaching with Compassion: An Educator's Oath to Teach from the Heart* (Maryland: Rowman & Littlefield, 2018), 45.

31. Keating, *Transformation Now!*, 16.

32. Berg and Seeber, *The Slow Professor*, 86.

33. Mountz et al., "For Slow Scholarship."

34. Jennifer Llewellyn and K. Llewellyn, "A Restorative Approach to Learning: Relational Theory as Feminist Pedagogy in Universities," in *Feminist Pedagogy in Higher Education: Critical Theory and Practice*, ed. Tracy Penny Light, Jane Nicholas, and Renée Bondy (Ontario, Canada: Wilfrid Laurier University Press, 2015), 21.

35. Maxine Greene, "Teaching as Possibility: A Light in Dark Times," In *Critical Pedagogy in Uncertain Times*, edited by Sheila Macrine (New York: Palgrave Macmillan, 2009), 89–90.

36. Llewellyn and Llewellyn, "A Restorative Approach to Learning: Relational Theory as Feminist Pedagogy in Universities," 15.

37. Peter McLaren, "Critical Revolutionary Pedagogy's Relevance Today," in *Critical Pedagogy in Uncertain Times*, ed. Sheila Macrine (London: Palgrave Macmillan, 2020), 219.

38. Quashie, *The Sovereignty of Quiet*.

39. Laura I. Rendón, *Sentipensante (Sensing/Thinking) Pedagogy: Educating for Wholeness, Social Justice and Liberation* (Sterling, VA: Stylus Publishing, LLC, 2012), 30.

40. Carl Phillips, *My Trade Is Mystery: Seven Meditations from a Life in Writing* (New Haven, CT: Yale University Press, 2023), 30.

41. Yuk-Lin Renita Wong, "Knowing Through Discomfort: A Mindfulness-Based Critical Social Work Pedagogy," *Critical Social Work* 5, no. 1 (2004): 4.

42. Sherry Turkle, *Alone Together: Why We Expect More from Technology and Less from Each Other* (New York: Basic Books, 2011).

43. hooks, *Teaching to Transgress*.

Chapter 1

Silence as a Problem

Many of us have a fear of silence in the classroom. As teachers, we often feel the urge to fill up the space, to fill up the silences. We ask our class a question, and often, if there's no response, we keep talking. We pack our syllabi so tight we stress about giving over too much time to "nothing," which is what moments of silence often feel like. Silence in the face of a question feels like the opposite of learning or the absence of learning, and so we push forward with more content, with rephrased questions, anything to fill the silence. In many ways, this is a sign of academic capitalism, where time equals money and productivity. And thus, each new silence feels like a failure.

What to do with this fear of silence? At the center of this book is the valuation and promotion of utilizing quiet in the classroom as a central pedagogical strategy. At the same time, tremendous cultural and institutional pressure is placed on faculty to engage their students with active participation. We want students to put their phones away and "reclaim conversation."[1] Many teachers, myself included at times, face resistance when encouraged to incorporate contemplative pedagogies, as quiet practices are associated with spirituality and/or emotion, both of which are marginalized in an institution organized around the norms of Western patriarchy.

And yet, as bell hooks writes, "accepting the decentering of the West globally, embracing multiculturalism, compels educators to focus attention on the issue of voice. Who speaks? Who listens?"[2] We often forget that silence isn't passive; deep and generous listening can happen in our classes—inside our silent students—but is often ignored through a preference for talk, which is seen as the pinnacle of insight. The institution of higher education has lofty goals that hope to lead us toward greater democratization and critical thinking. At the same time, there is no shortage of evidence for the impact of neoliberal policies that limits these ideological potentials, never mind the ways in which higher education is under attack in the political sphere.

There are many silences built into our institutions, into higher education; for example, those whose voices are ignored or silenced. This chapter will explore many of these silences, focusing on both students and teachers. The goal of this chapter is first to center students' voices and, thus, articulate the methodology behind this research, and second, to make sense of the historical processes that shape these problematic silences in the first place. Throughout, we will frame how to construct a praxis that chips away at these problematic silences and builds toward a strategic, self-reflexive, and engaged collective silence that facilitates a path for students to find the insightful possibilities of their quiet worlds.

This is a book about pedagogy that focuses more on classroom participation practices and participation assessment strategies. It is true that "curriculum is tied to power,"[3] but pedagogy is about much more than our curriculums. The pedagogical praxis of this book extends beyond the boundaries of curriculum and thus discipline, and speaks to teachers of all stripes. In addition, this work is grounded in a social justice lens. "Scholars point out that critical pedagogy can be seen as deeply theoretical, in need of living strategies to carry out its theoretical and conceptual goals."[4] The quiet practices outlined in this book are some examples of such "living strategies" that aim to challenge—historical, hegemonic—dynamics of power in the classroom. *Pedagogies of Quiet* takes seriously conversations about silence and power, takes seriously students' silences in the classroom, and engages with a praxis that values not just multiple voices entering the conversations but multiple strategies for approaching our conversations. The primary goal is to disrupt "talk" as the predominant route to classroom dialogue and to think of quiet as a route to student "voice."

Michelle Page, in her essay titled "LGBTQ Inclusion as an Outcome of Critical Pedagogy," writes that "critical pedagogy carries with it a diverse range of meanings and practices that are ever contested and evolving. As such, it is not a mechanistic series of steps to be followed."[5] At the same time, she poses the question that many of us have regarding pedagogical theories: What exactly do we do? As Page argues, we can—and should—tend to our curriculum as a strategy to deliver on this critical outcome. It is just as important to note that curriculum development is just one step in the process of transforming our classrooms toward equity. The other routes are through our classroom engagement strategies, our philosophy regarding participation, and our assessment choices, grading systems, and syllabus policies.

Given all these routes toward building a more just classroom, the focus here will be on classroom participation philosophy and assessment practices. We come into the classroom with values, which may be informal and/or unconscious or developed into a formalized classroom participation philosophy. As introduced previously, many of us have in our heads an idea regarding what a "good" classroom looks like. Or, more accurately, sounds like. As we exit the graduate classroom as students and enter the undergraduate classroom as teachers, we have creatively wild and wonderful fantasies about the kind of dialogues that would unfold under our tutelage in the classroom. As Elizabeth Ellsworth wrote, "the task of the critical educator thus becomes 'finding ways of working with students that enable the full expression of multiple 'voices' engaged in dialogic encounter."[6] This was the underpinnings of my personal fantasy: students in conversation as part of the long arc toward justice. It's been twenty years since I first brought that fantasy into my classroom. I've spent the past decade engaged in an ongoing process of self-reflection and working to meet students where they are. This book is about the process of interrogating this fantasy of dialogue and its impact on our pedagogies and thus our students' experiences in our classrooms.

Elizabeth Ellsworth wrote that "dialogue"—a "pedagogical practice fundamental to the literature on critical pedagogy"—is a "repressive myth that perpetuates relations of domination."[7] One of the ways that this has manifested in many classrooms is through silence: so many of our students do not engage in classroom talk and thus were and are left unheard. All the while, the "discourse on student voice sees the student as 'empowered' when the teacher 'helps' students to express their subjugated knowledges."[8] So if our students aren't talking, does that mean they are disempowered or that we have failed at our crucial task? Not so. Further, teaching introductory-level courses—a primary focus for those at small colleges, graduate teaching assistants, untenured faculty, part-time faculty, and/or those of us working at community colleges—is a space where engagement is necessary but "deep dialogue" might be premature. As we will see in later chapters, in the introductory classroom, when a discipline is still new, students are sometimes more hesitant to engage. This book is about them.

METHODS: CENTERING THE VOICE OF STUDENTS

Author Reflexivity

The practices in this book are a challenge to "traditional" teaching practices. Pedagogies of quiet decenter talk, encourage the value of quiet students, rely upon emotion, and recognize embodiment in the classroom. From where you sit, engaging with these practices (even if you are very interested in them) could feel like too big a risk depending on your institutional culture or your professional rank. The mythology of dialogue runs deep in educational cultures. It runs deep inside of me. And yet it is true that "reflexivity asks us to approach our work with epistemological unease because we are always at risk of reproducing categories that reify power."[9] As such, it is important that we question these hegemonic cultures and our positions within them that might hold us back.

These power dynamics are at play here as I make the case for pedagogies of quiet as a white person with a doctorate who is a tenured professor at a well-funded community college. I have vulnerabilities as well: I am an out lesbian, I appear young, and sexism is institutionalized. These vulnerabilities are shaped by the wider political winds of backlash (such as "don't say gay" and "antiwoke" policies) awash in the present historical era. While naming my intersectional location in the classroom and in society is important—for making sense of the methodology and conclusions of this project—what is most important is that this practice of reflexivity leads toward an attentiveness to the knowledge that our students bring to us.

While the goal here is to shine the light of focus onto the students' own understanding of their participatory experiences, my voice is still woven throughout. Reflexivity leads me to pose the question to my readers: Why listen to me? This book was inspired by my mistakes—which I will share with you here in brief—but more so, it was inspired by my students. Paige Sweet writes that "the familiar invocation to be 'reflexive' becomes a demand to center excluded knowledge and allow it to shift the object of study."[10] Thus, the story that unfolds in this section is in part an accounting of my positionality and part an accounting of my process of including my students' previously "excluded knowledge" into the space of pedagogical theory and, thus, the classroom, transforming our relationship to both. This book is about what happens when teachers step out of the way so that students' view of the classroom emerges as central, as the center, so we can create an equitable and shared learning space.

Picture this: a classroom with thirty-two students, all of whom professed great enthusiasm for being enrolled in the class. We are approximately four weeks into the semester. The goal for the day is to discuss a text using discussion questions shared with students prior to class, thus ensuring them extra time to consider their responses. The teacher opens the conversation with what she thinks are the "easy" questions: "What did you think of the readings?" "Did anything stand out to you?" "Were there any points of personal connection?" What follows is silence. Lots of it. Despite icebreakers galore, this class of thirty-two individuals had yet to show signs of coalescing into a chatty group. In addition, no one was showing up as an individual either. No vocal cords were being exercised; the space was utterly silent.

So what happens next? The teacher gets frustrated and asks the students if anyone has done the reading in an accusatory and demeaning tone. The teacher then attempts to cover up, or recover from, this shaming tone of voice by saying, "It's okay, you can be honest, as it will help me assess how to approach our time together today." The recovery can't fully accomplish what it sets out to, as the whiff of professorial shaming is still in the air, and the students remain disengaged (this word, disengaged, was what the teacher was thinking).

Fast forward through another week or so of silence, where the students continue to appear to be detached from the classroom, despite their physical presence. The teacher has prepared a mid-semester check-in form, hoping to get some information from her students to help her in her struggle to get them to talk. After class, reading the responses in her office, she fights off tears, as it's clear that she herself is (part of) the problem—in her students' eyes—as she has created a chilly classroom. They referred to their teacher as "intimidating" and they were uncomfortable with how their teacher responded to their comments, making them feel like they were "wrong" or "off track." While they didn't use the word "chilly," it was clear they were discomfited. Of course, "she" is me. I had to square this chilly reality with my feminist pedagogical goals.

This happened most days for this particular class—ask questions, no answers, rinse, and repeat. I tried so many tactics, some of which I am embarrassed to admit, all of which were grounded in frustration rather than sound pedagogy. I shamed them. I sat down, put my feet up, and said, "I can wait," thinking I was being funny or charming. I was not. I spoke, in scolding tones: "Did anyone do the readings?" or "I bet no one read the article again today." The anonymous feedback that I had collected from them made it clear that I had created an intimidating presence in the front of the classroom and that I was stifling their desire to participate.

By the semester's end, I fully realized I was the problem. I had been socialized into an academic context that I had yet to question: my pedagogical inheritance was harming my effectiveness as a teacher and, more importantly, my students' capacities to learn. I began to interrogate the building blocks of this pedagogical inheritance of mine, including ideas like the "best" students were the most talkative ones and the professor (and their syllabus and assessments) should be "hard." I was socialized into and taught from within a department of men who boasted of their first day of class tactics to scare fragile students out of their classes in the name of academic rigor. I was socialized into the fantasy of academic dialogue.

And yet I wasn't teaching graduate students, I was teaching introductory-level students at a community college. No better, no worse, but certainly a different context. Ultimately, I realized that the pedagogy I inherited through socialization in higher educational settings (not through formal training) was ill suited for this particular context. The diverse demographics that make up a community college alongside the needs of students—whether at two-year, four-year, or PhD-granting institutions—in introductory classrooms produce different requirements and thus should entail different pedagogical methods.

As I began thinking about how I might change my approach to teaching, I wondered if I could incorporate practices that engaged students without always requiring them to talk. Ultimately, however, I got them to "talk" through surveys: by asking them what they thought about classroom participation norms, their experiences in various classrooms, and the quiet practices I began to incorporate into my courses. This developed into the methodology for this project.

Research Site, Sampling, and Data Collection

The methodology that serves as the basis of this book started with the hope that I could engage all my students, whether they wished to talk or stay silent. One semester I tried something new in my classroom. I started using digital technology, which my students accessed primarily via their cell phones, to encourage students to answer questions in class without asking them to speak. I was curious how this practice impacted their learning, so I created a survey to inquire about their experiences with the program. Admittedly, I had no plans to give this survey more widely or across semesters, nor to author a book. Still, the project grew. I gave a professional development talk on my campus, and a few other faculty members began to use the strategies that I spoke of at my presentation. I recruited them to participate by sharing the survey with their students (Course Engagement Survey). From there, the project bloomed to include both field note data and data from student surveys.

Field note data was captured through recorded notes after classroom implementation of quiet pedagogical practices. As Phillippi and Lauderdale note, "qualitative field notes are an essential component of rigorous qualitative research," and field notes help to provide important descriptive details of the "study context."[11] In the context of this study, field notes provided additional details about the effectiveness of the classroom practices. While the survey data tells the story from the student perspective, the field notes capture the effectiveness from the lens of faculty.

In the midst of this project, the pandemic hit, and we were pushed out of our classrooms and onto Blackboard and Zoom. I adapted some of the quiet practices I had been using in the classroom, such as the study guide (see chapter 3) to the online context, and as in the case of the participation journal (see chapter 4), I created new practices. When doing synchronous online courses, I continued to use the digital technology I had come to rely upon in the physical classroom (see chapter 5). I also adjusted the survey to reflect the online context and these new practices. The survey queries are specific to the quiet practices utilized while also presenting broad questions that ask students to articulate what makes them feel cared for and/or connected to their classrooms. They were also asked to write about their experiences with verbal participation: Do they (like to) talk in class/on Zoom, why or why not, and for what reasons?

Prior to distributing any surveys, I received Institutional Review Board approval from my institution. The entire research project included the production and distribution of three sets of surveys. Even with that initial survey mentioned previously, I was focused on centering student voices and minimizing power differentials. I chose anonymous surveys as they seemed the best way to elicit honest feedback from students. Teachers interviewing current students pose a problematic power dynamic that could shape what the students share. I was attentive to and thus "able to minimize this potential conflict through my study design."[12] Surveys were given at the end of the semester. The college's online learning platform was not used, given the implications for disrupting anonymity; instead students completed the survey anonymously through Google Forms. Informed consent was built into the survey, and forms, where the student (who completed the survey) responded "no" to the informed consent question (about whether the student grants permission for their survey responses to be utilized in the study), were shredded.

In addition, given the number of students in our classrooms at the initial onset of this project—class sizes ranging from 35 to 150 students—a survey seemed the best way to hear from all of them. I incorporated both closed and open-ended questions to produce quantitative and qualitative data through the survey process. In addition, as previously mentioned, I gave a professional development talk on my campus, and four other faculty members—who taught English, psychology, and history—began using the strategies I spoke of at my presentation. I recruited them to participate by sharing the survey with their students (In-Person Class Engagement Survey).

The primary survey is about classroom culture and students' experiences with talking in class, focusing on student responses to a "quiet pedagogy" strategy incorporated by all the instructors administering the survey. During the pandemic shutdown, there was also a survey that focused on the participation journal assignment. Survey data comes from three sets of surveys:

1. Course Engagement Survey: Spring 2018–Fall 2019 in-person data set (N = 270)
2. Course Engagement Survey: Spring 2020–Summer 2021 online data set (N = 175)
3. Participation Journal Assignment Reflection: Spring 2020–Summer 2021 online data set (N = 275)

The first data set was given to students taking Introduction to Sociology, Introduction to Psychology, English 101, and The American Experience Since 1877. The second and third survey sets were administered only in the

COVID shutdown era and were only distributed to students enrolled in sociology courses. The third survey set provides rich details about the benefits of not just the participation journal assignment but about thinking about participation more broadly.

All told, 720 students participated in the survey process. Of those who were surveyed in the physical classroom, 270 participated. They answered questions about verbal participation alongside questions on the utility of classroom technology as a route to (quiet) participation. This data is explored in chapters 2 and 5. Once we made the shift to online learning, all the students surveyed were registered in sociology courses, of which 75 percent of the survey respondents were enrolled in Introduction to Sociology, while the other 25 percent were enrolled in Contemporary Families in the United States and the Sociology of Sex and Gender. 175 students participated in the survey about classroom participation (see chapter 2), while 275 participated in the survey that spoke directly to the participation journal assignment (chapter 4). A brief overview of the data through charts can be found in appendix A.

Like Mary Reda, who studied quiet students in her English courses in the early aughts, I did not design my study to "provide conclusive data about gender or race."[13] Demographic information *was* collected from students during the COVID era of the study, and the college tracks demographic information on the students enrolled in each course, so we can make some connections based on race and gender. That said, I did not design the study to make specific claims about the impact of various identities on students' experiences of their silences; rather, I wanted them to articulate the issues that shaped their experiences. If an identity marker—such as race, class, or gender—was salient for them, I wanted them to be able to articulate that without specific prompting. The goal was to allow students to be able to express their thoughts on classroom participation freely, without any guided or imposed (potential) impacts.

Data Analysis

All the open-ended data was coded using grounded theory coding strategies. This coding "shapes [the] analytic frame from which [I] build the analysis" and was completed in two phases: initial and focused.[14] The process relied upon "indigenous concepts,"[15] which is to say the focus was on the language that the students themselves made use of in their writing. When coding the open-ended questions, all the responses were read during the initial coding stage, one question at a time, and notable language was highlighted. From there, the focused stage included constructing a list of the prominent terms in each student's answer. Once this initial list was established, the task of the focus phase was to identify connections, patterns, and constructing themes;

these themes again relied upon the language students themselves used to describe their experiences.

The themes that emerged from the Participation Journal Assignment Reflection data (N = 275) are

- Time Management,
- Approaches to Studying,
- Processing Course Content,
- Emotions, and
- Student-Teacher Relationship.

These themes will be explored in depth in chapter 4. The themes that emerged from the Course Engagement Survey data (N = 445, including both online and face to face) are

- Socioemotional Considerations,
- Listening to Others,
- Processing Course Content, and
- Class Culture and the Professor

These themes will be explored throughout the text, in particular in chapters 2, 4, and 5. As is often the case with grounded theory, the researcher returned to the data on multiple occasions to assess these themes and to find further and deeper connections.

These coded themes are then used to organize the information that students provided through their open-ended survey question answers. The patterns that emerged from their data were so consistent that some of the student quotes shared within the text can appear repetitive, even though each quotation utilized contains the words of a single student. Some of the students provided short answers, while others elaborated, and both types of responses are included in the data analysis throughout the following chapters. It is these patterns that compelled the direction of the open-coding process.

Limitations

At the start, this study was not meant to be a larger project—a book no less—but instead an inquiry into whether the quiet pedagogical tactics used in class resonated with students. That the project has somewhat haphazard beginnings did shape its trajectory. At the same time, all research has limitations. We cannot explore everything all at once. For example, the first 270 Course Engagement Surveys did not include demographic information, while the last 175 Course Engagement Surveys did include demographic questions. Thus, we can assess the impact of identity categories such as race and gender on only a portion of the sample. This limits the ability to make some claims (for example, linking a specific comment from a student to their gender identity when that information is lacking), while still allowing other claims (for example, patterns among female-identified students for those surveys where such information was gathered). While sociological patterns can be found in the data that allow us to explore the potential impacts of race, class, and gender on our students' experiences, the utilization of a universal design framework means that our practices are designed to target institutionally marginalized students while benefiting all students simultaneously, future research would benefit from a more consistent and cohesive approach to gathering this data.

Another limitation of the study design, as a result of the sole reliance on anonymous survey data, is the inability to ask follow-up questions to ensure clarity or to dig deeper into the students' concerns. Future research would greatly benefit from focus groups and/or qualitative interviews with students; an embedded ethnography would also be a great direction for future work. Given that in this study the researcher was also the current teacher of many of the surveyed students, these more in-depth qualitative methods were not possible.

Finally, the data for this project does not cover all the quiet practices that are explored throughout the pages of this book. For example, while multiple technology platforms are utilized in the quiet classroom—Padlet and Perusall, for example—only one classroom polling software was included in the data. The survey set that inquires into the classroom efficacy of Mentimeter was implemented in the earliest years of the adoption of pedagogies of quiet in my own and my colleagues' classrooms and, as such, was the only platform included for that data set. Other quiet practices, from found poetry to crossword puzzles to the in-class writing portfolio, have been implemented with great success but do not yet have student-centered data to enhance the field note data. Future research would greatly benefit from more empirical explorations of these practices.

One key strength of this data is the centering of the student voice. As teachers, we regularly ask them to speak up in class, but here we have asked them to speak to their experiences with our expectations of talk. So they are granted voice in a conversation about student voices. As Sweet writes, "epistemic privilege illuminates the boundaries and binaries that make up social life."[16] One binary that is being challenged is that of the teacher as educator: we have a lot to learn from our students. Another is the idea that to speak is to be engaged and to be silent is to be disengaged. Silence functions in many ways, as students make clear in their data, and as is illuminated through historical analysis of power in the education system.

Patriarchal White Supremacy and the College Classroom

The community college students at the center of this book help us to understand whether and why they (do or do not) feel comfortable engaging in dialogue in the classroom. A challenge here is to figure out how to get to this place of critical, engaged dialogue in the face of students who are often uncomfortable—and thus opt out of—talking in class. Part of this work is engaging in a brief exploration of the macro-level and micro-level processes that function to silence students. This includes students' own explanations so that teachers can better strategize how to move forward in a way that gives students the space for quiet learning. We do all this while keeping a focus on skill-building, self-reflection, critical thinking, and engagement with peers.

To start at the macro level, much has been written about the neoliberal moment and the ensuing impact on higher education. In an institution whose aims are democratic, the capitalist meritocratic push toward credentialing has had a significant impact on the learning experience. Pedagogical constraints around time and curriculum, in particular from the push toward teaching to the test, have shaped professors' ideas around what can and what cannot be accomplished in the classroom, especially in the introductory classroom. As Llewellyn and Llewellyn write, "a higher education is no longer defined in terms of the knowledge and skills of democratic citizenship, but rather in terms of the attainment of the complex skills necessary for individual success in a global economy."[17] Certainly labor market skill attainment is a must, but something important gets lost as classroom time is rushed: (quiet) time for deep engagement.

This neoliberal push—and the structural dynamic of academic capitalism—has had a significant impact on how we organize our classrooms. It shapes our choices around content as well as our goals relating to assessment. As Berg and Seeber write, "corporatization has led to standardized learning and a sense of urgency," where productivity and efficiency are more highly valued than creativity and pleasure.[18] In this context, multitasking becomes a predominant pedagogical tool, even in the face of scientific knowledge that illuminates its futility. Instead students are expected to listen to lectures, read PowerPoints, and take notes—all at the same time—while being prepared to immediately respond to any questions posed by their professors. Knowing what we do about the pitfalls of multitasking, it's no wonder we are often faced with a room full of silence following a question: so often our students are still busy writing down the last sentence we spoke without time to fully listen to our question.

Students feel this sense of urgency coming from their professors. Most of the students in this study referenced a more subtle impact, though they were concerned about being disrespectful and "talking over others" or because they felt "awkward to interject during a lecture." A few of them mentioned that there wasn't a lot of time given to ask/answer questions, so not speaking in class was more a requirement than a choice. In an introductory course where we often feel the push to cover as much material as possible, to give a sufficiently broad overview of our discipline, we might be more at risk regarding this neoliberal rush toward productivity.

There are other ways that academic capitalism shapes our understandings of classroom participation. Susan Cain refers to "the New Group Think" that encourages cooperative working and learning and that directs us toward "an increasingly popular method of instruction called 'cooperative' or 'small group' learning."[19] In higher education, there are big pushes for utilizing practices such as the "think-pair-share" approach to learning where the "share" part of the equation is seen as the most important and is what receives the most allotted time. As Frambach et al. write, "one of the educational tools in student-centered education is small group work, where students are expected to actively engage in critical discussions about learning topics, problem cases, or projects."[20] Cain points out that talking in class is seen as a valuable sign of leadership skills, and thus the business model of leadership shapes how we see our talkative, and our quiet, students.[21]

This operates as a (potential) unconscious bias in our classrooms where the talkative students are seen by teachers as "better," as more engaged, and as the "good" students. It also emerges from the hidden curriculum of Western culture. Frambach et al. posit that "several authors have contended that this type of interactive and independent behavior reflects typically Western values, such as individualism and a focus on verbal interaction."[22] Western culture is deeply entrenched in our classrooms and, alongside academic capitalism, shapes the lack of (time for deep) classroom participation.

Racism, another structural dynamic at play, also produces many classroom silences. Norms around verbal and nonverbal communication are grounded in a Western, white cultural habitus that values politeness, for example, over justice.[23] In writing specifically about Black girls' experience in the classroom, Caldera (citing Morris) "suggest[s] that silencing occurs when a Black girl is denied the privilege of acknowledging her whole self."[24] This denial often emerges as a result of the ways in which patriarchal white supremacy is embedded into our beliefs that the rational mind prevails in the classroom; where emotions, especially those expressed by women in general, and women of color in particular, are seen as out of place. This view results in those students feeling out of place in our classrooms.

At the same time, sometimes participation practices that effectively silence students actually emerge from the requirement to talk. Tokenism can be forced upon students who are called on by teachers in order to speak to an issue for which they are presumed to be experts. This practice shapes students' unwillingness to speak up, as they work to avoid having to be the one to educate the room.[25] For example, Duquaine-Watson points out that single mothers are often called upon to speak to political issues relating to single motherhood. She argues that "this type of singling out, or 'spotlighting' is a classic form of 'othering' that stigmatizes individuals of a particular group by treating them as different from 'regular' or 'normal' students."[26] This practice of othering emerges from teachers' unconscious biases, while also being grounded in our standardized practices of verbal participation that lead us to call on students to speak to the issues we raise as we teach. This highlights that embedded within the ways we structure classroom participation are complex and harmful dynamics of the white racial habitus.

Alongside research into the institutionalization of racism in higher education, feminist scholars have long identified silence as a problem. Women's historical exclusion from social life and women's invisibility in male-dominated spaces have led to both scholarship and social media memes about dynamics from mansplaining to men taking women's ideas and presenting them as their own. As DeVault and Ingraham write, "silencing, the more active form of the term [silence], is taken to refer not just to quieting, but also to censorship, suppression, marginalization, trivialization, exclusion, ghettoization, and other forms of discounting."[27] This allows us to see two important dynamics: one, that power is organized to value voice, and two, that patriarchal white supremacy, in the service of power, denies voice to women and people of color.

Given the role that unconscious bias plays here, it's a requirement of social justice educators to analyze our own intersectional location within historical and current dynamics of power—especially from within the specific location of our institution of employment. In addition, we must remain reflective of our classroom practices and assessments in addition to our curriculum.

> Curriculum and pedagogy have been employed as an instrument to colonize individuals into Eurocentric American hierarchical practices that include culture, values, and understanding; thus, as educators and cultural workers, reflection is imperative to recreate oneself and the practices utilized in education.[28]

Reflection is central to social justice scholars' capacity to unlearn the ways in which patriarchal white supremacy has been embedded in our practices. Each of us is operating from within this macro-level context, as well as from within the unique dynamics of our local community, our specific institution, and our individual classrooms. The argument presented here posits that a student-centered, critical pedagogy must explore the ways in which power and silence intersect, so as to use this knowledge to enhance and increase student engagement and participation. This, in turn, improves their experiences in classrooms as well as their overall success.

Silencing the Body

One place that power and silence intersects is in the body. Feminist and contemplative scholars have started a conversation inside the academy about the Western ideology of the mind-body split. Further, a path to reintegration of mind and body is central to the contemplative pedagogical approach as well as social justice education at large. The mind-body split, which was institutionalized into the academy during the Enlightenment, is the ideological framework for patriarchal white supremacy. Grounded in Aristotle's "great chain of being," Enlightenment thinkers posited the "rational" mind as the quality that renders (some) humans a superior species. Per this logic of inequality, animals—the rung below humans in Aristotle's chain—are driven by instinct, by the body, and are thus seen as inferior. From here, so the thinking goes, we get the belief system that associates the mind with men, white people, and superiority, while the body is tied to women, people of color, and inferiority.

The belief that the mind and body were "separate" spheres—just like the belief that the public and private are distinct spheres—and the ensuing association between mind and superiority and the body and inferiority serves as the ideological force behind patriarchal white supremacy. Disrupting this system in the classroom thus requires a reintegration of mind-body, and the incorporation of the body—including emotions—into our teaching practice. As Beth Berila argues, "contemplative practices enable students to cultivate emotional intelligence, learn to sit with difficult emotions, recognize deeply entrenched narratives they use to interpret the world, cultivate compassion for other people, and become more intentional about how they respond in any given moment. All of these abilities can transform dialogues about power, oppression, and privilege from intense reactionary debates into more relational, empathic, and reflective experiences."[29] These abilities—as will be outlined in later chapters—also transform students' classroom participation, their focus on/in the course, and their overarching experience in class.

A restorative approach to teaching acknowledges "that non-verbal communication modes may be used in the classroom. . . . For example, silence, or the right to listen more than tell, is critical to any learning process."[30] This was also made clear by the students surveyed for this project, as will be outlined in later chapters. This feminist approach, grounded in a feminist ethics of care, highlights that the classroom is a crucial space for engagement with antioppressive tactics that encourage a creative—and quiet—praxis. These nonverbal approaches reflect a challenge to the mind-body split, an ideology that has been central to patriarchal dominance. Instead feminist pedagogies argue that we must engage the body more fully by incorporating the physical sensations and emotional reactions that students and teachers bring into the classroom, and that the classroom brings out of us.

Feminist scholarship has shed much light on the ways in which Enlightenment ideologies have functioned to dismiss women's experiences and ideas through the binary of the "rational" male and the "emotional" woman. The mind-body split of patriarchal white supremacy has disrupted the learning practices of all students, while functioning as a particularly oppressive structure for historically marginalized students. This binary results in a dehumanizing approach to learning and knowledge production that excludes the "outsider-within"[31] knowledge of women of color, of Indigenous students, female and femme identified students, and other historically marginalized students. Hooks writes of her experience as a professor:

> It was difficult to maintain fidelity to the idea of the intellectual as someone who sought to be whole—well-grounded in a context where there was little emphasis on spiritual well-being, on care of the soul. Indeed, the objectification of the teacher within bourgeois educational structures seemed to denigrate notions of wholeness and uphold the idea of a mind/body split, one that promotes and supports compartmentalization.[32]

Western culture has a practice of associating the masculine with talking and the mind, while the devalued feminine is linked with listening and the body. This hurts our students. If we deny our wholeness, as hooks makes clear we are encouraged to do, we will bring the mind-body split into our classrooms, thus denying our students' ability to explore their own whole, full capacity and humanity, and find ourselves (unintentionally) reinforcing patriarchal white supremacy.

The Chilly Climate in the Classroom

Carrying this focus on how silence and power intersect invites us to explore how silence shows up in the classroom. This matters, given that silence can be both oppressive and expansive. To explore this further, Kelsey Blackwell's concept of "conversational architecture" is relevant here. She argues that there is a "hidden architecture that creates any group discourse. Each new voice that shares in a group dialogue builds this architecture, and its structure determines how we speak, what is said, and who is invited to participate. Though we might not realize that such structures exist, we've all experienced their confines."[33] Attention to the conversational architecture of our classrooms require that we reckon with the patterns that emerge: "Who leads the conversation? Whose opinions incite head nods and agreement and whose seem to go unnoticed? Who speaks first? Who speaks last?"[34]

And I would add, importantly: Who doesn't speak at all? What tones are utilized when speaking, especially the teacher's tone? What methods of nonverbal communication predominate? Why do we (sometimes) value listening to others while being inattentive to our own inner voices, our own inner quiet? Why do we (sometimes) value speaking at the expense of listening? These questions lead us into an exploration of classroom silence and silencing, reflecting on how our unspoken values and habits shape what's possible in the classroom.

Students also make it clear—as we will see in chapter 2—we must engage these questions. Teachers set the tone of the class not just through our syllabus but through our "conversational architecture," and as such our informal communication and nonverbal communication play a central role. For example, one student explained that they are sometimes uncomfortable with verbal classroom participation, "especially if the teacher seems annoyed." Sometimes we are transparent about our frustration. But more likely, our often unconscious nonverbal cues shape students' level of comfort with classroom engagement. And, as outlined earlier in this chapter, I know that I have been this annoyed teacher and that most often the annoyance stemmed from my own expectation that students speak. This aspect of my own conversational architecture didn't shift by pushing them into talk, but when I changed my expectations to value their silence, and the dynamics of their inner quiet. Thus, it's important that we widen our pedagogical lens to incorporate an awareness of the classroom architecture and, thus, the kinds of silence(s) we are building.

Participation expectations, and in some cases participation grades, are often an important part of the conversational architecture of the higher education classroom. Each of us organizes our class around both spoken and unspoken cultural norms around student participation, such as hands should be raised before speaking, one should speak only when called upon, students should expect to be called upon at any time, and there should only be one speaker at a time, among others. There are deeper dynamics involved as well, such as how we go about reprimanding students who violate these expectations and whether we do so publicly and equitably. Further, teachers often have their own sense of time, such as how much time is allotted for a question and thus how many students get to chime in to the discussion before the class moves on to another subject. This is why a few of the students wrote in their survey comments that they sometimes don't speak because another classmate had already said what they had planned to say or that the conversation had already moved on. Part of this, too, is the norms we set about whether or not it's acceptable to go "off topic" or whether we are strict to stay on "schedule."

All of these factors overtly and covertly shape the learning spaces that our students are operating from within, and as teachers, we need to be cognizant of the structures and spaces we are producing.

One example of conversational architecture that I've observed in classrooms are the socially stigmatizing behaviors of students who express problematic reactions to classmates with disabilities. Stigmatizing microaggressions such as whispers, giggles, and tuning out are some of the ways I've seen temporarily able-bodied students respond to, for example, neurodiverse students. These microaggressions are a component of the conversational architecture and make clear that in such spaces no one is free from the criticism of their peers. This fear of judgment and its impact on classroom discussions is evident in the data that will be explored in later chapters in this book. It also highlights the various pathways to silencing—to students' silences— that (might) exist in our classrooms.

Reflecting on the role that power plays in constructing conversational architecture, Blackwell writes that "when the designers of a conversation are white, often white men, we may forget to examine the architecture of the discussion because these are the architects we're all most familiar with."[35] We are also so familiar with ourselves as teachers that we might forget to examine our own role in constructing the conversational architecture of our classrooms. As I stand in front of the room, I bring to bear the power that comes with my whiteness, with my degree, and with my role as professor. So, for example, if I respond to the aforementioned belittling microaggressions of my temporarily able-bodied students by shaming them, I am perpetuating the unequal power dynamics of the space and further limiting the potential of my classroom as a space of deep dialogue.

This resonates deeply with feminist understandings of the chilly climate and the impact of this coldness on female-identified learners. There is important work that highlights the various practices that produce the chilly climate for women: the chilly climate is "a result of a variety of overt and covert behaviors of faculty and students, including faculty calling on men more than women, faculty and students making stereotypical comments about women's intellectual abilities, and faculty taking men's contributions more seriously than women's."[36] There is also intersectional work that hones in on specific groups of women, for example, how the chilly climate impacts single mothers in community college classrooms whereby "inattention to their needs . . . contributes to an institutional climate in which single mothers and their particular needs simply are not addressed."[37] Of course, there are many more intersections to remain mindful of.

This inattention to some students' needs shapes the knowledge produced in our classrooms. Critical pedagogy calls attention to the social construction of knowledge and to "how and why some constructions of reality are legitimated and celebrated by the dominant culture while others clearly are not."[38] In this way, we can shed light not just on the knowledge production that happens in our classrooms as we teach but on the dominant discourse of classroom participation that impacts our praxis. McClaren calls attention to the role that critical pedagogy plays in exposing the gendered dynamics of the hidden curriculum, such as men speaking more often than women and men's regular interruptions of women, and makes the case that "most teachers try hard not to be sexist,"[39] but that students still come to learn these gendered lessons. At the same time, the critical pedagogue is focused on what the students are learning about male dominance and on exposing the ideological power structure at play in the hidden curriculum, but much of the theory neglects to dive further into the role of the professor and our pedagogy.

We must carry our understanding of the hidden curriculum into our analysis of the conversational architecture of the classroom, and how it is shaped by the chilly classroom. As Lee and McCabe point out, often our goal as teachers is to increase the classroom participation of everyone, and while this is a worthy goal, they argue that "it is also important to examine participation rates of varying social groups—in other words, to view college classrooms as social sites and pay attention to who speaks and who listens."[40] Like Susan Cain, they make clear that classrooms value those who speak more than those who listen, while also opening up the space to think through the various roles that silence plays, and can play, in our classes. For example, it is clear from the body of literature on the chilly climate that patriarchal gender norms shape male-identified students' classroom practices. Male-identified students are more likely to dominate the conversation, to interrupt other students and the teacher, and to speak out of turn. Of course faculty responses to these male-identified students' patterns of behavior often function to both produce and reinforce this aspect of the chilly climate. This renders femme- and female-identified students and those with subordinated and marginalized masculinities silenced.[41]

The values that we, as teachers, bring into the classroom can perpetuate these dynamics. That is, when we value talking more than listening, we create a value system that opens the door to the chilly climate, whereby male students come to be more valued as they dominate the "sonic space" of the conversations.[42] Further, because the classroom privileges the rational mind in knowledge production, the "feminine realm" of emotions and the body are ignored as central to learning and knowledge creation. Thus, the chilly classroom isn't only perpetuated through faculty's (gendered responses) to students' classroom participation but also by the values we bring through our classroom participation ecology.

For example, in the middle of one of my courses a student began to cry in response to a very moving TED Talk by Chimamanda Ngozi Adichie. During the ensuing conversation about hegemonic power dynamics this student did not engage in any verbal discussion, and it would be easy to discount her experience as participation. When students are graded for participation, a show of emotion during a conversation about a difficult—and personal—subject matter isn't often included on the list of "activities" that earn students participation points. And yet it was clear from the observation of this classroom that the student was engaged and participating through a deep listening practice. Learning requires vulnerability—any moment of change does—and this student was engaging the content with vulnerability. That said, not only are emotional displays typically not valued in the classroom, they are more often than not discouraged, feared, and/or ignored. As faculty, we are socialized into a framework that encourages us to respond to "rational" rather than "emotional" displays from our students as if the two are separate.

As patriarchy plays a central role in the construction and perpetuation of the chilly climate, it should be noted that heteronormativity is intimately tied up in patriarchal dynamics. Thus, it isn't just women—cisgendered and transgendered—who experience such a climate. Research also documents a chilly climate for LGBTQ students.[43] For example, Whitehead and Gully write, "studies have since confirmed and extended these findings by highlighting how unfair treatment by instructors, loss of support from peers, and intra-community discrimination figure significantly in LGBTQ+ students' negative perceptions of the campus climate."[44]

Examples of this "unfair treatment" highlight how faculty are also shaped by the hidden curriculum, through, for example, our reliance on gendered—and binary—language. This puts us at risk for causing (unintentional) harm in our classrooms. For example, when we routinely make informal references to the language of heterogender,[45] such as "men" and "women," "husbands" and "wives," or "mothers" and "fathers." Attention to this linguistic aspect of the chilly climate should make us more aware of the heteronormative terms we rely upon, while encouraging us to shift toward gender-neutral terms (people, parents, spouses).

This intersectionality is a component of the patriarchal gender binary. As such, a heterogendered classroom discourse is yet another component of the chilly classroom. While we might be inclined to think that we aren't one of the "bad" teachers, it's crucial that we always keep our eye open for our own biases. Race, class, gender, sexuality, and ability are all identity categories that shape students' lives inside the classroom and that shape their experiences with both talk and silence.

White Racial Habitus

Heterogender is not alone as a prevailing force of classroom silencing. White supremacy shapes these climactic dynamics as well, where students of color often feel "othered" in the classroom, and where norms of whiteness—such as accent—produce internalized oppressions that shape students' classroom participation. Often students' silences are valid responses to both macro- and micro-level oppressions. As Llewellyn and Llewellyn argue, "things [are] not said for many reasons: being too vulnerable, resentment that other oppressions were marginalized, feeling the burden as a minority to 'educate' students and the professor, and concerns about distorted communication."[46] As a result, students have learned to use silence as a method of self-protection. The concept of habitus is helpful here. Michael Messner, for example, frames his understanding of the classroom through Bourdieu's concept of habitus, where he argues that the structure of the classroom is shaped around a "white guy habitus" that privileges both the feelings and experiences of white male professors and white male students.[47]

This white (guy) racial habitus shapes our pedagogical practices in complex ways, ranging from our valuation of talking over listening, to whose interruptions are allowed, and to our assessment practices. As Asao Inoue writes, the white racial habitus is built into our writing assessment practices and in "linguistic agreements" that result in "whiteness and white racial formations [that] historically are closely associated with SEAE [Standardized Edited American English] and dominant discourse."[48] Many of us are not aware of the ways in which the language that we speak—and assume others know as intimately as we do—impacts our classroom and students.

Further, what is often ignored is the role that these linguistic assumptions play in shaping our grading and assessment practices and thus in the perpetuation of the white racial habitus of our classrooms.[49] As one student surveyed for this project said of an experience with a teacher, my "professor of history was . . . verbally aggressive and . . . intimidating. I was even afraid [to] turn in papers because I just don't want to be close to him. . . . I was terrified of putting my thoughts in the writing [and being misunderstood]." This student was grappling with both verbal and nonverbal communication in the context of a white racial habitus that made turning in written papers an intimidating experience, both physically and linguistically.

The white racial habitus also shapes our participation norms. While Inoue speaks of the writing ecology, the same logic holds true to the participatory ecology of the classroom, where students are perceived as rational beings and failures are seen as individual failures.[50] Teachers' expectations about vocalization and leadership are shaped by the Western context, where "students are expected to show rather assertive behaviors, as speaking up, asking questions, and challenging the opinion of others, and students' responses to this may vary between cultures thereby shaping learning processes and outcomes in different ways."[51] That is, we have one hegemonic participatory, cultural expectation, while our students come to us from varied cultural contexts. We have first-generation students, English language learners, international students, Indigenous students, nonbinary students, and clinically depressed students (among many others), and yet we often apply one (Western) standard to participation: they need to talk in class. And when they don't, it's often seen as an individual failure.

One way this is manifested is through the professorial practice of blaming students. Even if we only do this in our heads, when we assume that students' lack of participation comes from boredom, disengagement, cell phones, or too much partying, we fail to recognize the cultural and structural dynamics that are at play in their lives. For example, when students are quiet because they are tired, we could see that through the lens of the individualized white racial habitus and blame the student for not getting enough rest. We could also take a compassionate approach, rather than blame, but one that still frames the issue through the lens of this racialized habitus (that is, encouraging the student to get more rest while not shaming them for being tired in your classroom).

On the other hand, when seen through the lens of the structural, this requires that we recognize the role that white supremacy plays not just in our participation ecology but in the students' exhaustion. As Kay Barrett points out, "people of color are not allowed rest. That disavowing of rest [is] directly sourced by white supremacy . . . to have the privilege to slow down, to excavate, and to just be creative—there's a hierarchy on who gets to have those things."[52] That is, structural racism, patriarchy, ableism, heteronormativity, and capitalist systems of profit and time shape what lives in our students' bodies and how those bodies live in our classrooms.

An example of the impact of the white racial habitus on students comes from some of their comments around verbal participation. Some of the stated fears students have around speaking in front of others emerge from classroom cultural and linguistic norms: classroom linguistic norms in addition to binary cultural norms around "right" and "wrong." As one student stated in their survey response, "English is not my native language and I like things to be perfect." And as a result, this student limits their verbal participation. English language learners can sometimes "take a longer time in their thought processes," producing a context whereby "instructors sometime misjudged the silent nature of their students."[53]

In addition, Jane Hill notes that "people who function as fluent bilinguals in their inner sphere become so anxious about their competence that sometimes they cannot speak at all."[54] This anxiety is clear in students' responses: one student said that "my native language is not English. Although I have been qualified to take courses at Harper, I know that my accent is strong, and I am afraid of being not understood." Pedagogies of quiet, and the practices that make up this framework, give multilingual students and English language learners a space to go where they can evade these social, oppressive forces while also creating a classroom context that serves to deconstruct and dismantle the forces of the white racial habitus.

Faculty Moves to Innocence

Many academics see themselves as experts in their fields and, in some cases, experts in understanding social inequality. This sense of expertise can create a feeling of being beyond reproach on any related matters, whether the content of our specific disciplines or more generally inequality in higher education. This could lead some of us to believe that as a result, we are exempt from participation in systems of inequality. Often we see teaching itself as an act of social change. In other words, some scholars, including myself, don't always recognize the ways in which we perpetuate inequities and cause harm. Those of us in the social sciences and humanities, in particular, might think things like: "I teach Patricia Hill Collins's canonic text *Black Feminist Thought*, so I'm on the 'right' side of social inequality." Many of us were taught in graduate school by a homogenous group of faculty, and the faculty who hired and socialized us into the tenure track likely believe(d) in their own "goodness,"[55] despite also engaging in oppressive practices such as equating academic rigor with being "hard."

Many scholars now recognize and challenge this bias. Robin DiAngelo, for example,[56] calls out the idea of the "good," "liberal" white people who see themselves as outside the realm of racisms' harms. One of the most significant critiques of critical pedagogy is similar—that critical pedagogues see themselves as "better than." Elizabeth Ellsworth writes, "the contortions of logic and rhetoric that characterize these attempts to define 'empowerment' testify to the failure of critical educators to come to terms with the essentially paternalistic project of traditional education"[57] and further posits that we must recognize the limitations that we bring into the classroom. In line with feminist standpoint theories, Ellsworth makes clear that faculty members who espouse critical pedagogy and who are adamant about disrupting hegemonic dynamics in both their classrooms and society still engage in their teaching from a particular standpoint. She continues to say, "I cannot unproblematically bring subjugated knowledges to light when I am not free of my own learned racism, fat oppression, classism, ableism or sexism. No teacher is free of these learned and internalized oppressions."[58]

This plays out in other academic contexts as well: classrooms, academic conferences, shared governance meetings, graduate advisor offices, and online discussion boards. The hierarchy of higher education—from the elite, prestigious institutions to community colleges, to rankings such as R1, M3, and technical schools—shapes our experiences in complex ways that we are often unaware of at the classroom level. I was, for example, warned by my graduate advisor about the (implied negative) impact of my community college teaching aspirations on my career trajectory, just as I was warned that my curriculum vitae that included published scholarship focused on the LGBTQ community might be "too gay" to land a good job.

In the context of academic conferences, many scholars perform what Michael Armato calls "academic masculinity," a form of the patriarchal dividend that men experience in higher education.[59] He makes clear that while institutions of higher education produce much scholarship that problematizes and directly challenges patriarchal white supremacy, they are still structured by the very same systems they critique. Armato describes an experience at a sociological conference where the "academic gaze" was mobilized to "effectively frame those of us in the room as all-knowing and without prejudice and separating us from the people 'out there.'"[60] The people Armato describes in his study reflect the men—all white—who socialized me into my teaching profession; like the one who felt "his knowledge allow[ed] him to transcend the forces that exert so much control over less enlightened men."[61] This drives home the requirement that we engage in reflexivity and are willing to explore our own unconscious biases, including our beliefs that we have no biases.

Patriarchal white supremacy, in the form of "academic masculinity," is what shaped the hallway conversations about students that formed the backdrop of many of my experiences with informal socialization while going through the tenure process. These conversations included a plethora of arguments about students and their many "failures." Personally, this was at the peak of attention to and media coverage of the "Millennial generation," which only served to add fuel to the fire. Students were said to be entitled, lazy, disengaged, glued to their phones, uncaring, and unmotivated. They were framed by colleagues as horrible readers, writers, and thinkers. These were the same colleagues who would boast about scaring away students on the first day of class to weed out those students deemed uncaring or unmotivated.

Many of us were taught through these same scare tactics, by professors who spent the first day of class talking about how much reading, writing, scientific research, and/or artistic endeavors we'd have to do for their course. When we aren't otherwise taught to teach, we might be apt to recreate these practices in our own classes. Many writers have pointed out that graduate programs often do not train graduates in pedagogy and teaching skills, thus leaving us prepared, at best, to teach as we were taught. In higher education, this lack of teacher training[62] can lead to our being slow to implement student-centered practices.[63] As O'Shea Lane writes, "the K–12 educational system has long known that teacher preparation is a key to student success; however, this notion is just beginning to permeate in higher education institutions."[64] This means that in the vacuum of formal pedagogical training, informal socialization remains prominent.

Thus it is important to call attention to studies from the past few decades that make clear that gossip and complaints play a central role in informal faculty socialization. As Lauren Vargas wrote, "complaining about students happens in teachers' lounges and copy rooms all over the country. Teaching is hard work. But complaining about students is not only toxic for teachers' feelings about their work (and therefore their longevity in their jobs). It's detrimental to students."[65] This strategy—referred to in this book as faculty "moves to innocence"—reproduces power dynamics by shifting any blame connected to classroom problems onto students and other teachers. It's a form of NIMBY—not in my backyard—in the higher ed classroom. As Vargas points out, this produces a level of toxicity that harms students, especially in light of the structural constraints shaping their lives. One participant in an often-cited study from the late twentieth century on new faculty socialization reported the following:

> No, no one has said much about teaching. Mostly, I've been warned about colleagues to avoid. A lot of it is gossip and complaining. I can only think of two specific things that have been said about teaching here. One is how bad the students are . . . about how unprepared and unmotivated they are. The other one, that maybe two people mentioned, was a warning about the need to set clear rules and punishments on the first day of class. All in all, I'm pretty disappointed with the help I've gotten.[66]

This faculty member's experience in the 1990s mirrors my own experience in the 2010s. Still to this day there are senior faculty telling us to be hard, in the name of rigor, and to associate all that's wrong with the classroom with the students that walk through the doors.

These conversational shifts can be understood as faculty "moves to innocence."[67] From the perch of the tough expert demanding that students climb up to his level, to the complaints about the lazy, entitled, and internet-ruined "kids these days," to the all-knowing arbiter of (in)equality, faculty persistently shift the attention to the "other." As Tuck and Yang argue, "moves to innocence" are practices that allow a dominant group to maintain or restore beliefs in our own innocence despite the realities of our complicity in systems of inequality and structural violence.[68] Referencing Janet Mawhinney, they argue that "moves to innocence" are "strategies to remove involvement in and culpability for systems of domination."[69] In the classroom, this would look like faculty who recreate the chilly climate and the white racial habitus while blaming students—or high school teachers, or administrators, or any "other"—for the ensuing silences those climates produce.

As stated, the work of a "move to innocence" is to displace responsibility and in turn displace reflexive action. The focus is on making the dominant group feel better about, and ignore, their privileged relationship vis-à-vis systems of power. In the context of settler colonization it's about "making moves to alleviate the impacts of colonization"[70] without any real engagement with decolonization in the form of land redistribution; as they argue, "this violence is not temporally contained in the arrival of the settler but is reasserted each day of occupation."[71] For example, higher education is great at opening conferences on stolen land with a land acknowledgment but with no real or sustained conversation about how the land in question is harming or serving Native communities.[72]

Moves to innocence in higher education are about attempting to address structural racism, for example, in the form of achievement gaps and hiring practices without acknowledging our own role in having produced these dynamics, particularly in the form of our pedagogy. In the academy it's about the ways in which the chilly climate can be perpetuated through our teaching practices that normalize a white racial habitus and hegemonic masculinity—being a hard teacher, being rational, being the expert—while denying that we contribute to such structural inequities.

These structural inequalities shape our students' daily lives. Our students at both community colleges and universities bring complex lives into the classroom; certainly quiet in the form of mindfulness practices would be of benefit for them, as Song and Muschert suggest. And still, when scholars write about students, in particular about their levels of distractedness, they write, as an example, "[the students] lacked focus, were distracted by communication devices, or perhaps . . . they had never been taught how to push back distractions from their consciousness in favor of focused attention and engagement with their activities."[73] In my experience with digital technologies, all of us—students and faculty alike—face these dynamics of distraction. Despite our own inclusion in the realm of the distracted, this structural dynamic is often blamed on individual students and those other people out there (teachers, parents) who neglected to teach students how to harness their focus.

There are two things of note regarding the previous explanation of students' distractedness, both of which highlight how we engage in faculty moves to innocence. First, excluded from this list of reasons are the lived realities of some (many) of our students, especially first-generation students, first-year students, and those at the community college level: they are working two jobs, are engaging in familial care labor, and are managing bodies, including illness, all amid the general business of daily life. This was especially true in the era of COVID campus shutdowns. These distractions cannot be pushed into the "problems with modern technology" box of our students' classroom "problems."

Second, this exploration lacks professorial reflexivity in that there is no space granted for the possibility that the teacher's pedagogy is one (potential) cause of the distraction. That is, Song and Muschert rightly posit contemplative pedagogies as an antidote to students' distraction, but they don't ponder the role that our noncontemplative pedagogies (for example limited time for questions, an overreliance on PowerPoint, or long lectures) play in helping to produce the distractions in the first place. Instead they stick with the well-used shift to the cell phone–addicted "kids these days" trope.

I engaged in such moves to innocence all semester during that aforementioned fall of 2017. In addition to the blame and shame tactics I've already outlined, I was still deeply invested in Nicholas Carr's argument that Google was making *them* "stupid," all while my expert knowledge shielded me from this cultural pattern. While Carr centered himself in his piece, making arguments such as "what the Net seems to be doing is chipping away my capacity for concentration and contemplation,"[74] I saw this trend as impacting my students while (magically!) excluding me and my teaching praxis (unconscious bias hard at work). In particular, I had high expectations for participation but had been offering no classroom space for contemplation.

"Deep teaching"[75] is an antidote to these concerns, and *pedagogies of quiet* are a form of deep teaching. Central to a praxis of deep teaching, and grounded in feminist principles, is the idea of reflexivity. Dewsberry writes that "deep teaching [is] the constant, critical reflection practitioners apply to their awareness of self and student, as well as the degree to which this reflection informs the practice of an equitable pedagogy."[76] In 2017, I accused my nontalking students of being ill prepared for class, and despite the shame I felt wash over me during and after these moments of accusation, I continued to look for explanations outside myself. Rather than face this dynamic of shame and blame head-on, I continued to ignore this reality. I was not living out my values through my pedagogy; I was not deep teaching but instead relying on my own "moves to innocence."

Opening up to our responsibility and our vulnerability—to our underlying fears of failure for example—is a necessary component to *pedagogies of quiet*. AnaLouise Keating outlines "intellectual humility as an open-minded, flexible way of thinking that entails the acknowledgment of our inevitable epistemological limitations, the acceptance of uncertainty and the possibility of error, and intense self-reflection."[77] Faculty vulnerability is grounded in feminist theories and serves as a counter to faculty moves to innocence. In response to the embeddedness of the patriarchal white supremacist socialization many of us received, rather than aiming to be rational and hard, quiet pedagogues see our role as more embodied, challenging the mind-body split of Western Enlightenment ideologies, which are central to structures of inequality. We open up our classroom space to new and quiet ways of participating, allowing for more voices to be heard.

Silence as a Problem: Conclusion

We must make visible the inequities of our praxis so as to build a healthier, more equitable participation experience. Pedagogies of quiet are an excellent intervention around these institutional concerns as we use silence that leads to an engaged inner experience where students can express their ideas without their ideas being publicly judged or assessed as "right" or "wrong." Using silence so that students can tap into their inner quiet engages all students as whole people. This understanding of quiet pulls from Kevin Quashie's articulation in his work *The Sovereignty of Quiet*:

> In everyday discourse, quiet is synonymous with silence and is the absence of sound or movement, but for the idea of quiet to be useful here, it will need to be understood as a quality or a sensibility of being, as a manner of expression. This expressiveness of quiet is not concerned with publicness, but instead is the expressiveness of the interior. That is, the quiet of a person represents the broad scope of his or her inner life.[78]

Quiet is not an absence but a presence; a presence full of possibility. The classroom is not an apolitical or decontextualized space of experience and as such it can be used as a "stay against the social world."[79] As will be explored in the chapters to come, pedagogies of quiet offer students an educational space where they can be released from their fear of judgment as well as from actual public responses (that can be perceived as judgmental). This space is offered through silence, giving students the time to engage with their inner quiet, as well as through classroom engagement assignments that can be accomplished either silently, anonymously, or both, allowing them the opportunity to participate and shift past or through these fears of social judgement.

Pedagogies of quiet, like other feminist pedagogies, shine "a light on hegemonic masculinities, which attempt to disassociate teaching and learning from emotion and the [realm of the] embodied."[80] One way that we make this shift is through empowering students' voices by way of multiple routes—rather than a singular verbal standard—to participation (to be explored further in the coming chapters). The students surveyed for this project illuminate some of the complex ways that students' emotions shape their classroom experience, in particular, their relationship to verbal participation. Knowing these emotional realities helps us to develop tools to build pedagogies that reflect and care for students' embodied experiences in classrooms.

Pedagogies of quiet incorporate feminist—and sociological—arguments that we are not autonomous but rather exist in an interdependent relationship and must attend to this reality in our classrooms. Not doing so serves to reinforce our students' feelings of discomfort and disconnect and thus their silences. While we cannot alleviate their discomfort, we can use quiet participation practices that build their capacity to sit with discomfort and to more effectively engage with their classmates and the course material. In the process, this praxis seeks to illuminate and dismantle some of the problems of patriarchal white supremacy in higher education, while building something whole and quietly freeing.

NOTES

1. Sherry Turkle, *Reclaiming Conversation: The Power of Talk in a Digital Age* (London: Penguin, 2016).

2. bell hooks, *Teaching to Transgress* (Oxfordshire, England: Routledge, 2014).

3. Michelle Page, "LGBTQ Inclusion as an Outcome of Critical Pedagogy," in *The Critical Pedagogy Reader*, third edition, ed. Antonia Darder, Marta Baltodano, and Rodolfo D. Torres (Oxfordshire, England: Routledge, 2017), 347.

4. Page, "LGBTQ Inclusion as an Outcome of Critical Pedagogy," 348.

5. Page, "LGBTQ Inclusion as an Outcome of Critical Pedagogy," 350.

6. Elizabeth Ellsworth, "Why Doesn't This Feel Empowering? Working Through the Repressive Myths of Critical Pedagogy," *Harvard Educational Review* 59, no. 3 (1989): 309.

7. Ellsworth, "Why Doesn't This Feel Empowering?," 298.

8. Ellsworth, "Why Doesn't This Feel Empowering?," 308–9.

9. Paige L. Sweet, "Who Knows? Reflexivity in Feminist Standpoint Theory and Bourdieu," *Gender & Society* 34, no. 6 (2020): 924.

10. Sweet, "Who Knows?," 926.

11. Julia Phillippi and Jana Lauderdale, "A Guide to Field Notes for Qualitative Research: Context and Conversation," *Qualitative Health Research* 28, no. 3 (May 2017): 381.

12. Mary M. Reda, *Between Speaking and Silence: A Study of Quiet Students* (New York: SUNY press, 2009), 10.

13. Reda, *Between Speaking and Silence*, 15.

14. Kathy Charmaz, *Constructing Grounded Theory*, 2nd ed. (Thousand Oaks, CA: Sage Publications, 2014), 113.

15. Reda, *Between Speaking and Silence*, 15.

16. Sweet, "Who Knows?," 925.

17. Jennifer Llewellyn and K. Llewellyn, "A Restorative Approach to Learning: Relational Theory as Feminist Pedagogy in Universities," in *Feminist Pedagogy*

in Higher Education: Critical Theory and Practice, ed. Tracy Penny Light, Jane Nicholas, and Renée Bondy (Ontario, Canada: Wilfrid Laurier University Press, 2015).

18. Berg and Seeber, *The Slow Professor* (University of Toronto Press, 2018), 8.

19. Susan Cain, *Quiet: The Power of Introverts in a World That Can't Stop Talking* (New York: Crown Publishing, 2013), 77.

20. Janneke M. Frambach, Erik W. Driessen, Philip Beh, and Cees PM Van der Vleuten, "Quiet or Questioning? Students' Discussion Behaviors in Student-Centered Education Across Cultures," *Studies in Higher Education* 39, no. 6 (2014): 1003.

21. Cain, *Quiet*.

22. Frambach et al., "Quiet or Questioning?," 1003.

23. Robin DiAngelo, *Nice Racism: How Progressive White People Perpetuate Racial Harm* (Boston: Beacon Press, 2021).

24. Altheria Caldera, "Toward Wholeness: Anzaldúan Theorizing Used to Imagine Culturally Accepting Educative Spaces for Black Girls," in *Teaching Gloria E. Anzaldúa: Pedagogy and Practice for Our Classrooms and Communities*, ed. Cantú-Sánchez, Margaret, Candace de León-Zepeda, and Norma Elia Cantú (University of Arizona Press, 2020), 42.

25. Rita Kohli, "Breaking the Cycle of Racism in the Classroom: Critical Race Reflections from Future Teachers of Color," *Teacher Education Quarterly* 35, no. 4 (2008).

26. Jillian M. Duquaine-Watson, "'Pretty Darned Cold': Single Mother Students and the Community College Climate in Post-Welfare Reform America," *Equity & Excellence in Education* 40, no. 3 (2007): 234.

27. Marjorie L. DeVault, *Liberating Method: Feminism and Social Research* (Philadelphia: Temple University Press, 1999), 177.

28. Vivian García López, and Vivian García López, "The Struggles to Eliminate the Tenacious Four-Letter 'F' Word in Education," *Counterpoints* 422 (2012): 315.

29. Beth Berila, *Integrating Mindfulness into Anti-Oppression Pedagogy: Social Justice in Higher Education* (Oxfordshire, England: Routledge, 2015), 15.

30. Llewellyn and Llewellyn, "A Restorative Approach to Learning," 21.

31. Patricia Hill Collins, *Black Feminist Thought: Knowledge, Consciousness, and the Politics of Empowerment* (Oxfordshire, England: Routledge, 1990).

32. hooks, *Teaching to Transgress*, 16.

33. Kelsey Blackwell, "Why People of Color Need Spaces Without White People," *Arrow Journal*, August 9, 2018, https://arrow-journal.org/why-people-of-color-need-spaces-without-white-people/, 6.

34. Blackwell, "Why People of Color Need Spaces Without White People," 6.

35. Blackwell, "Why People of Color Need Spaces Without White People," 6.

36. E. J. Whitt, M. I. Edison, E. T. Pascarella, A. Nora, and P. T. Terenzini, "Women's Perceptions of a 'Chilly Climate' and Cognitive Outcomes in College: Additional Evidence," *Journal of College Student Development* 40, no. 2 (1999): 110.

37. Duquaine-Watson, "'Pretty Darned Cold,'" 234.

38. Darder, "Pedagogy of Love," 58.

39. Sheila L. Macrine, ed., *Critical Pedagogy in Uncertain Times: Hope and Possibilities* (New York: Springer Nature, 2020).

40. Jennifer J. Lee and Janice M. Mccabe, "Who Speaks and Who Listens: Revisiting the Chilly Climate in College Classrooms," *Gender & Society* 35, no. 1 (2021): 34.

41. Robert W. Connell and James W. Messerschmidt, "Hegemonic Masculinity: Rethinking the Concept," *Gender & Society* 19, no. 6 (2005).

42. Lee and Mccabe, "Who Speaks and Who Listens," 33.

43. Brian T. Ivory, "Little Known, Much Needed: Addressing the Cocurricular Needs of LGBTQ Students," *Community College Journal of Research and Practice* 36, no. 7 (2012).

44. Melvin Whitehead and Needham Yancey Gulley, "LGBTQ+ Matters and the Community College: Policy and Program Considerations for Students, Faculty, and Staff," in *Rethinking LGBTQIA Students and Collegiate Contexts: Identity, Policies, and Campus Climate*, ed. Eboni M. Zamani-Gallaher, Devika Dibya Choudhuri, and Jason L. Taylor (New York: Routledge, 2019), 124.

45. Chrys Ingraham, "The Heterosexual Imaginary: Feminist Sociology and Theories of Gender," *Sociological Theory* (1994).

46. Llewellyn and Llewellyn, "A Restorative Approach to Learning," 21.

47. Michael A. Messner, "White Guy Habitus in the Classroom: Challenging the Reproduction of Privilege," *Men and Masculinities* 2, no. 4 (2000).

48. Asao B. Inoue, *Antiracist Writing Assessment Ecologies: Teaching and Assessing Writing for a Socially Just Future* (South Carolina: Parlor Press LLC, 2015), 29.

49. Inoue, *Antiracist Writing Assessment Ecologies*.

50. Inoue, *Antiracist Writing Assessment Ecologies*, 49.

51. Frambach et al., "Quiet or Questioning?," 1003.

52. Kay Ulanday Barrett, "To Hold the Grief & the Growth: On Crip Ecologies," *Poetry Magazine*, January 2022, https://www.poetryfoundation.org/poetrymagazine/articles/156938/to-hold-the-grief-the-growth1-on-crip-ecologies, 319.

53. Krishna Bista, "Silence in Teaching and Learning: Perspectives of a Nepalese Graduate Student," *College Teaching* 60, no. 2 (2012): 78.

54. Hill, "Language, Race, and White Public Space," 479.

55. Ozlem Sensoy and Robin DiAngelo, *Is Everyone Really Equal?: An Introduction to Key Concepts in Social Justice Education* (New York: Teachers College Press, 2017).

56. Robin DiAngelo, *Nice Racism: How Progressive White People Perpetuate Racial Harm* (Boston, MA: Beacon Press, 2022).

57. Ellsworth, "Why Doesn't This Feel Empowering?," 307.

58. Ellsworth, "Why Doesn't This Feel Empowering?," 308.

59. Michael Armato, "Wolves in Sheep's Clothing: Men's Enlightened Sexism & Hegemonic Masculinity in Academia," *Women's Studies* 42, no. 5 (2013).

60. Armato, "Wolves in Sheep's Clothing," 588.

61. Armato, "Wolves in Sheep's Clothing," 590.

62. Terrell E. Robinson and Warren C. Hope, "Teaching in Higher Education: Is There a Need for Training in Pedagogy in Graduate Degree Programs?," *Research in Higher Education Journal* 21 (2013).

63. Daniel Z. Grunspan, Michelle Ann Kline, and Sara E. Brownell, "The Lecture Machine: A Cultural Evolutionary Model of Pedagogy in Higher Education," *CBE—Life Sciences Education* 17, no. 3 (2018).

64. Jill O'Shea Lane, "Lived Experiences of New Faculty: Nine Stages of Development Toward Learner-Centered Practice," *Journal of the Scholarship of Teaching and Learning* 18, no. 3 (2018), https://doi.org/10.14434/josotl.v18i3.23373, 2.

65. Lauren Vargas, "Complaining About Students Is Toxic. Here are 4 Ways to Stop," *Ed Week*, June 11, 2019, https://www.edweek.org/teaching-learning/opinion-complaining-about-students-is-toxic-here-are-4-ways-to-stop/2019/06.

66. Robert Boice, "New Faculty as Teachers," *The Journal of Higher Education* 62, no. 2 (1991): 155.

67. Eve Tuck and K. Wayne Yang, "Decolonization Is Not a Metaphor," *Tabula Rasa* 38 (2021).

68. Tuck and Yang, "Decolonization Is Not a Metaphor."

69. Tuck and Yang, "Decolonization Is Not a Metaphor," 69.

70. Tuck and Yang, "Decolonization Is Not a Metaphor," 63.

71. Tuck and Yang, "Decolonization Is Not a Metaphor," 65.

72. Elisa Sobo, Michael Lambert and Valerie Lambert, "Land Acknowledgements Meant to Honor Indigenous People Too Often Do the Opposite—Erasing American Indians and Sanitizing History Instead," *The Conversation*, October 7, 2021, https://theconversation.com/land-acknowledgments-meant-to-honor-indigenous-people-too-often-do-the-opposite-erasing-american-indians-and-sanitizing-history-instead-163787.

73. Kirsten Younghee Song and Glenn W. Muschert, "Opening the Contemplative Mind in the Sociology Classroom," *Humanity & Society* 38, no. 3 (2014): 316.

74. Nicholas Carr, "Is Google Making Us Stupid?," *Atlantic Monthly*, July 2008, https://www.theatlantic.com/magazine/archive/2008/07/is-google-making-us-stupid/306868/.

75. Bryan M. Dewsbury, "Deep Teaching in a College STEM Classroom," *Cultural Studies of Science Education* 15, no. 1 (2020).

76. Dewsbury, "Deep Teaching in a College STEM Classroom," 173.

77. AnaLouise Keating, *Transformation Now!: Toward a Post-Oppositional Politics of Change* (University of Illinois Press, 2012), 16.

78. Kevin Quashie, *The Sovereignty of Quiet* (New Jersey: Rutgers University Press, 2012).

79. Quashie, *The Sovereignty of Quiet*.

80. Sara C. Motta and Anna Bennett, "Pedagogies of Care, Care-Full Epistemological Practice and 'Other' Caring Subjectivities in Enabling Education," *Teaching in Higher Education* 23, no. 5 (2018): 633–34.

Chapter 2

It's Not All Talk

Listening to (Quiet) Students

Many of us have had—dare I say all of us?—plenty of moments as teachers, standing in front of a room full of students who won't speak. Some of us are compelled to encourage speaking because we have participation grades and don't want our quiet students to perform poorly. Others of us do so because we've been socialized to value gregariousness and extroversion. For many of us, it's both of these dynamics. Facing silence in the classroom can feel like a failure. Like Holmes, I've had many moments in class where "those moments of silence in the room [are] when I as the instructor question [my] pedagogical approach."[1] Pedagogies of quiet are an alternate approach in that they are a way to reframe the silence as a solution and not problem. Rather than come up with more ways to push the quiet students into verbalizing, pedagogies of quiet use these silences toward an academic advantage. We don't just allow them, we encourage them, we cultivate them, and we value them, even if doing so feels like swimming upstream.

Given that I have yet to meet another teacher who hasn't struggled with or been frustrated by quiet students—it's been the topic of many of my own department meetings—it's stating the obvious to declare that we aren't alone. It is, however, important to note that students notice and are impacted by these silences as well. Comments such as, "if it seems as if I'm the only one participating I will stop" proliferated in their survey responses. This makes it clear the process is cyclical and that the classroom is relational. That is, classrooms are built around expectations for verbal participation from teachers, and thus the ensuing silences that follow make both faculty and students uncomfortable. As one student put it, "it can be awkward if everyone in the room is silent as well." So, then, should we just barrel through those moments, striving for the kind of dialogue we often see as crucial for critical thinking and social justice, or should we rethink our approach? The argument presented here supports the latter.

As was made clear in chapter 1, speaking doesn't always result in being heard. Through observational data a pattern emerges whereby those students who talk too often can also become those who are most ignored. It's not uncommon for the rest of the class to roll their eyes when these "too much" participators raise their hands (again). These responses (the verbal snickers and the nonverbal eye rolls alike) in turn create a culture of judgment that further silences all students, lest they find themselves on the receiving end of such rudeness. The students in this study were in tune with their levels of participation—too much or too little—and also wanted to be sure that their contributions matter. As one student put it (and others expressed similar sentiments), "I only talk if I feel I have something valuable to add to the conversation." Many of them are willing to talk, but only within the context of amenable social conditions.

In the context of introductory classrooms, sometimes teacher and student goals do not align. When students are brand new to the content matter, listening is often a preferred learning method. Of course, this could also be habit, as our hierarchical, Western educational culture encourages the approach of professors filling up their (silent) students with knowledge. As one student put it, "often I find my comment or verbal addition to the class asinine. My speaking does not provide any additional information or benefit. It's better to let the professor do their job. So as I am the student, and they are the teacher." As pedagogies of quiet aim to dismantle binary thinking's pull on our classrooms, we can see both dynamics at play: a culture of and preference for listening rather than speaking, in the introductory classroom especially.

Both scholarly and empirical evidence reiterate the ideas that many faculty rely upon when engaging with their students and constructing their classroom praxis. The students themselves report awareness of teachers' expectations—they know we want them to talk (of course, this is obvious when we ask them questions!). The scholarly literature in turn points toward the devaluation of silence, and how silences can reflect both privilege and oppression.[2] In particular, most teachers see students' silence as a sign of disengagement.[3] Further, scholarship that presents the students' viewpoints on their classroom silences are limited; where they do exist, they focus on the international student experience and rely more on faculty perceptions.[4] This chapter aims to address this gap. Here we will explore students' relationship to classroom speaking—general classroom participation, not formal public speaking assignments—and provide a student-centered justification for pedagogies of quiet.

The association between participation and verbalization is a longstanding norm in higher education. For faculty who include participation in their assessment practices, such participation is most often measured through the frequency of students' verbal engagement. Susan Cain argues that practices like this emerge from a culture that has come to value extroversion at the expense of a very fruitful and creative introversion.[5] Further, verbal participation is seen to be more readily measurable, and this is in line with the productivity outputs that have come to be most valued in the context of academic capitalism. Bob Jessup argues that the neoliberal classroom is shaped by "new methods of teaching and research, such as exploiting new or enhanced information and communication technology . . . and seeking to cut costs and boost efficiency by standardizing learning and commoditizing education."[6] In this vein, classroom participation has become standardized, and our singular understanding of participation a commodified outcome of the educational process. In the current cultural and historical context it seems that the equating of verbalization and participation has become taken for granted.

At the same time, as will be detailed in the next chapter, existing pedagogical theories do point us toward pedagogies of quiet. Contemplative pedagogy certainly leads the way, but so to do antiracist and feminist approaches, along with critical pedagogy, such as those organized around compassion and love. As Antonia Darder writes, building on Paulo Freire's body of work, "educational practices powered by a radical love also create the conditions where students can explore their cultural histories, which can also enhance their individual expression in the classroom."[7] Pedagogies of quiet urge us to see this kind of exploration as requiring silent spaces for students to attune to their inner quiet, as preparation work for engaged dialogue, and so as to come to know themselves (as critical thinkers). That said, the most important nod in support of this approach comes from students themselves. The community college students in this study—all students enrolled in 100-level, introductory courses—tell us directly the value of pedagogies of quiet.

The data presented in this chapter highlight that there are some patterned reasons as to why students don't verbally participate. It also makes clear that if our pedagogical approach is inclusive of quiet, it will be much more inclusive of all of our students. As Cain points out, introverted students often feel left out and devalued, despite the evidence that "college students who tend to study alone learn more over time than those who work in groups."[8] Creativity flourishes amid quiet, in solitude, and our students deserve that time in our classrooms; we should push against the grain—against the rush that we feel working in neoliberal institutions—and cultivate the space and time for pedagogies of quiet.

Students note a multitude of reasons for not participating in class, some of which are grounded in their experiences in their bodies—personality traits and mental health, for example—while others have more to do with the social conditions within which students are operating. These reasons warrant serious consideration. According to the American Psychological Association, "more than 200,000 children lost a parent or primary caregiver to COVID-19."[9] The report continues, reiterating that homelessness, food insecurity, and poverty, among other structural forces, "can lead to stress-response patterns that are known to underlie mental health challenges."[10] The alarm about youth mental health has been raised, especially during the pandemic, and since the release of the Center for Disease Control's 2023 report on teen mental health. Directly and indirectly, the students in this study also tell us that these stressors and mental health concerns, among others, are shaping their classroom silences. All their reasons for their silences point us toward the justification for adopting pedagogies of quiet.

THE CHILLY CLIMATE AND CLASSROOM PARTICIPATION

As outlined in the methodology, students were asked both open-ended and closed questions about their feelings and perceptions around verbal classroom participation. When asked if they felt comfortable with verbal classroom participation, 15 percent of those students surveyed said a flat out "no," and the patterns that emerged from their reasoning centered on shyness, introversion, mental health, and fears of judgment. Pedagogies of quiet are strategies that aim to engage these students in classroom participation, without forcing them into verbal engagement when they aren't prepared or comfortable doing so. Given that we all have had at least a few students, if not many, each semester who *never* speak, it's important to know why they don't so that we can (re)assess how to reach and teach them. Yes, they are taking our tests and writing our papers, and in this way we can evaluate their learning; still we aren't (always) capturing the informal process of learning. This, of course, is what class participation is all about: creative and engaged—and sometimes messy and embarrassing—meanderings toward content mastery.

It has been made clear that gender plays a significant role in classroom participation, with women experiencing a "chilly classroom" that functions to the benefit of male students. In the data gathered for this project, women were (8 percent) more likely to respond to the question "Do you usually participate verbally in class?" with a static "no" response, while men were much more likely to state "yes" or "depends." Women often experience more doubt as a result of patriarchal dynamics in classroom participation.[11] And yet it's important to note here that for both male-identified and female-identified students, "sometimes" was a more oft-given response than "yes" or "no," making clear that there is further nuance to explore, within and beyond male dominance, in relation to student silences in participation. As gender scholars point out, there are hierarchies among men and women, rendering some men, for example, subordinate and/or marginalized.[12]

Among those who identified as male, the students who were not comfortable talking in class were men of color, highlighting the impact of "marginalized masculinities."[13] Men of color were more concerned with being judged by others; white men expressed more agency, such as framing their silence as a moment-to-moment preference. For example, one student who identified as a white male said that sometimes "I just don't feel like talking." In other cases, the white men framed their silence as a teacher problem, not a personal problem. 41 percent of white men said that they didn't want to be the only one talking.

On the other hand, 11 percent of those who identified as women of color reported being uncomfortable talking in class (that percentage was higher for those who identified as white women, at 16 percent). In another study, it was reported that women are more likely to experience microaggressions and often feel "criticized for their behavior."[14] These scholars shared the experience of a white woman who reported her assertiveness often makes her feel dismissed as being "too loud" or a "bitch."[15] In the current study, women were apt to report that they didn't like being the center of attention. 37 percent of women, as compared to 21 percent of men, reported that their classroom silences were shaped by fear, anxiety, shyness, and discomfort. Among white students (12 percent), there was a pattern of assertive language—"I'm fine talking" or "I have always been extremely outgoing and have never been shy of participating in class"—that was muted among students of color (fewer than 2 percent).

It is evident from other scholars' research that the chilly classroom also shapes students of color, international students, and LGBTQ students in varying ways, and with similar results to the gendered dynamics already discussed.[16] The students in this study were not asked direct questions about their race, class, or gender. This was not a study designed specifically to explore microaggressions or the chilly climate. The direction of the surveys was to allow students the opportunity to explain (without prompting or guiding questions) why they don't feel comfortable speaking in classrooms. In their answers, very few of them directly named race, class, or gender as drivers of their experience. And yet patterns do exist in the collective responses. A few students (1 percent) directly addressed discomfort around stigmatization emerging from language norms and the white racial habitus. Student responses that referenced classrooms as an "unsafe space" were focused on teachers' responses more so than their own identities. Other comments illuded to their identities, but these patterns are implicit not explicit. These inequities lurk in the (institutional and personal) background of their experiences and concerns.

The classrooms in this study, along with college classrooms across the United States, are statistically female dominated. A greater proportion of enrolled college students are women, and yet the chilly classroom persists.[17] In addition, even as more students of color are enrolling in higher education, research highlights how students of color are often highlighted in marketing materials while their actual needs are ignored.[18] This highlights the structural nature of patriarchal white supremacy and thus the importance of heightened attention to our pedagogies. As Tovar notes, "it has been noted that our educational system is particularly apt at recognizing specific cultural competencies commonly associated with the dominant culture, and compensates those individuals who already possess valuable forms of capital."[19] Talk is a kind of social capital, and in classrooms it predominantly accrues to men, to cisgender people, to the temporarily able bodied, and to white people.

Teacher reflexivity is crucial here, as the gendered, racialized, and ethnocentric chilly classroom emerges not just from the larger institutional context within which we are operating, but from us: those of us in the front of the classroom. Without realizing it, teachers' attempts to encourage classroom verbalization can sometimes result in further silences. We act as gatekeepers and as such we have a "determining role in either reproducing or interfering with the reproduction of class, racial, and gendered inequality."[20] Pedagogies of quiet direct us toward interference.

Survey Data: What Students Have to Say

What Students Have to Say About Their Teachers

Western culture, with its deep roots in hierarchical systems of inequality grounded in the superior/inferior binary, produce many taken for granted ideologies that become embedded into our classroom praxis. Often we are unaware of these ideas and their impact, such is their insidious nature. One such idea is the binary logic that presupposes an opposition between public and private. When operating from within this binary as teachers, we see our own work in the public context: public education for a public good. This leads to seeing the classroom as a public space where the goal is to get students out of their private shell so as to connect to and build a group experience.

Public spaces are often thought about through the lens of the collective. In the classroom, this comes through in our pedagogical focus on team building, icebreakers, and think-pair-share exercises, where often the "pair and share" component of the exercise gets the most attention. These practices are grounded in multicultural education theories and critical pedagogies alike. Central to developing critical thinking skills, and the tools to live and work in a globalized world, is the capacity to engage in dialogue in diverse contexts. At the same time, large groups can also be spaces where group identity can come to be oppressive, as when students are treated as tokens and expected to do the work of representing their group identity and educating the class.

And yet, as explicated elsewhere, students need us to do this community building. For many of the students surveyed for this project, discomfort with their peers was a central reason for their choosing not to participate in class. Whether their peers are uncomfortably judging them or if that's the perception our students have of each other, it's part of our task as teachers to create a space—or spaces—for classmates to get to know one another and build trust. Quiet practices, such as a found poetry exercise or the class playlist/mixtape (see chapter 3), are opportunities for students to engage with each other without having to be in the oft-dreaded "spotlight," thus giving them more breathing room to build comfort. In this process of trust building we are prescient of our students' vulnerabilities and implementing practices that hold them with care while also reaching toward engagement and connection.

That being said, pedagogies of quiet require that instructors use a mirror to explore the impact of our own human fallibility—our vulnerability—on our classroom culture. The students in this study have clearly had experiences in classrooms like the one outlined in chapter 1. Interestingly, the students who are outright uncomfortable with talking in class did not express the same level of concerns around classroom culture. Rather, they were focused inward: mental health, personality, fear, and discomfort. It was the students—83 percent of them—who were more apt (the "sometimes" and "yes" groups) to feel comfortable with participation that talked about the impact of others—and in particular their teachers—on their comfort levels. One student who is sometimes comfortable talking in class said that they lose this comfort because "some professors attitude/personality can make answering questions uncomfortable." Another "sometimes" student wrote, "when I know what I wish to share with the class is in confidence, then I love to participate. There's nothing worse than thinking you are correct and then you're hit with the 'mmm . . . not quite' response from your professors."

There is a problematic feedback loop at play here. Teachers expect verbal responses while at the same time are, in some cases, responding to students' participation in stifling and/or stigmatizing ways. In moments such as these, we (teachers) are helping to produce the silences that we dread. We are human. We get frustrated and insecure. Developing a practice of self-awareness is crucial if we want to avoid taking these emotions out on our students. Further, as stated previously, it's very challenging to move away from our expectations around talk and dialogue. It takes consistent focus and effort on our part to develop comfort with quiet participation. I am deep into writing this book and still facing this hurdle in my classrooms. On the other hand, as we will see in later chapters, the flexibility, compassion, and value embedded in quiet practices allow us to tip the balance (toward involvement) for those quiet students, while benefiting all students.

For example, if we want to ask the class a question about the content we've just presented so as to assess student comprehension, a quiet approach c/would include a few minutes for all students to write down their answer, followed by an opportunity to share their answer via classroom technology. All of their answers would then be displayed on the screen in the classroom. This entire process—taking up approximately five to ten minutes—happens in silence, giving students time to think through their own answers and then to read and ponder their classmates' responses. This preparatory work opens up the space for verbal engagement while also creating a culture where all of the students' responses are valued rather than (unintentionally) diminished. Mistakes can be made and trust can be built without the public messiness that students deeply fear, and that (sometimes) comes with verbal participation. We want students to "use their own existing knowledge and prior experience to help them understand . . . new material; in particular, [we want them to] generate relationships between and among the new ideas and between the new material and information already in memory."[21] Jumping directly into dialogue, according to students, is not the ideal route if this is our goal.

QUIET PRACTICE 2A: CROSSWORD PUZZLE REVIEW EXERCISE

Using an online crossword puzzle generator, this exercise brings both play and engaged thinking into review exercises. To use quiet as a strategy that builds toward greater comfort with talk, I give students ten to fifteen minutes to complete the crossword, in silence, using their notes and textbook. The principle here, of course, is that it's easier to talk when you already have some thought out and completed ideas to work with. From there, I have them pair up with a classmate to compare their work. After this, we get back together as a large group to complete the crossword together. At this point I free them from the expectation that they must raise their hands before they speak. Another approach is to have them do all the work without any talking—sometimes with soothing lo-fi music in the background—and compete (for dollar store gifts, campus gift cards, or simply for pride and fun) to see who can get the most answers in a certain amount of time. These crossword puzzles then become tools for studying for quizzes and exams; I always share a blank copy on the campus learning management system for future access.

As such, to be reflective of our position in the classroom isn't just about our power in relation to our students or our intersectional identities and the biases that emerge from our specific relationship to structural power. We want our students to be willing to make mistakes in the classroom while in many cases failing to acknowledge our own or, worse, being hard on ourselves in a way that doesn't help us grow and improve. As Kaufman and Schippers remind us, we must extend the compassion we are so often willing to offer our students to ourselves. Now, let me be clear about my own vulnerability all those years ago: I knew that I was a part of the communication problem in my classroom, but instead of facing that head-on, I ran away from the vulnerable feelings that were evoked—namely, failure—by blaming and shaming my students instead, and "shame is an effective method of silencing."[22] My initial unwillingness to be fully vulnerable led me to throw those midsemester check-in forms I sought away, so now I can only report on them anecdotally. But I know my students said, in various ways, that I was intimidating, too quick to shift away from and disregard their comments, and too impatient. They found my responses to their comments too corrective and thus preferred silence over the risk of feeling, as one student phrased it in survey data for this project, "put in their place."

To shift beyond this troubled space I had to become willing to let go of my defensiveness, my attachment to being the expert, to being right, and instead explore my own insecurities as well as my expectations that speaking equals learning. I still struggle with this. I still find myself having moments where I interpret silent students as my own personal failure. A quiet class can still trigger an internal belief that "class didn't go as well as I expected" or that a teaching tactic "didn't work as I hoped." Just as our students have wild and rich inner dialogues, so do we, and as such, to be reflective we must include attention to our own inner worlds, with all their rich feelings and emotions. Personally, after standing in front of that quiet class week after week, it became clear that I had some issues to address. Imposter syndrome is real for us teachers, especially for those of us who are female, young (appearing), queer, disabled, and/or people of color. As Taylor and Breeze comment, "academic imposter syndrome resonates with—yet rarely explicitly names—these structural inequalities."[23] From within this structural location, and with these emotional and institutional vulnerabilities, it can be hard to challenge the pedagogical status quo. My own fear of failure kept me from listening to the wisdom that my students had to offer me through their silence (and through their feedback on those forms!). In time, as I opened into a willingness to be reflexive, and to face those comments, I came to value my students' full humanity and thus their silences.

Regarding professorial accountability and our impact on the culture of our classroom, students have strong feelings. A common refrain from their survey responses was directly about the teacher/professor's role in creating an unwelcome space for classroom participation (as I had done in the past and still work to avoid in the present). Certainly some students do like to participate in class. As already stated, 35 percent of the students surveyed said that they are comfortable speaking in class. One student stated that she participates, unless she's not yet familiar with the material, because she "like[s] building a rapport with [her] teachers." At the same time, even those students who walk into our classrooms already comfortable with speaking in class note the importance of the teacher in shaping this comfort. In the words of another student, "the instructor makes all the difference in every aspect of the class. I find I engage more in a class when the instructor is open to it and into her students."

Students didn't always have a concrete language around why some professors feel "open" while others don't. But when they did pinpoint a concern, it was around our responses to their classroom verbalization. Comments such as "the professor makes me feel stupid for my comment or question" could just as likely have been what was reported on my midterm check-in survey from those years ago. Students have an understanding of when there is an "unwelcome instructor" of if there is "not [a] nice teaching environment." Certainly, a limit of survey data is the lack of follow-up questions, so we cannot extrapolate, in each circumstance, as to what specifically makes these students feel unwelcome (and it could differ from student to student). This is an area for future research.

Some students did give us a window into this, however, as they went into more detail in their survey comments. One student—someone who is usually comfortable talking in class—wrote that "in previous experiences in school, however, I would feel uncomfortable speaking if the instructor or classmates created an environment of judgement and looked down upon the student if they did not deem their participation as 'correct' according to their standards and/or expectations." One of the benefits of quiet classroom practices is that they help to dismantle this "environment of judgment," as well as to shift the "standards and/or expectations" into a shared rather than hierarchical relationship.

For example, the combined utilization of classroom technology and the participation journal (both practices are introduced in chapter 3 and outlined in detail in chapters 4 and 5) gives students opportunities to engage in classroom participation, verbally and in silence, in class and outside of class, and with terms that they help to set (such as what counts as participation). When asked in the survey "What makes you feel cared for in your class?" students said things like, "[my teacher] allowed us to write reflections explaining why we might not have done our best this week," that "[the teacher] writing comments in response to something we said in our journals made me feel that [my teacher] was genuinely trying to engage with every single student," and that "her direct commentary made me feel heard, and made me feel more comfortable opening up." Thus, we can "hear" from all students without forcing them into (stressful) verbal classroom responses. The care and relationship development that happen outside of class shape how students experience life inside the classroom.

That said, we can enter into our classrooms aware that students can sense an "unwelcome space," as one student reported, and remain aware of our own role—from body language, to tone of voice, to assessment practices, and more—in this process. We can remain mindful that some students have said of their teachers that "sometimes the professor or teacher makes me feel bad for answering" and think through how we might bring more compassion to our dealings with our students as they are verbally participating. We can unintentionally cause these harms through our devotion to the content—for example, our commitment to the right answer—and while it is of absolute import that we maintain our ethical commitment to teaching our disciplines, there is a way to strike a balance between a culture of care and a culture of critical thinking and content mastery. Students' silences instruct us to shift toward this more balanced direction, and we can use structured, engaged silences to help build this culture of care.

In addition to some students mentioning an unwelcome feeling in the classroom, students referenced that their verbal comments were not always encouraged because they felt their teacher to be rushed and in a hurry. This is another way that academic capitalism and the pressures on our time shape our classroom culture, and this clearly impacts students' comfort level with verbal participation. A few student comments highlight this:

- "With so many students in class there's often not enough time; conversation has already moved on, so I don't participate."
- "[There is] not enough space in the conversation."
- "My teacher doesn't give that many opportunities to participate."

This makes clear that we must take seriously Ellsworth's point that, "while critical educators acknowledge the existence of unequal power relations in classrooms, they have made no systematic examination of the barriers that this imbalance throws up to the kind of student expression and dialogue they prescribe."[24] These power relations are shaped by teachers' actions at the micro level, the macro-level forces of capitalism, as well as the politics of patriarchal white supremacy, and they can manifest in impatience, for example, in those moments when a question we've asked is met with silence, which we then respond to by moving on, erasing the silence with our own voice, or through forcing an unwilling participant to speak. In this latter circumstance, we might rely on our unconscious biases, picking on a student we already know to speak in class, facilitating the dominance of just a few voices in the participation ecology.

Another student brings this point home in addressing the way that power shapes their silences. They wrote on their survey that

> at [this institution] specifically I've learned to stay quiet after certain . . . debates. It honestly is a different environment, mostly good, though. I am from the city . . . I went to public schools and graduated from a great public high school, but I have lived in some of the worst neighborhoods most my life. The way SOME students/staff view "those people" from "those parts" of the city shows me how little minded they are so I don't speak on certain topics. (Emphasis in original)

Rather than risk being transformed into an "other," this student chooses silence. We might, as teachers, have access to "academic masculinity"[25] or we might respond with "white fragility"[26] or some other "move to innocence,"[27] but the fact remains: especially those of us who work at predominantly white institutions, this could be us or our colleagues. The patterns that emerge from the survey data presented here illuminate the role faculty play in shaping students' discomfort and cannot easily be brushed off as one-offs because of "bad apples." Collectively, teachers are a sociological force shaping students classroom experiences.

As a result of the oppressive structures that shape students' choices in speaking up as well as their silences, giving grades for verbal participation presents its own challenges and is something that is discouraged in pedagogies of quiet. Some students are direct in their comments on verbal participation grades: "I don't like participation points, I think they're unnecessary." Others go about in a roundabout way, with one student stating that

> I am just a really quiet person, so speaking up is very challenging and causes a lot of stress for me. If I absolutely have to, such as if my grade requires participation, then I will speak up, but otherwise, I usually don't say much, and if I have questions, depending on the professor, I either email them, stay and ask them one on one, or just struggle on my own. Classmates usually make me unwilling/uncomfortable to speak in class, kids are just usually rude, or I feel judged by them, so it's easier to just stay silent.

This quote highlights that students have questions and ideas and ways of engaging that they hold on to tightly rather than share. It also highlights that in students' worldview, as shaped by their classroom experiences, participation equals verbalization. This is how silence comes to be understood as a problem. Clearly, though quiet, this student is engaged. That said, in addition to some aspects of their personality, this student also makes a crucial point about silence as both oppressive and emancipatory. Most of us have been witness to our students being rude: we've all seen the eye rolls and the whispers and witnessed the verbal and nonverbal communications of teenage immaturity. Shared, communal silence frees them from this social judgment.

So the question is: What are we doing to create a culture that diminishes these kinds of power dynamics? How can we engage with pedagogies of quiet to create a more equitable and comfortable culture? One way that the Western binary of superiority/inferiority shows up in classrooms is through students' own internalized responses. Our students—all of us, really—can feel that their comments are "less than," or at least come to feel that way through interpreting their classmates' informal banter as communicating this inferiority to them. In this way, giving students spaces out of the spotlight of their peers can function to build trust and community through silence, where they can focus on accessing their inner quiet and their inner strength. In their quiet moments they can access, and we can encourage, positive self-talk, deep listening, and content engagement.

Further, given the role of the professor in creating the classroom culture, engaging in reflexivity and acknowledging our own vulnerabilities are a key component of this praxis. The encompassing philosophy of a quiet pedagogy encourages us, too, to allow for moments of quiet, including in relation to our responses to our students. We can give ourselves a moment of quiet pause to think through a compassionate response to our students' comments. We can give them—and us—quiet moments of freedom to express ourselves without verbal commentary, free to focus not on the peanut gallery but on developing our ideas and knowledge.

What Students Have to Say About Processing Course Content

It's common for many faculty to pause in the midst of a lecture and ask students if they have any questions. From there, it's common for students to remain silent, to shake their heads "no," and for the teacher to swiftly move on, back into the lecture. It is admittedly hard to "wait through the quiet of apparent indecision."[28] Silence can sometimes be a jumping off point for us to move students into small groups so that they can talk to each other about the content, in the hopes that these conversations will deepen their engagement. At the core of these methods is the professorial hope that our students are processing the course content.

The premise is that through student verbalization we will find the proof that we need: the proof that they are learning. At the same time, the data presented here makes it clear that silences can be just as productive. In the words of Hamelock and Friesen, silence can reflect the crucial moment "in which the student is crossing a threshold between the comfort of what is 'no longer,' and a moment of attainment or awareness that is 'not yet.'"[29] Which is to say, the absence of verbalization is as intimately connected to their learning, to their engagement with the material, as their speaking. What if sometimes students have, in the words of one, "nothing to say," and what if that were, for a moment even, okay? For many of the students in this study, this was precisely the case.

When asked why they don't participate in class, it was clear that students were using silence as a strategy to think through what they were learning and wanted this to be a quiet, internal process (rather than an out loud, verbal one). Overall, 34 percent of students registered in an online course said that they preferred not to speak in class when they were not (yet) comfortable with the material. The discourse that emerged from their open-ended responses was phrased in various ways, though the general theme was consistent. For those students registered in a face-to-face course at the time of their survey, 59 percent of students chose "not (yet) comfortable with the material" as one of the barriers to their verbal participation. When asked an open-ended follow-up question, 32 percent referenced their familiarity and/or comfort with the course content as a factor that shapes their classroom participation.

Another pattern emerged from this data. Some students stated that they were flat out unwilling to participate in class. Or, put another way, when forced to participate, they will, but when given the choice they will not. These "no participation" students were less overtly concerned with content mastery. While 65 percent of them selected understanding of the content as a barrier, only 1 percent of them wrote about comfort with course content in the open-ended follow up response. These "no" students framed their experience through a mental health lens; 56 percent of these students said that anxiety, depression, or mental health shaped their participatory experience. 76 percent of them reported they were too shy or introverted to speak up. On the other hand, 69 percent of students who are "sometimes" comfortable with participation—those students whose willingness to engage verbally is conditional—selected "not (yet) comfortable with the course content" as their barrier, while 33 percent of them raised the issue in their open-ended follow-up statements. Finally, those students who are the most comfortable with participation referenced content mastery as the primary reason for their silences: 41 percent of face to face and 46 percent of online. These "yes" percentages are lower in part because of the higher no response rate to the follow-up question (25 percent of the "yes" students skipped the open-ended question that asked for more details about their [dis]comfort).

Regardless of their overarching (dis)comfort with verbal engagement, many students made it clear that their reasons for opting out of participation stems from the complex ways that they engage with the material; faculty "moves to innocence" aside, this particular silence can be a sign of active participation. One student frankly states that they don't participate verbally in class when they "don't know the content well enough," while another states that they are "stuck in thought." Oftentimes when teachers ask questions, the seconds-long pause we offer afterward doesn't leave enough time for students to get unstuck or to get to a place where they know the material better. A student who is sometimes comfortable participating explicated that when she is quiet, when she doesn't participate, it's because of her relationship to the content:

> I usually verbally participate if I understand the material and want to expand on something. When I don't, it is because I don't understand the material as well and I am better at working out things in my head and not aloud. If I am called on to participate when I don't understand it makes it even worse and discourages me.

This student's comment highlights a central tenet of quiet pedagogy: our praxis needs to recognize that not all student engagement can be captured when we only rely on verbal participation. Instead we need to allow the time and space for students to engage with their inner quiet so that they can work things out, on their own, in their heads.

While some students will participate in these moments—"I speak when I'm confused about what we are learning"—most opt to wait. In fact, more students surveyed here reported that confusion about the topic decreased—rather than increased—their willingness to participate. They said that they won't speak up "when [they're] confused about what we are learning." They stated that when they were "unsure" or in "doubt" or "not comfortable," then they remain silent rather than speak up. This certainly points us in the direction of future research, to explore why students often prefer to struggle alone. Context is also important here, and as such, this context should drive our pedagogical approach.

First-generation and first-year students, at two-year and four-year institutions alike, are key constituents of a social justice educational approach. As Pratt and colleagues write regarding first-generation students, "in addition to financial stress, at-risk students are less confident about their academic ability and report anticipating difficulty with forming relationships with their on-campus peers."[30] This argument is empirically supported by these students; pedagogies of quiet take this reality to heart and provide first-year and first-generation students the (quiet) space to enter into academic conversations at a pace that is appropriate to their content exposure and experience level. We don't see this is as a lack or a gap but rather a learning approach that acknowledges students' human need to consider new ideas prior to (graded) requirements for dialoguing.

In some cases, this silence is as much about education culture at large as it is about an individual student's needs. Western culture is awash in binary logic, and one way this shapes our institutions and classrooms is through the belief in either a "right" or a "wrong" answer. Certainly, a math class, a history class, an art class, and an anthropology class might have their own disciplinary logics around how many answers there are to any given question. But the teach to the test context of the neoliberal university is pushing a rigid culture that stifles the process of learning. This forces educators and learners alike to push through or ignore the messy and creative realities of making mistakes along the way, all in the name of getting the "right" answer, the "right" test scores, and thus the institutional right to continue to operate as a place of learning.

These institutional forces have a significant impact on student participation. For example, one student stated that they don't like to participate, especially when "I feel like my idea isn't correct or is somewhat useless." Another student posited that "I want to know my answer is correct before speaking." These students have been socialized into a context whereby it's "normal" for them to believe that their ideas could be incorrect or that their ideas are useless, or that the "correct" answer comes *before* speaking rather than *through* speaking. Sentiments such as this one abound in the data collected here, making it clear that there's a sociological process at play. Students aren't taught to see their untested ideas as useful, particularly in a system that values test scores, GPAs, and credentials more so than critical engagement with the world of ideas.

While some students are outright unwilling to speak until they know the "right" answer, others express significant doubt about any and all answers. They don't feel their answers are ever "right." It is this doubt, this fear, that shapes their unwillingness to verbally participate in class. Students made comments such as "I'm afraid my ideas won't contribute much to the discussion" and "I am afraid to make mistakes." Many others say they don't speak in class because they "doubt [their] answers." The words to highlight here are "afraid" and "doubt." As previously stated, these doubts are not uncommon—nor problematic—for first-year and first-generation students. English language learners and students of color, as reported in other studies, feel similar doubts that emerge from the ways in which ethnocentrism and racism shape their experiences and others' perceptions of them.[31] Our students walk into our classrooms with these fears and doubts, and without a pedagogy that challenges this cultural pattern, they will leave our classrooms with these same feelings. All students deserve the time and space to discover and access their cultural capital and to be socialized into the college context.

This fear of the wrong answer, in addition to being impacted by oppression and ethnocentrism, is at least partially shaped by the ways in which higher education has become organized around a market logic. Values such as "productivity, efficiency, metrics, [and] data-driven value" shape decisions both at the administrative level and in classrooms.[32] In this way, the "right" answer is seen as the necessary data for students to feel a sense of worth, either on the test or, more relevant here, when participating in class. The neoliberal university can be a cutthroat environment. The stressful dynamics of competitive capitalism, as embedded in higher education, shape students' beliefs in their own capacities from within institutions that aim to "promote a 'technically trained docility.'"[33] It is from within this space that students' fears of making mistakes—a form of this docility—lead to their silence. As Henry Giroux writes, "missing from neoliberal market societies are those public spheres—from public and higher education to the mainstream media and digital screen culture—where people can develop what might be called the civic imagination."[34] In the quest for the "right" answer, students fail to engage their imaginative capacities.

A culture of efficiency shapes many aspects of students' responses about classroom participation. Here are a few comments from students about why they (sometimes) don't speak in class:

- "I struggle to put my thoughts into words."
- "I overthink the answer which makes me nervous."
- "I have a hard time being concise."
- "I don't want to go off topic."

All of these responses reflect students' perceptions that there is not enough space—or time—in the classroom for uncertainty, nor for long-winded, prolonged responses or discussions. Some pedagogical approaches certainly welcome these "diversions," but they often speak to an upper-level institutional context. Becky Thompson writes that

> what students have taught me is that inviting the body into the classroom can't be a onetime thing. It can't be an intellectual exercise. I can't afford to skip steps in making this invitation real. For form and content to be in sync, I need to pay attention to both of them each day, see how they align themselves. I have to counter my worries that precious time will be lost if I make space for the body. I have to stop rushing. This is hard.[35]

She acknowledges that as teachers it's hard for us to allow extra time—for getting stuck, engaging in dialogue, or for embodied "interruptions"—and yet it's a crucial step for the slow pedagogue, for the social justice educator, for the contemplative. At the same time, while some work in a 200-level course with a teaching assistant, many other teachers are working without such support in high-volume introductory level classes. As such, pedagogies of quiet encourage the incorporation of the space not just for embodiment but for meta-cognition and other quiet pedagogical approaches that are useful and relevant to first-year and/or first-generation college students.

Here we are expanding these pedagogical conversations—slow professors, embodied professors, critical professors—with the aim to disrupt this culture of efficiency while providing students with the tools to increase their comfort with the inevitable feelings of uncertainty that come with learning. Indeed, in my observations—of my own classrooms and my colleagues—students often lose focus when there's a prolonged engagement between a single student and the instructor around a question. In addition, faculty often encourage those students who ask "too many" questions to come to office hours, so as to save class time for the required content. These patterns are related—students sense teachers' discomfort with straying too far from their lesson plan and thus self-police their potential "rambling" distractions. And yet, always, our students' thoughts are still there, and one of the aims of pedagogies of quiet is to balance what we see on the exterior with the realities of students' interior lives. Learning is primarily understood through a verbal lens, and as a result, we don't capture these internal daydreams as learning moments.

Daydreaming (in class) is something that can (by some) be seen as "wasted time." Sun and Shek reported daydreaming as an informal but still problematic classroom behavior.[36] Because teachers are apt to feel like we don't have enough time, we scramble to avoid wasting this precious commodity. Time is crucial to learning, and it is also something that is stripped from us as a result of academic capitalism.[37] Many students reported that they don't speak up in class because they haven't had the sufficient time to process and make sense of the material that they are learning. "Time is a key coercive force in the neoliberal academy,"[38] and this is evidenced in our rush to move through the material, offering only brief moments for questions or comments.

Even when we do give students the opportunity to delve more deeply—through a think-pair-share activity, for example—we put time structures around the experience and rush to end this time once we sense that the students are no longer talking about the question(s) at hand. Time, in this way, becomes a central tool for the silencing of students.[39] The slow professor movement, however, "urges that we act with purpose, cultivating emotional and intellectual resilience to the effects of corporatization in the academy." [40]

One student puts it this way:

> I take time to process, I have anxiety, and I'm generally quiet-ish. I enjoy learning and I want to participate but it's not always comfortable to speak up

and sometimes questions don't always feel welcome. My least favorite thing teachers did in in-person class was when they'd talk at us for a long time, then pause five seconds to ask if there's any questions—how can I process what the teacher's taught and then unexpectedly ask a question before the five or seven seconds are up. (And yes, I understand many teachers are on a time limit and that lectures are a part of college "learning"—doesn't mean I think they're helpful to me.)

It is clear from this student's comment that they want to participate, but don't feel they have adequate time to either process the material or to interject into the conversation. Often as teachers, we have an expectation that students will speak up immediately, and when they don't, we move on. We don't offer up prolonged, productive silence. Instead we push through it, creating a culture of time—in particular, a perception that we lack sufficient time—that leaves many students feeling that their ideas and questions are unwelcome.

In my experience, this also relates explicitly to the 100-level context, whether we are teaching at a two-year or a four-year university. For those of us who aren't teaching majors and/or graduate students, where our goal is for breadth not depth, nor have we developed the interpersonal relationships that emerge in such a context, we are at heightened risk to rely upon this more "coercive" form of time that functions so well in academic capitalism. When our primary task is to teach introductory courses, we feel a greater pressure to get through "all" of the material (whatever that "all" means in our disciplinary context).

What, then, is needed to shift these dynamics? Giroux argues that "the question of what kind of education is needed for students to be informed and active citizens in a world that increasingly ignores their needs, if not their future, is rarely asked."[41] But here we will again pose this question. Pedagogies of quiet are useful here for two reasons. One, they give students the time they need to deepen their understanding of the material and to find some confidence in both their process and their ideas. Two, they give teachers the tools to counter the neoliberal culture and to produce a classroom culture that values process as much as outcome.

It's a remarkably simple and valid explanation for student reticence toward verbal participation: they just don't know the content well enough. Sure, as evidenced in the discussion of socioemotional considerations in chapter 5, some of this has to do with a fear of judgment, but that doesn't explain it all. Some students need more time with the content in order to be prepared for verbal participation. One student wrote that they don't participate in class when they "just feel like what I have to say isn't correct." Another student went into more detail: "For me, there's always the fear of being incorrect

> **QUIET PRACTICE 2B: MID-CLASS CHECK-IN**
>
> The purpose of this practice is to disrupt lecture and discussion, to create time and space for students to quietly reflect on the material they are learning. Use a "scales" option in your classroom technology platform and provide a few concepts/ideas that were presented/discussed in the first thirty minutes of your class. Ask the question, "Which topics, concepts, or ideas to you want to spend more time with?" Whichever option gets closest to "strongly agree" becomes the topic for an on-the-fly exercise, where students type into your polling software of choice anything they remember about that topic so that the instructor can get a sense of where the students are with the material. From there, based on the patterns that emerge, the instructor can present any clarification through a brief lecture to be followed up with a writing prompt for some quiet reflection. This will ensure that students have had ample time to digest the material that they stated they wanted more time with.

especially in a classroom setting. Other times it's usually because I do not know enough about the topic to speak on it or have an opinion."

While this could be understood through the lens of fear and judgment, it can also be extrapolated that when these students gain more confidence in what they are learning—when they feel like what they have to say is "correct" or in line with the content—they will be willing to speak up. Quiet pedagogies give them both the time to develop their learning and the direction to look inward, focusing on their thoughts and ideas, while reflecting on their accomplishments over time, thus building their confidence (more on this in chapter 4).

What Students Have to Say About Classroom Size

Many of the students in this study made it clear that they want to have more time with the material they are learning before they are ready and willing to speak to those subjects among their peers in class. There are also plenty of other factors that shape their willingness to speak. Disrupting hegemony in our classrooms can be facilitated through engaging dialectically with the ideas of "public space" (school, the classroom) and "private lives" (our students' inner world, their humanity, life outside the classroom), as both are always at play in our online and physical classrooms. To allow for our full humanity to be on display, we must acknowledge the ongoing inner life that shapes all of our experiences in learning spaces, students and teachers alike. In fact, using strategic silence so as to welcome this quiet is a data-driven way to engage students, enhance participation, and embrace a compassionate classroom; a "culture of care."[42] The students surveyed for this project reiterated that classroom culture is crucial and that we must hold ourselves accountable as the curators of this culture. The "conversational architecture,"[43] as it is shaped by patriarchal white supremacy, can easily become a chilly climate for our students. The physical architecture can play a role as well.

One clear pattern that emerged from student responses regarding classroom culture had to do with the size of the classroom. This was especially the case for students who were surveyed in face-to-face courses (those surveyed while enrolled in online courses did not note class size at the same rates). For the students surveyed in face-to-face courses, 13 percent of them checked a large classroom as a barrier to their comfort with verbal participation. For students who reported not being comfortable with participation, 35 percent were concerned with class size, while only 14 percent of students who were (usually) comfortable with talking reported this same concern. The follow-up comments make it clear that the more peers there are in the room, the more social judgment is possible, thus this class size–driven fear.

It's important to address this and give it some space here, because so many of us are—or were, prior to the COVID pandemic, and likely will be in the future—teaching in larger classrooms with 100-level students, and yet much of the pedagogical literature engages with student discussions through the lens of small groups, advanced level, and/or seminar-style classrooms. One study, for example, reflected that "it seemed that over the short few weeks together, we were forming a family of 17."[44] This piece of scholarship on contemplative pedagogies is remarkably insightful, but we have to think through how to translate what's possible with seventeen students into what's possible with fifty or one hundred and fifty students.

Many felt that the larger the class, the more likely they were to refrain from verbal participation. And it wasn't always out of a sheer refusal: as reflected in one student's comment, a larger class makes it "hard to speak up," especially for those with a "soft voice." Others said that it was difficult to feel connected in larger classes. One student put it this way: "if the class is very large it is hard to always stay connected and speak up." For those of us well versed in teaching large lecture survey classes, we've seen this play out, often leading to teachers' offering up minimal time for discussion, as previously discussed. In the context of the banking model of education, this is a structural constraint that most of us are unable to fully address. At the same time, through pedagogies of quiet, we can broaden our understanding of classroom participation beyond the traditional verbal question and answer sessions to deepen engagement from within the constraints of a large classroom (see chapter 5).

While the students in this study expressed greater concerns about speaking up in larger classes—and though we do not have an operational definition of what makes a class large—smaller classes come with insecurities as well. In my experience, the intimacy of a smaller class can be just as silencing. In this context students need more community and trust building before they are willing to engage in discussion. In either case, whether large or small, students reported that it was hard for them to speak up when they didn't know their peers. This would be an excellent place for future research to explore the qualitative and quantitative difference between verbal participation in small and large classes, as well as the ways pedagogies of quiet can be useful in both contexts. What we do not need to do, however, is assume that because a student isn't talking that they aren't engaged, as listening is a crucial way to engage in the learning process.

What Students Have to Say About Listening

Deep listening is an emerging theme in the social justice literature. As discussed in chapter 1, speaking but feeling unheard, in addition to being denied a voice, are strategies for dominant groups to maintain power. Marjorie DeVault wrote that

> the social relations of speech, listening, and acknowledgement are embedded in a larger hegemonic discourse. As Lugones suggests, some things can be effectively said—that is, heard by particular others—while other messages intended by speakers are often misheard or unacknowledged. This observation suggests that the problem is not merely one of participation, but of how the "conversation"—through its organization, forms, and traditions—excludes the particular things that cannot easily be said and heard. A radical challenge to "silencing" would need to identify these forms and traditions, and actively seek some counter-hegemonic praxis with the potential to interrupt traditional relations of speech and authority.[45]

This hegemonic conversational structure is certainly at play in (some of our) classrooms, as evidenced by students' articulation of their discomfort with verbal engagement. Through student-centered data, pedagogies of quiet aim to push us beyond the surface of classroom participation into a deeper understanding of the complex dynamics at play, including our students' external reactions and their inner worlds. In doing so, we hope to "interrupt traditional relations of speech and authority" in the classroom, granting students more agency over the ways in which they participate in class, allowing for more to be said and heard.

As such, disrupting these power dynamics requires not just that we give people a voice but that we take the time and give attention to listening.

Pedagogies of quiet recognize that listening is as crucial to learning as speaking. In fact, rather than framing listening and speaking as being diametrically opposed (one is either speaking or listening), we understand that listening to *ourselves* is a crucial component in learning because we are always "speaking" in our minds. Both are integral processes that should be equally valued in the classroom. Renita Wong writes that "this integrated concept of language or logo, with its semantic roots encompassing both listening and speaking, was gradually 'reduced by half' in the course of Western history to primarily represent 'vocalization' and 'sound and voice,' which comes to shape all the rational pursuits."[46] Framed through Western patriarchy, voice is associated with the rational masculine sphere, while listening is seen as a more feminine, emotive process. As such, listening—except when listening to the expert—came to be devalued, *as participation*, in the classroom.

Students, however, challenge this Western patriarchal framework. While listening to others was a minor theme that emerged from one data set—only nineteen students, in explaining their discomfort with verbal participation, made the direct case that they would rather listen to others—the theme did emerge, inadvertently, in responses to other survey questions. In response to questions about the classroom technology used in face-to-face classes, students very strongly appreciated being able to hear from (more) others. For those students surveyed in the online context, many mentioned the online platform used for engaging with their classmates as a key component of their connection to the course. Students enjoy listening to their classmates!

Scholars argue that deep listening is about listening to self, to others, and to the social environment,[47] and the students in this project support this approach. A few of the students surveyed made the case that they sometimes don't speak in class because they are busy listening, and often they did so by framing the issue through the lens of learning values. While one student said directly that "I would rather just listen," without specifying whom they are listening to—the teacher, their classmates—others make the case more pointedly, by stating that "I would not say that I'm uncomfortable or unwilling [to speak up in class], but instead I see value in listening to what other people have to say." This matters to pedagogies of quiet, as the goal is to broaden participation beyond the verbal realm. As such, listening matters and should be equally valued as a crucial component of students' participatory experience in class.

As it is the case that vocalization is connected to a Western worldview of patriarchal white supremacy, it's also important to point out that listening—and deep listening in particular—is seen as a central leadership quality of Indigenous communities. That is, as there are multiple pathways to knowledge production, there are also multiple pathways to learning. To disrupt Western ideologies of inequality in our classrooms we can look to other forms of knowledge about (good) pedagogy. Further, indigenous understandings of deep listening are really about fostering "community and reciprocity,"[48] which are central aims for most instructors. Susan Cain's research on introversion bear this out as well: leadership doesn't have to be loud, it can be quiet.

In this case, what students are pointing to is important. They are pointing toward a pedagogy that gives students the space to make sense of their own thoughts in relation to what others are saying. That is, our students (often) know their own thoughts—living in our bodies as we do, we are all most familiar with our own thought processes—and prefer to stay silent so that they can hear and consider what other people have to say. As a practice of deep listening, they are making the case that we should see students' silences as productive. As Kerri Laryea writes, deep listening is a "practice of listening deeply to one's self, others, and world in order to change or deepen one's understanding and way of being in the world."[49] This highlights the active engagement of deep listening, where students are attentive to their own thoughts and ideas in relation to others at the micro and macro levels.

One student asserts that "I like to hear what everyone else's ideas are." They are articulating this process of engagement with a diversity of ideas, in order to develop their own thinking and to learn the course content. At the same time, we need to recognize that if all of our students are hoping to listen, then no one will be speaking. The push toward pedagogies of quiet isn't about shifting our allegiance from speaking to listening; it's about finding a way to balance and value both as necessary to learning and to rethink our expectations around participation as a result.

At the same time, most teachers know from experience that there are those students who like to dominate the conversation. Some of the students in this study were aware of their own tendencies to dominate and as a result explained their classroom silences through this lens: "I want to give others a chance to speak." Seen in this way, some students' silence in the classroom is a gesture of consideration. Others, however, frame it through the lens of being unheard in statements such as "I feel like no one is listening to me when I answer." So often we make assumptions about what our students' motivations are, but unsurprisingly the discourse of "kids these days" and the faculty moves to innocence we sometimes rely upon aren't present when students explain their own reasons for not participating in class. While some students did mention the need for sustenance—food, coffee, sleep—and a few of them admitted to disinterest—all told, only 1 percent of students explained their lack of participation through the lens of mood, (dis)interest, or a lack of basic needs—in cases such as the one previously quoted (a student wanting to ensure other students space to speak) there is a generosity that is sometimes ignored by teachers.

At the same time, the need to listen, or preference for listening, to others is a sign to teachers that we need to help cultivate our students' sense of agency. Pedagogies of quiet, and the social justice implications of their use, will be explored further in later chapters, including the role of developing our students' sense of agency in their learning experiences. That said, when students talk about why they don't participate in class, what they say about their silences are instructive toward this end. One student, for example, said that "I assume others understand the material better" and that they'd rather listen to those who know more, while another states, "when I am not confident about my answer, I usually [don't] respond and carefully listen to others and compare mine with them." Still another student explains, "I doubt myself and I think that I do not know the correct answer, and I also like to hear other people's explanations and opinions and that helps me solidify my answers and opinions and a lot of the times helps explain things." There's a balance to be found here, in respecting students' desire to listen to others (classmates and teachers both) as a central component of the learning process and in working through their doubts. While deep listening is an important goal for student participation, it's also important to find ways to cultivate students' confidence in what they do know and their comfort with what they do not yet know.

Deep listening is important to social justice education because it opens up more room in our classrooms to create the space and time for historically marginalized groups to speak and to be heard. As one student said, "I like to hear what everyone else's ideas are," making clear that our students emphasize the importance of attending to diverse perspectives. At the same time, they see listening as central to learning. One student writes that "I'd rather listen so that I can learn." No matter how they frame their desire to listen, they make it clear that it's integrally tied to their learning. Students' classroom silences aren't necessarily a sign of passivity, as some might assume, but are signs that our students are active agents in their own learning and are choosing to listen as a part of that process.

Sometimes we might appear to be quietly listening, but really what is happening on the inside is loud, and we aren't really listening. Instead we are planning what we want to say when it is our turn to speak. Deep listening, then, is a skill that needs developing. Deep listening is a key praxis of pedagogies of quiet, and as such, we are encouraged to rethink our automatic associations between classroom participation and talk. Shared silent time in the classroom gives students the space for cultivating a quiet that is internally loud, and thus they are more able to be present to listen to others when it is time to talk. Inclusive teaching strategies call for attentiveness to student voice, in particular so that marginalized students aren't excluded nor privileged students riding the waves of the normative.[50] Pedagogies of quiet expand on this inclusiveness by acknowledging that students' deliberate silences are a valid component of their voices while also opening up the space for more student voices (such as the introverted and the anxious) to enter into conversations.

What Students Have to Say About the Body

Teen anxiety is on the rise: "The prevalence of anxiety is as high as 35% in tertiary students," and that was before COVID disrupted our lives.[51] 44 percent of teens reported that they were persistently sad in 2021.[52] There is a lot of focus on girls' mental health, especially in relation to social media use, but boys are struggling too, as evidenced, for example, by the rates of young men perpetrating mass shootings. All of this points to the stressors in our students' lives and the ways that these stressors manifest in the body, and how the body impacts student success. Pascoe, Hetrick, and Parker report that "[students] with higher self-reported anxiety and depression symptoms were found to achieve poorer grades on examinations."[53]

Whether students are comfortable with verbal participation or not, they come into the classroom with bodies, and those bodies have fluctuating heart rates, sweat glands, and blushing cheeks. For many of us—myself included—the prospect of speaking in front of a group instigates these physiological responses. For some of us, we can use our breath or some positive self-talk to push through and speak up anyway; for others, they shut down. One student who is sometimes comfortable talking in class mentioned her physiological response: "Sometimes even if I have the correct answer I struggle to speak out, afraid of how people will react, whenever I need to talk in class my heart races, hands get sweaty and shake, and I often have to rehearse what I will say." This embodied response to verbal participation makes clear the benefits of pedagogies of quiet: when students are rehearsing their responses, they aren't listening to what anyone else has to say and thus could miss out on key learning moments. Cultivating spaces for quiet, on the other hand, allows for students to "rehearse" in a space of collective quiet. Students can then engage with their central nervous systems prior to verbal participation and without having to miss out on the opportunity to listen to others.

Another physiological component often mentioned by students comes as no surprise in the context of twenty-first-century capitalism and the meritocratic push of the neoliberal academy: students are tired and burnt out. This is likely the case across the board, but for the students in this study, exhaustion is enhanced by both work and family responsibilities. In the United States, it has been reported that approximately half of all full-time students are employed and around 85 percent of part-time students are employed.[54] Nationally, 30 percent of community college students are working forty-hour work weeks in addition to their schooling.[55] At this local institution, 56 percent of students are working either full or part time. Anecdotal experience at the midwestern community college that is the focus of this study also illuminates that many of the students surveyed here are actively involved in unpaid family labor.

During and since the shutdown phase of the pandemic, conversations about work-life balance have flourished. And yet those conversations rarely shed light on the ways that educational attainment shapes our feelings of imbalance. When asked what matters more, being a student or a worker, 64 percent of community college students stated that both were equally important; only 31 percent said that being a student was most salient.[56] Thus, it comes as no surprise that students report that they are "too tired" or "zoned out," as explanations for their lack of classroom participation. Other ways this was reported were through the language of energy. One student said that they usually do participate in class, except when they are "feeling too low energy," while another stated that they sometimes don't participate because they "need coffee." A simpler way of articulating this was the student who said that they don't participate because they "just don't want to talk."

Work and family life might shape the energy level students bring into the classroom, while the classroom itself produces its own physiological experience. Regarding the physiological impact of verbal participation, a few students talked about how they don't like to be the center of attention, and while they didn't elaborate on this in terms of the physiological experience—such as increased heart rate, tight chest, shaking hands, sweating—they frequently associated this kind of attention with anxiety. One student stated that they "don't want to draw attention to" themself, while another wrote that "being called on the spot gives me anxiety." Another student is more direct when expressing that "my social anxiety will not let me speak in front of the class." These responses highlight some of the complexity of our students' embodied experiences, and how their body's response to social conditions impacts their interest and willingness to engage in verbal participation. As we will see in the next chapter, pedagogies of quiet can address this issue in two ways. First, we can use contemplative silences to help students calm their central nervous system. Second, we can give alternate pathways to participation that don't evoke these same anxieties and the associated physiological discomforts.

Conclusion: Shifting into Silence

When students state that they like working through their ideas in their head, it makes clear that silence can be utilized to facilitate an engaged and participatory quiet. Which is to say, allowing some silent space in class for students to think through the material on their own allows them to cultivate the possibilities of their inner world and to develop their own ideas and questions about the material. In addition, students make it clear that the overvaluation of "talk" is a potentially perilous path, especially for those of us whose primary task is to teach 100-level students. Because we aren't teaching majors or graduate students, rather, we are the ones introducing new subjects and new ideas to new students, so it's crucial that we create a classroom space that encourages rather than discourages their capacity to engage with (new) ideas.

One theme in this data regarding classroom culture and professor accountability allows us to see the complexity of "silence as power; silence as gendered; silence as oppression; silence as protection; and silence as expression of identity."[57] What are the implications of the explanations that the students in this study provide—listening to others, processing course content, socio-emotional considerations, and classroom culture—in relation to these more broad categorical understandings of silence? It's clear in the data presented here that silence can be seen and understood through all of these lenses and that we can use pedagogies of quiet to minimize the problematic silences—disempowering, gendered, oppressive—and encourage the individually and socially empowering ones, while also remaining cognizant of the relationships among them.

A common refrain that emerged was that students didn't talk in class because their classmates were also silent. Echoing the collective, one student wrote that "when the rest of the class tends to be quiet I also tend to remain quiet unless I know someone else that is in that class. Personally, I am socially awkward as is so being in a class where no one else wants to talk makes me feel very awkward to speak up when I want to." Working with these students so as to value silence means transforming an awkward silence into an active but quiet place and space; it means cultivating the silence for a productive quiet. From there, we build and use planned silences and an engaged quiet mind to create a more comfortable pathway to student success, which can still include moments of verbal participation.

Students' perceptions and experiences matter. And, taken as a group, when exploring the patterns that emerge, they tell us that sometimes, it's okay to be quiet! Introductory-level students need more (quiet) time: to develop relationships with their peers, their teachers, and all the new ideas their course work is exposing them to. Using silence as a shared strategy that functions so as to allow all students time and space to find and strengthen their inner worlds helps them develop both confidence and critical thinking. This is the jumping off point into the coming chapters where we illuminate the pedagogical practices of quiet pedagogies.

NOTES

1. Ashley J. Holmes, "'Being Patient Through the Quiet': Partnering in Problem-Based Learning in a Graduate Seminar," *International Journal for Students as Partners* 4, no. 1 (2020): 41.
2. Merilee Hamelock and Norm Friesen, "One Student's Experience of Silence in the Classroom," *Norm Friesen*, July 2012, https://www.normfriesen.info/papers/ihsrc2012.pdf; Ange-Marie Hancock, *Intersectionality: An Intellectual History* (Oxford University Press, 2016).
3. Jing Hu, "Toward the Role of EFL/ESL Students' Silence as a Facilitative Element in Their Success," *Frontiers in Psychology* 12 (2021), doi: 10.3389/fpsyg.2021.737123.
4. Krishna Bista, "Silence in Teaching and Learning: Perspectives of a Nepalese Graduate Student," *College Teaching* 60, no. 2 (2012).
5. Susan Cain, *Quiet: The Power of Introverts in a World That Can't Stop Talking* (New York: Crown Publishing, 2013).
6. Bob Jessop, "On Academic Capitalism," *Critical Policy Studies* 12, no. 1 (2018).
7. Antonia Darder, "Pedagogy of Love: Embodying Our Humanity," in *The Critical Pedagogy Reader*, third edition, ed. Antonia Darder, Marta Baltodano, and Rodolfo D. Torres (New York: Routledge, 2017), 102.
8. Cain, *Quiet*, 81.
9. Zara Abrams, "Kids' Mental Health Is in Crisis. Here's What Psychologists Are Doing to Help," *American Psychological Association*, January 1, 2023, http://www.apa.org/monitor/2023/01/trends-improving-youth-mental-health.
10. Zara Abrams, "Kids' Mental Health Is in Crisis. Here's What Psychologists Are Doing to Help," *American Psychological Association*, January 1, 2023, http://www.apa.org/monitor/2023/01/trends-improving-youth-mental-health.
11. Joan V. Gallos, "Gender and Silence: Implications of Women's Ways of Knowing," *College Teaching* 43, no. 3 (1995).
12. Robert W. Connell and James W. Messerschmidt, "Hegemonic Masculinity: Rethinking the Concept," *Gender & Society* 19, no. 6 (2005).
13. Connell and Messerschmidt, "Hegemonic Masculinity: Rethinking the Concept."
14. Adele Lozano, Jörg Vianden, and Paige Kieler, "'No, Teach Yourself!': College Women's Expectations for White Men's Awareness of Privilege and Oppression," *JCSCORE* 7, no. 1 (January 2021): 27.
15. Lozano, Vianden, and Kieler, "'No, Teach Yourself!'" 28.
16. Bista, "Silence in Teaching and Learning"; Rita Kohli, "Breaking the Cycle of Racism in the Classroom: Critical Race Reflections from Future Teachers of Color," *Teacher Education Quarterly* 35, no. 4 (2008).
17. Lozano, Vianden, and Kieler, "'No, Teach Yourself!'" 13–45.
18. Dian Squire, Bianca C. Williams, and Frank Tuitt, "Plantation Politics and Neoliberal Racism in Higher Education: A Framework for Reconstructing Anti-Racist Institutions," *Teachers College Record* 120, no. 14 (2018): 4.

19. Esau Tovar, "The Role of Faculty, Counselors, and Support Programs on Latino/a Community College Students' Success and Intent to Persist," *Community College Review* 43, no. 1 (September 2014): 50.

20. Tovar, "The Role of Faculty, Counselors, and Support Programs on Latino/a Community College Students' Success and Intent to Persist," 51.

21. Alison King, "From Sage on the Stage to Guide on the Side," *College Teaching* 41, no. 1 (1993): 30.

22. Melissa Febos, *Body Work the Radical Power of Personal Narrative* (New York: Catapult, 2022), 22.

23. Yvette Taylor and Maddie Breeze, "All Imposters in the University? Striking (Out) Claims on Academic Twitter," *Women's Studies International Forum* 81 (2020), https://doi.org/10.1016/j.wsif.2020.102367, 1.

24. Elizabeth Ellsworth, "Why Doesn't This Feel Empowering? Working Through the Repressive Myths of Critical Pedagogy," *Harvard Educational Review* 59, no. 3 (1989): 309.

25. Michael Armato, "Wolves in Sheep's Clothing: Men's Enlightened Sexism & Hegemonic Masculinity in Academia," *Women's Studies* 42, no. 5 (2013).

26. Robin DiAngelo, *White Fragility: Why It's So Hard for White People to Talk About Racism* (Boston: Beacon Press, 2018).

27. Eve Tuck and K. Wayne Yang, "Decolonization Is Not a Metaphor," *Tabula Rasa* 38 (2021).

28. Holmes, "'Being Patient Through the Quiet,'" 41.

29. Hamelock and Friesen, "One Student's Experience of Silence in the Classroom"; Hancock, *Intersectionality*, 1.

30. Ian S. Pratt, Hunter B. Harwood, Jenel T. Cavazos, and Christopher P. Ditzfeld, "Should I Stay or Should I Go? Retention in First-Generation College Students," *Journal of College Student Retention: Research, Theory & Practice* 21, no. 1 (2019): 107.

31. Bista, "Silence in Teaching and Learning"; Kohli, "Breaking the Cycle of Racism in the Classroom: Critical Race Reflections from Future Teachers of Color," *Teacher Education Quarterly* 35, no. 4 (2008); Pratt et al., "Should I Stay or Should I Go?"

32. Henry A. Giroux, "Public Intellectuals Against the Neoliberal University," in *Qualitative Inquiry—Past, Present, and Future*, ed. Norman K. Denzin and Michael D. Giardina (Oxfordshire, England: Routledge, 2016), 4.

33. Giroux, "Public Intellectuals Against the Neoliberal University," 4.

34. Giroux, "Public Intellectuals Against the Neoliberal University," 3.

35. Becky Thompson, *Teaching with Tenderness: Toward an Embodied Practice* (University of Illinois Press, 2017), 40.

36. Rachel C. F. Sun and Daniel T. L. Shek, "Student Classroom Misbehavior: An Exploratory Study Based on Teachers' Perceptions," *The Scientific World Journal* (2012) pages, https://doi.org/10.1100/2012/208907.

37. Riyad A. Shahjahan, "Being 'Lazy' and Slowing Down: Toward Decolonizing Time, Our Body, and Pedagogy," *Educational Philosophy and Theory* 47, no. 5 (2015).

38. Shahjahan, "Being 'Lazy' and Slowing Down," 491.
39. Holmes, "'Being Patient Through the Quiet.'"
40. Maggie Berg and Barbara K. Seeber, *The Slow Professor* (University of Toronto Press, 2018), 90.
41. Giroux, "Public Intellectuals Against the Neoliberal University," 3.
42. Llewellyn and Llewellyn, "A Restorative Approach to Learning: Relational Theory as Feminist Pedagogy in Universities."
43. Kelsey Blackwell, "Why People of Color Need Spaces Without White People," *Arrow Journal*, August 9, 2018, https://arrow-journal.org/why-people-of-color-need-spaces-without-white-people/.
44. Malgorzata Powietrzynska et al., "Holding Space for Uncertainty and Vulnerability: Reclaiming Humanity in Teacher Education through Contemplative | Equity Pedagogy," *Cultural Studies of Science Education* 16, no. 3 (2021): 951–64, 957.
45. Marjorie L. DeVault, *Liberating Method: Feminism and Social Research* (Philadelphia: Temple University Press, 1999), 183.
46. Yuk-Lin Renita Wong, "Knowing Through Discomfort: A Mindfulness-Based Critical Social Work Pedagogy," *Critical Social Work* 5, no. 1 (2004).
47. Laura Brearley, "Deep Listening and Leadership: An Indigenous Model of Leadership and Community Development in Australia," in *Restoring Indigenous Leadership: Wise Practices in Community Development*, second edition, ed. C. Voyageur, L. Brearley, and B. Calliou (Alberta, Canada: Banff Centre Press, 2015).
48. Brearley, "Deep Listening and Leadership."
49. Kerri Laryea, "A Pedagogy of Deep Listening in E-Learning," *Journal of Conscious Evolution* 11, no. 11 (2018), https://digitalcommons.ciis.edu/cgi/viewcontent.cgiarticle=1078&context=cejournal, 2.
50. Bryan M. Dewsbury, "Deep Teaching in a College STEM Classroom," *Cultural Studies of Science Education* 15, no. 1 (2020).
51. Michaela C. Pascoe, Sarah E. Hetrick, and Alexandra G. Parker, "The Impact of Stress on Students in Secondary School and Higher Education," *International Journal of Adolescence and Youth* 25, no. 1 (November 2019): 105.
52. Eric Levitz, "Four Explanations for the Teen Mental-Health Crisis," *Intelligencer*, March 27, 2023, https://nymag.com/intelligencer/2023/03/4-explanations-for-the-teen-mental-health-crisis.html.
53. Pascoe, Hetrick, and Parker, "The Impact of Stress on Students in Secondary School and Higher Education," 105.
54. The Condition of Education, 2020, https://nces.ed.gov/programs/coe/pdf/coc_ssa.pdf.
55. The Center for Community College Student Engagement, 2020, https://cccse.org/sites/default/files/WorkingLearner.pdf.
56. The Center for Community College Student Engagement, 2020.
57. Maureen A. Mahoney, "The Problem of Silence in Feminist Psychology," *Feminist Studies* 22, no. 3 (1996).

Chapter 3

Silence as a Solution

Social Justice Education and Pedagogies of Quiet

One day in a face-to-face class in 2021 I could tell that my students—masked and six feet apart—were overwhelmed by life outside the classroom. At the start of class the air felt heavy, and in my experience this feeling is an early indicator of a quiet class. Left alone, this feeling could lead to less verbal participation. As evidenced, earlier in my career I would have banged my head against the wall for the duration of class trying to get them to verbally engage. Now, while I still struggle with this pressure to create talking students, with pedagogies of quiet I can lean into the moment and work with the silence rather than against it. To assess where they were at, I used a classroom technology tool (explained in detail in chapter 5) that produces a word cloud in response to my chosen question, "How are you feeling?" If I had asked this question verbally, at this point, I would have heard from just a few of them; using this technology, the majority of the class responded, and the screen filled up with words like, "tired," "hungry," and "stressed."

With this real-time data, I asked them to close their eyes. I explained to them that closing their eyes had two benefits: the first was that it lessened social embarrassment (to know that no one was watching them), while the second is that it helps them develop focus. With their eyes closed, I encouraged them to locate tension in their body (neck, eyes, shoulders, etc.) and to engage in any movement that might release some of that tension. To conclude, I guided them to take one big, deep inhale, and one long exhale. From there, I had them open their eyes and reminded them how important it is to take care of themselves in the midst of busy lives and global pandemics. The entire exercise took around five minutes and eased the heaviness while bringing them together into a shared experience. Even without talking, this shared experience cultivates community and connection. This transition time from the hallway to the course content helped create a more engaged presence; the quiet facilitated greater focus and thus participation.

Silence, as utilized in the aforementioned practice, can cultivate a shared, grounding experience. Rather than silencing, such a practice builds up both individual students and the collective. That said, relying on silence is going against the pedagogical status quo. Teaching is an inherently political enterprise, and the classroom is a site where oppression can be (re)created, while at the same time a site of (potential) emancipation. Scholars from a multitude of theoretical traditions have explored the ways that Western systems of inequality have become embedded into higher education. Whether we realize it or not, this inequality can invade the "mood" of our classrooms. Some of the students in this study reported having teachers that make them feel unwelcome: one student, for example, reported an instance when a teacher laughed at them in response to their answer to a question. In light of such moments, it comes as no surprise that fewer than 40 percent of them do feel comfortable speaking up in class.

At the same time, scholars have engaged with theoretical frameworks and practices that function to deconstruct oppression so as to build democratic classrooms full of possibility. One such approach, critical pedagogy, like the slow professor movement, aims to disrupt hegemonic systems inside the classroom, in students' lives, and in the social world at large. For example, scholars argue that critical pedagogy is a route toward greater inclusion.[1] Inclusion, by way of classroom participation, is a central preoccupation of most teachers and deeply informs pedagogies of quiet. We want to hear from as many of—all of—our students as possible. We want their lives to become embedded in the knowledge production process.

While critical pedagogy research brings dialogue and discussion to the fore, it also, subtly, points in the direction of pedagogies of quiet. For example, Michelle Page's case study focuses on one teacher's classroom conversations around LGBTQ texts and lives. One of the primary examples that Page highlights starts with an "opening journal assignment."[2] Neither Page nor the teacher included in her study emphasize the journaling component; rather, they highlight the ensuing classroom discussion as the prized outcome of the pedagogical practice.

The clear question that comes to mind, however, is: What would the discussion have been without the quiet that preceded it? Without giving students a chance to live in the wild space of their quiet imagination—and writing and journaling about their ideas—would they have as much to say? One of the students who participated in this study wrote of one of the quiet practices that will be explored in these pages, "[it was helpful] because it gives students that might have a lot to say a chance to express their thoughts without speaking in front of everyone." Another student said, "the journal was a little time consuming but I do believe it helped me to write down my thoughts and connect to where I was struggling." Often what students project verbally doesn't reflect the full scope of what's going on inside their brains. Thus, presented here is another reading of Page's case study: the moments of quiet and the journaling that preceded the discussion are a crucial component of the impact of the praxis and must be brought center stage.

Our students have complex lives with alive and humming bodies and minds. Much of this vibrancy and activity is left unattended to when we frame participation solely through the lens of what students verbalize. Song and Muschert rightfully point out that so often in our classrooms "outward engagement has not been sufficiently connected with inward practices."[3] The goal of pedagogies of quiet is to build this connection: to develop a classroom praxis that facilitates "inward practices" so as to deepen students' critical thinking and emotional regulation and to enhance their experiences with "outward engagement." In this chapter we will explore the pedagogical foundation of this quiet approach and then conclude with a brief overview of the many practices that I have utilized in the classroom so as to facilitate quiet teaching.

PEDAGOGIES OF QUIET AS INTERSECTIONAL PEDAGOGY

Intersectionality is a key concept in both feminist and antiracist theory. The goal of intersectional analysis is to explore the complex ways that power functions in people's lives, as shaped by multiple axes of inequality; intersectional scholars explore in both breadth and depth the nuances of the general and the specific. Black feminist theorists and the "third-world" scholarship of the authors of *This Bridge Called My Back* were central in shaping theories of intersectionality as a response to the silences among mainstream—white, middle-class, cishet—feminism.[4] The pedagogical literature has been slow but keen to explore students' intersectional identities and the impact on their classroom experience. Nichols and Stahl, for example, write that "within university institutions, shaped by privilege and oppression, gender and race become 'intersecting factors that negatively affected' the academic experience for women."[5] Like the Black feminists that preceded them, educational scholars note the ways that race, class, and gender intersect to shape the experiences of students, as reflected, for example, in a nonbinary student in this study who reported that having "always felt different" has shaped their discomfort with classroom participation.

Intersectionality is also a useful concept in thinking about how to construct a socially just classroom praxis. Rather than deploy contemplative pedagogy, or critical pedagogy, or feminist pedagogy, we can instead use an intersectional lens to explore the ways in which these approaches overlap, and the ways in which power in the classroom is shaped by pedagogical practice. That is, an overreliance on one "type" of pedagogy could lead to the same kinds of silences that were created by a universalizing framework of gender (for example, that of the mainstream white feminist movement). Pedagogies of quiet reach wide to construct an approach that bridges students' multiple and various salient identities with strategies that emerge from the intersections of the contemplative with the critical.

Further, different pedagogical approaches often point in the same direction, even if indirectly. For example, Mountz et al. write that "we situate slow scholarship within a feminist praxis that positions self-care and the creation of caring communities as a means of 'finding ways to exist in a world that is diminishing.'"[6] This argument itself is intersectional—making an argument for slow scholarship as feminist—but it also connects deeply with contemplative pedagogies through its grounding in care labor. As Barbezat and Bush argue, contemplative practices in the classroom result in "personal gains" including "psychological well-being," while also revealing "our connection to others, and many practices are focused on the development of empathy and compassion."[7] Pedagogies of quiet directs this care and compassion to students, and to ourselves, encouraging us to be gentler toward ourselves as we navigate our classrooms and work to align our values with our classroom practices. What all these social justice–oriented pedagogies have in common is care for both self and community and for exploring our interconnectedness in the world. No matter the subject matter we teach, pedagogies of quiet allow us to carry forward all these principles—slowing down, contemplative moments of silence, and critical explorations of power dynamics—into a cohesive classroom strategy.

In all ways, mindfulness allows us to realize our values and enhance our awareness of what's happening for our students. All people engage in complex negotiations around managing stigma,[8] and in the classroom self-censorship is a central tactic used by the students in this study as a part of this process. One student wrote that not being comfortable with the material impacts their willingness to speak. They elaborate: "Sometimes I'm not sure what the teacher wants to hear when they are giving a lecture and ask a question, and so I might not answer because I don't know and don't want to get it wrong. I think it's maybe about disappointing people, both teacher and peers." In order to avoid this feeling of disappointment, this student, along with the others who expressed similar sentiments, chooses to refrain from speaking. Staying "out of the spotlight" was another often mentioned preference that highlights students' stigma management and self-censorship.

For these students, classroom silence is a chosen strategy for self-protection; often, though not exclusively, it is protection against responses from others, and a culture of perfection, that make them feel diminished. This is where we work to push away from oppressive silence and toward an expansive and connecting experience of quiet. As teachers, we can feel this pressure to be perfect as well. Whether we are conscious of it or not, our own inner dialogue is coding our class sessions (such as, "not my best day") and the students in them as "disengaged" or "good." As a contemplative practice, pedagogies of quiet can help faculty and students alike manage these aspects of our inner world and their impact on our teaching and learning. As Kevin Quashie argues, there is tremendous power in quiet, power that is restorative, inspiring, and, most important, humanizing.[9]

This intersectional lens allows us to see that pedagogies of quiet meet up in all these spaces: antiracism work meets universal design meets the feminist ethic of care meets the compassionate core of contemplative practices. And at these intersections, this pedagogical strategy reaches all of our students and lets their inner worlds, their imaginations, run wild. Pedagogies of quiet allow all of us to be more fully human in the classroom while deepening student engagement with their learning practices and the course content they are learning. It also gives teachers room to engage reflexively with their teaching praxis. A survey respondent wrote that a quiet practice (classroom technology outlined in chapter 5) helped to add "depth to concepts that may not always be easy to understand," while multiple others commented that it more effectively allowed them to "see what others think." The structured space of quiet in the face-to-face classroom facilitated this diversity and depth.

Classroom experiences with quiet students, coupled with the COVID-19 pandemic, have made clear that we must maintain a flexible pedagogy; we must always be ready to change and adapt. This requires an openness to explore and upend our overreliance on some tactics (lectures, vocal participation) and to rely upon a multitude of creative practices that fall under the rubric of pedagogies of quiet (and that will be explored later in the chapter). Just as Shahjahan does in his work on "being lazy" and slowing down, a restorative feminist approach is critical of "academic capitalism" and the Western dictate of the "rational learner."[10] In response to this context, and in reliance on an intersectional pedagogical approach that bridges multiple theoretical paradigms, pedagogies of quiet function to create a learning environment where everyone can thrive—students and professors—and where everyone has agency in relation to what they are learning. This facilitates complex critical thinking experiences and skills that are useful across disciplinary and institutional contexts, including the workplace.

This strategy is especially useful in the context of entry-level courses, where deep relationships between students and course content, in addition to between student and teacher, have not yet been built. Whether we are part-time instructors, work at a four-year teaching college, are graduate assistants at major public universities, or are professors at a community college, many of us are shaped by this relational dynamic; while we mentor our students in a variety of ways, we might not develop the kinds of relationships with students that come from mentoring a student through a major capstone experience or graduate studies. Pedagogies of quiet are a praxis that works especially well for students who are in their first-ever college class who've yet to be acclimated to, as one example, the Socratic method. Thus, pedagogies of quiet also aim to center students who are often left out of the (pedagogical) conversation: first-year students, introverted students, anxious students, historically marginalized students, first-generation students, and community college students.

As discussed previously, the majority of the students surveyed for this project are women and people of color, and this reflects the demographics of the institution, of which 49 percent identify as nonwhite, 56 percent as first-generation, and 57 percent as female.[11] Further, as will be explored in more detail, one of the primary barriers to participation that students articulated was around having a shy and/or introverted personality, as well as anxiety, depression, and other mental health concerns. And since the pandemic, especially, mental health concerns among adolescents are on the rise.[12] Revisiting this demographic and empirical data reminds us of the need to utilize an intersectional framework, as our students' feelings and needs are shaped by myriad social and psychological factors. Quiet is a strategy that bridges these complexities, allowing for those who feel silenced and those who choose silence to feel connected and engaged with their classmates, their teachers, and their course content. In this way, an intersectional approach necessitates integrating a universal design framework.

Universal Design

Universal design is an educational logic that most often is applied to reach students with disabilities, but a historical look at the education system means we can broaden this understanding. Absolutely, we need to ensure that our modes of teaching reach our neurodiverse students, our deaf and hard of hearing students, and our blind students (as examples). But invisible disabilities abound, so we must also consider our anxious students, our depressed students, and now our grief-stricken students and our COVID long-haulers: "In considering intersectionality, the issue of disability must be mentioned here, where the expectation of academic speed disadvantages certain groups, particularly those with a hidden disability (such as mental health issues, HIV/AIDS, and epilepsy."[13] Further, we must do all of this with an intersectional lens, knowing that among all these aforementioned students, so often left out and behind, are historically marginalized people: Black and Indigenous students, nonbinary students, and bisexual students (as examples).

Further, universal design approaches challenge the notion that the student is the "problem" and instead see the classroom as the site of change. As Grier-Reed and Willams-Wengerd write, "by ignoring the need to design (from the ground up) inherently 'open' or accessible spaces and pedagogical practices, traditional approaches to teaching and learning ignore the principle that it is the institution or classroom environment that is limited (or disabled), not the student."[14] This tracks with dominant discourses around achievement "gaps," where students—usually students of color—are seen as "missing" something that "traditional" (read: white) students possess. Ayala and Contreras capture this problematic framework and, using empirical data that centers students' voices, make the case that students enter our classrooms with varying cultural capital, and urge educators to rethink our relationship to hegemonic assumptions about "the normative cultural capital [that is] conducive to academic persistence and attainment."[15] In this way, adopting a universal design framework for our classes allows teachers to challenge this dominant discourse, allowing for students to benefit from the capital that they do bring into the classroom, even as what each student brings may differ from others.

Quiet pedagogies encourage this framework, in particular in relationship to classroom participation. We seek to disrupt a dominant framework of verbal participation to create a more expansive participatory ecology that allows students multiple—and many of them quiet—ways to enter into classroom dialogues and engagement with course content. As Tobin and Behling write, "for some students, speaking up in class causes paralyzing fear," and many of the students in this study confirmed this. As a result, these authors argue that universal design for learning practices should encourage choice and options, so that "students [can] be active members of the teacher/student process through means that worked for them."[16] In this way, choice is an important aspect of the universal design approach, as adopting a both/and approach to participation (and assessment) facilitates the process of removing learning obstacles.[17]

Students have varying needs, and our pedagogy needs to reach all of them. For example, students who are not comfortable talking in class had different priorities regarding their explanations for this discomfort as compared to those students who are comfortable talking in class. The "no" students (those who said they were not comfortable) focused on personality, mental health, and judgment from their peers and/or self-comparison concerns. In the survey, students were asked to provide additional comments regarding their feelings about speaking in class. The students who replied "no" when asked if they were comfortable speaking in class provided additional comments that focused on concerns for how they might be perceived by others. This pattern was the most significant in the data: 100 percent of the comments included sentiments around social comparisons and (potential) stigmatization. Those surveyed in a face-to-face class mentioned this concern 74 percent of the time. The "no" students were also the most likely to highlight having a shy or introverted personality and/or mental health concerns: 76 percent of them reported being shy or introverted, while 56 percent said their mental health kept them from feeling comfortable speaking in class.

On the other hand, those students who do feel comfortable talking in class had differing priorities. For the surveyed students who were enrolled in a face-to-face class, only 10 percent of them reported that their mental health impacts their participation. 40 percent of them said that being shy or introverted did impact them, but they still preferred to speak. These numbers were consistent for those enrolled in online courses as well. For these students, their primary concern was their relationship to the content: they are comfortable talking in class *unless* they are not (yet) comfortable with the material. This is where the data leads us to center the introductory classroom and first-year college students, as they are more likely to be unfamiliar with the course content and therefore potentially less inclined to speak in class.

Despite these varying concerns, the overwhelming majority of them responded positively to the quiet strategies that were utilized in their courses. The face-to-face students were asked if the classroom technology (to be explored in depth in chapter 5) that facilitated moments of collective silence helped their learning experience. Only 1 percent of them said that they did not find it helpful. For the online students, they were asked if the participation journal assignment—another quiet strategy explored in chapter 4—aided their learning experience. When asked if the assignment helped them to stay focused on the course, 81 percent said yes; 79 percent of the students encourage the continued use of the assignment. What stands out here is that though not all students, for example, feel that shyness or introversion are an impediment to their verbal participation, the vast majority of them had a strong preference for these quiet practices, thus highlighting their universal design. Some students like to talk in class, while others very strongly do not, but pedagogies of quiet engage them all.

Utilizing a universal design framework in social justice education is especially crucial at institutions that see significant numbers of first-year and first-generation students, such as the institution where the present data was collected. The range and variability of our students' experiences and needs are increasingly diverse across these contexts, and thus our pedagogies must meet this diversity. And as Grier-Reed and Williams-Wengerd highlight, universal design and culturally competent pedagogy can be paired effectively to address the diverse needs of our students. They highlight that the social setting in which learning happens sets the stage for what is possible, and as such we must tend reflexively to our praxis in order to reach and value all of our students by offering multiple pathways to successful engagement.[18]

Critical and Contemplative Pedagogy

Universal design is grounded in the desire for collective educational empowerment; it's not alone among pedagogical theories in sharing this value. Critical theory, in particular, with its focus on dialectical thinking, provides us with a framework for thinking of silence as both a site of oppressive power—as a problem—and also, simultaneously, a route to a solution. As Peter McClaren writes, "the dialectical nature of critical theory enables the educational researcher to see the school not simply as an arena of indoctrination or socialization or a site of instruction but also as a cultural terrain that promotes student empowerment and self-transformation."[19] Pedagogies of quiet recognize this dialectic and its impact on both faculty practice and student experience. As such, we are focused on providing more space for students to engage with their inner worlds, to explore the impact of their learning on their lives and the impact of their lives on their learning. Thus, we carry with us into the classroom an understanding (as outlined in chapter 1) of how silencing functions—and which of our students might experience its most oppressive impacts—while also seeing the emancipatory value in collective silence, a shared experience of a silence with clearly stated educational goals.

Critical theory aims to help students build the intellectual tools to analyze their society and their social position within that society. Pedagogies of quiet, too, are grounded in a similar emancipatory project—for example, acknowledging and working to dismantle the chilly climate—though our focus is on pedagogical practices of classroom engagement and participation. The focus here is on bringing more students into the conversation through a broad understanding of participation that values silence as much as talk. Our goal is to help students navigate the social, emotional, and physiological aspects of learning so as to enhance their relationship to course content.

Course content plays a significant role in students' comfort level with verbal classroom participation. For students who are comfortable speaking up in class—35 percent of the students in this study—in those moments when they choose not to speak, their relationship to the course content was their primary concern. The students who were surveyed in face-to-face classes placed this as their top concern (42 percent); for those surveyed in an online course, 46 percent of them stated that their comfort level with the material impacts their classroom participation habits. For those students who are sometimes comfortable participating, comfort with the material clearly tips

QUIET PRACTICE 3A: LESSON/LECTURE BREAK

After presenting material for thirty minutes (based on a seventy-five-minute class), give students a writing prompt that allows them five minutes of freewriting time to review what they've just learned. For example, prompt your students to make a list of five key ideas that were just presented to the class, in their own words. Then have them select one of those ideas from the list and expand it into a short paragraph. Have the students take a picture of their writing and submit the photo to the instructor electronically (so the writing stays in the students' notebook). This is a useful strategy in the context of emerging AI technology. Then have the students share one point on their list via your preferred classroom polling platform so that the whole class can see what everyone else came up with. From that collective list the teacher can then facilitate a verbal discussion and find an entrance point back into the day's lesson/lecture. This functions to give students more time to process the material and to establish their own thoughts about the content while it is still fresh in their minds, aiding learning and avoiding memorization. It's also a window into their classmates' ideas, but without requiring that everyone speak up.

the balance. 69 percent of these students said that whether they spoke or not depended on their knowledge related to the topic of the day. Introductory courses, of course, are full of students who don't yet know the content at hand. As a result, verbal participation may not always be in the best interests of the students, in particular when there are alternate options that more effectively serve to create learning moments: A quiet freewriting exercise, as one example, is useful strategy to replace our habit of asking students to verbalize their comprehension.

With our goals of comprehension and critical thinking, it's important that we apply a critical lens to our own often relied upon classroom engagement practices. It's important that we shine the lens of analysis on to the habituated practices that we bring into the classroom. Critical pedagogy's focus on tackling oppressive social structures, and their micro- and macro-level impact, is primarily directed toward a praxis of content and dialogue. Most of the scholarship that emerges from this tradition focuses on what we (should) do as professors but often leaves out the *how* of the equation. While there is attention to process, to understanding that learning is as much about process as outcome, the overarching focus is on outcomes and, in particular, on social change outcomes.

While both critical theory and contemplative pedagogy are grounded in a commitment to challenging and dismantling systems of inequality, contemplative pedagogies more effectively integrates a focus on both outcomes and process. For example, as Beth Berila argues, "mindfulness is an important component of [an education that works against oppression] because it takes us beyond the cognitive into embodied transformation at both the individual and collective levels."[20] So while the attention is still on teaching that disrupts hegemony and oppression, the incorporation of mindfulness allows for a *process* that handles this learning, and the students doing the learning, with care.

Contemplative pedagogy is a theoretical framework that fosters an approach to education that incorporates self-reflection, introspection, and what Arthur Zajonc calls "the 'epistemology of love.'"[21] There are a range of practices that fit within the rubric of contemplative pedagogies, from movement and embodiment practices to journaling and mindfulness meditation.[22] The overarching goal of this pedagogical approach is to bring contemplative practices further into the "mainstream" of higher education. This is grounded in "the belief that bringing contemplative practice into the academy would have pedagogical and intellectual benefits and that contemplative awareness can help to create a more just, compassionate, and reflective society."[23] Research on contemplative practices makes clear that there is a range of benefits, from focus to increased self-compassion and access to flow states.[24]

Social justice education, of which critical pedagogy is a leading theoretical framework, aims for both micro-level and macro-level social changes. Focusing as we are on individual classrooms, pedagogies of quiet tend toward a micro-level focus: our individual students, our specific classrooms, and our unique institutions. While we recognize that small changes can ultimately lead to and reinforce macro-level shifts, there's lots of fertile ground to explore at the micro level. Pedagogies of quiet—as will be explored in detail in later chapters—can enrich students and help them to "better connect on an emotional, meta-cognitive, psychological, and creative level."[25] Coupled with transparency, this tack can also attend to sociological conditions both in the classroom and in the world at large, with an eye toward equity and justice.

Contemplative practices have been especially useful during COVID-era teaching. As my classes transitioned to fully online in March 2020 I utilized a compassionate contemplative pedagogy in my approach to online learning that students really responded to. My strategy was simple: most days throughout the week I would post an announcement on the course page (that was also emailed to students) that presented self-care as an important part of the learning process; this was always positioned in relation to the week's content.

As Hill explains it, "contemplative pedagogy aims to build students' capacity, deepen understanding of complexity, generate compassion and resiliency, and explore their human nature and inner world."[26] These tools are of the utmost importance during a global pandemic—or any other crisis that impacts our lives, from racial violence to war—as they allow students to sit with the realities of the world and how they impact their experiences in the classroom. Hill goes on to write, "ultimately, the goal is for students to gain empowerment in their learning, in themselves, and in the world. But, we first must pause to authentically recognize and relate to our own capacities in the present global crisis while recognizing and respecting the students' capacities as well."[27]

Students reported that this contemplative approach—that was always tied in an intersectional understanding of their lives—facilitated their experience in the course. This is affirmed by others who relied upon a contemplative praxis during COVID shutdown, as evidenced by Conboy[28] and Pucino.[29] When asked in this survey what aspects of the class made them feel cared for or facilitated their feelings of connectedness to the course, many of them commented on these check-ins. In the words of one student:

> I do not have enough words to say how comfortable and cared for I felt by [my teacher]. She checked in with her students on a daily basis and was always available and more than happy to help her students in any way possible. She constantly reminded us that she was there for us no matter what and if we needed anything, to please reach out to her. She also made sure to provide office hours and live bi-weekly review sessions, which made an online course feel personalized and engaging. [She] reminded us to breathe and that we are not alone in these challenging times. She was simply always there for her students, and it means beyond the world to feel so supported during such times of isolation.

This student's commentary on connection makes it clear that mindfulness is an impactful pedagogical strategy. We can see here how faculty mindfulness—manifested as regular check-in announcements to students through the course learning platform—along with encouraging students to engage in quiet and caring practices for themselves (breathing, stretching, connection to others) helps students stay connected to the course and, thus, the course content. While this was especially useful during the pandemic, ongoing global and local crises mean that students continue to live their lives in the context of stress. This praxis is both compassionate and critical, as it presents a challenge to the hegemonic structure of higher education.

There are many critical theorists who bring this contemplative approach to bear on their work. Antonia Darder writes, "embracing the rightful place of the body in the classroom requires a view of students as integral human beings. It is this integral view that is negated within banking education, where a more complex understanding of the body and its significance to students' intellectual and political formation is absent."[30] Pedagogies of quiet take this up, centering the body as a force in the classroom that requires more intentional attention. So much of the learning process is shaped—and interrupted—by the ongoing experiences of the body. Students' heart rates, their hunger pangs, and their internal mental chatter are always with them and are a part of the learning team. Pedagogies of quiet do more than bring the body into our lens of awareness, we incorporate these internal processes into our assessment practices and thus our approach to classroom participation.

This is one of the many places where pedagogies of quiet bring critical and contemplative pedagogies into conversation. We bring the critical lens to the fore, to explore the impact of the Western worldview on the education system and students' lives, while also pulling in contemplative pedagogy's similar lens, as applied to the (Western) body. As Wing explicates, "other forms of knowing and transformation through the body, emotions, and spirit have been submerged under the 'discursive rationality' paradigm that privileges the mind in categorizing and normalizing the world, an epistemic bias of the Enlightenment in European history."[31] Pedagogies of quiet work to address this impact so as to build toward equity and emancipation.

In light of all the stressors in students' lives, contemplative pedagogues make the case for the many benefits of mindfulness in the classroom.[32] One of them is that contemplative practices in the classroom can help students engage with difficult content. Those difficulties could be in relation to helping students to process reactions to learning about various types of social violence to helping with processing difficulties associated with complicated mathematical algorithms. A second benefit is that mindfulness practices facilitate a path to greater openness, allowing students to attain "academic detachment from their own knowledge systems" and to "cultivate . . . a greater emotional resilience and tolerance for divergent points of view."[33] I would add to this that contemplative practices can also help students (all of us) to detach from their own entrenched ideas, such as whether or not they are "good" at or "like" a certain subject (for teachers, we can explore our own ideas around whether a certain participation strategy is "good" or "the best"). This is a common block that students experience in our classrooms, as they bring with them preexisting ideas about their abilities and interests regarding the subjects we are teaching and they are intending to learn.

Pedagogies of quiet build on this contemplative push for incorporating mindfulness practices into the classroom, though I don't equate mindfulness practices with meditation practices. Barbeatz and Bush write in their indispensable text on contemplative pedagogy that the approach "include[s] both simple and complex concentration practices that sometimes require periods of calm and quiet and sometimes sustained analytical thinking. The critical

> **QUIET PRACTICE 3B: AN
> EXPANDED STUDY GUIDE**
>
> In my Introduction to Sociology class I have always used a study guide, and for years now I have had students submit that study guide for points, using a labor-based grading approach. I have expanded upon this assignment to incorporate the principles of pedagogies of quiet. Namely, I wanted to create space for students to engage with the discipline's ideas but also, separately, their own ideas. For each short answer question that I pose on the study guide I have students respond in two ways:
>
> 1. As the discipline would answer the question. This comes from their notes, their textbooks, and their additional readings.
> 2. Through the lens of personal connections and critical thinking. Here the students are encouraged to connect the ideas to their life experiences, to engage with their skepticism, and to ask follow-up questions.
>
> This additional step—part two—encourages students to think about the content on a deeper level, as well as to explore their own thoughts, concerns, and questions in a space that is separate from the perspective of the discipline. This means that students can quietly explore both the new ideas and their humanity, engaging critically with the material rather simply regurgitating the "right" answer. Having this practice space also functions to prepare them for discussions that might come up in class.

aspect is that students discover their own internal reactions without having to adopt any ideology or specific belief."[34] They make clear that the reliance on mindfulness, or silence, is a secular practice aimed at developing critical thinking skills; empirical data supports this, as will be illustrated throughout the pages of this book. There are many different approaches to silence in the classroom, so it's important for us to retrain our teacher brains so that we can more regularly see silence as an educational net positive. As I've reiterated throughout this book, this has not been easy for me—I still have days where I find my internal dialogue telling me my students are too quiet—and it has required the same work that's typical when building new habits (practice, practice, practice). Whether we are incorporating intentional quiet practices in class or using the approach as a lens to value all of our students, including the less—and non—talkative ones, silence provides a range of benefits.

Pedagogies of quiet allow us to expand upon Peter Kaufman's argument that "if educators fail to welcome students into the process of creating knowledge and constructing social reality, then our efforts [as critical educators] will be futile."[35] I contend that the goals of critical pedagogy are enhanced through a linkage to the contemplative, where "contemplative pedagogues strive to treat students and the educational process with humanness and compassion"[36] and where it is slowly being recognized that contemplative pedagogy can be used as a "vehicle for social change."[37] Through practices grounded in quiet we can bring to the fore a path that illuminate *how* to bridge the contemplative and the critical into a single, quiet approach. One thing that is sorely needed in this process is time, in particular, a reshaping of time through the lens of quiet.

Slow Professor Movement

A multitude of different pedagogical genres can be framed in conversation to build a strong theoretical argument in support of silence as a social justice pedagogical strategy, and here we will add another: the slow professor movement. As previously stated, teachers are a significant cause of silencing in the classroom. As noted, I have had to face my own moments of creating an intimidating, silencing atmosphere, often masked through a joking demeaner. While students make clear their distrust of their classmates (see chapters 2 and 5), faculty also play a significant role in both enforced, oppressive silencing and the silencing of student self-censorship. Personally, this most often happened through my approach to lecturing. In teaching an introductory class, it was my belief early on in my career that I need to introduce as much as I could, and thus my lectures included few moments of silence and were in turn silencing. When I gave students the opportunity to enter the conversation, to speak, the time was so sparse they seldom took up the offer. The slow teaching movement addresses this problem head-on.

Maurice Holt, one of the first major proponents of the slow teaching movement, wrote that, "in the context of education, the form of schooling espoused under the banner of standards demonstrates the same deterministic thinking that governs the production of fast food."[38] As a result of this neoliberal push toward the standardization of teaching and testing, Riyad Shahjahan calls for a pedagogy of laziness, wherein "being lazy" is seen as a pathway to reimagine the classroom in ways that allow for us to "slow down, be mindful, and embrace present moments."[39] When, for example, I provide a brief interruption in my lectures to ask students a question—and in so doing only allow the time for two or three students to answer—I am stifling and, thus, silencing my students. But instead, I (we!) can offer *all* students five to ten minutes of silence to engage in a quiet exploration of their own answer(s) to the question(s). A student-centered approach asks this of us: that we slow down our "typical" pace, in particular in introductory classrooms, so as to shift out of a learning context in which "many of our . . . students . . . memorize the material, 'regurgitate' it on the exams, and forget it so promptly and completely that no mental nourishment remains."[40] Instead let's incorporate quiet, balanced nourishment; let's push against the forces of (capitalist) time.

As we know, time (or a lack thereof) can be a component of the silencing forces of the chilly climate. For example, to think of time as a negative force in relation to pedagogy, the obvious first thought is about content and how much pressure we experience—both internally and externally—regarding the amount of content we cover in a class period, in a quarter or semester. As a result of this pressure on content, when pressed for time, it tends to be the more creative endeavors that get pushed aside. This is much like self-care in the midst of one of life's challenges: it's often what's most needed but the first to get cut from the schedule.

For instance, my first semester back in the classroom after the COVID shutdown I was teaching a blended course, which included one weekly face-to-face session. Despite the access to online video lectures, I regularly found myself weighted down by the internal pressure to ensure content absorption. As a result I struggled to resist the urge to relecture what they had access to online when we were in person together. When I succumbed to this pressure, the more creative plans I had for a given session often got pushed aside. One practice (outlined shortly), found poetry, kept getting delayed as I told myself, "we will do that next week." When I finally did the exercise during the last class session of the semester, I felt immediate regret, because the students were connected to the assignment and produced great work, but there were no more classroom opportunities to try it again. If I had engaged in the practice of "laziness," or of a "not do" slow approach, I would have provided ample opportunities for quiet pedagogies such as found poetry and allowed my students the time and space to explore the expanses of their quiet inner worlds.

The slow professor movement as a whole focuses on engaged creativity and critical thinking through "timeless time" and the ability to "escape from time."[41] In pedagogies of quiet, this is done not through the oft-relied-upon methods of teaching and learning like lectures and structured small groups but in more exploratory shifts away from traditional content delivery, such as giving students fifteen to twenty minutes of freewriting time around a current event (that may or may not be related to the topic at hand) or having them engage in a meta-cognition practice prior to an exam rather than review the

QUIET PRACTICE 3C: FOUND POETRY

Select one to two pages from the text that will be discussed on the day that you are doing this quiet practice. Make copies of this page and hand it out to all the students. Start by providing the students with the larger context of the pages/excerpt you have chosen. From there give them the time to read the excerpt. Once they have all read the excerpt, give them the found poetry instructions:

- Read the excerpt and highlight words in the text that stand out to you as important to the overarching ideas of the piece. Or just select words that speak to you, that are meaningful for you.
- Using the words that you highlighted, construct a poem that, while shorter than the original excerpt, still conveys some of the original meaning of the text.

Once all the students have written their poems, you can have them share via classroom technology or verbally. You could also have them submit their work to the instructor. From here the teacher can move the class into a discussion of the meaning of the excerpt, as well as the new insights that were raised through the students' poems. An option for further reflection is to have the students freewrite about how they felt writing the poetry and to write about the meaning behind their crafted poem. In technical classes or disciplines that do not rely heavily upon textual analysis this can be done with the syllabus as an orientation and community-building exercise or with a current event (news or web) article that connects to the course content.

material in a more "rational" way. Further, Seeber and Berg argue that this leads to a "pedagogy of pleasure," something that I was able to witness as my students, on that last day of the class mentioned previously, finally got to engage with the content through found poetry.[42]

My initial resistance (and, to be transparent, this internalized voice hasn't gone away for good) to practices such as these is that they would take away from the required task at hand, but through my own lived experience, and in the data from over five hundred students, these practices clearly function to build the kinds of relationships—to the content, among students, between students and teachers—that don't often come in 100-level, introductory lecture courses. Importantly, the practices that I've come to rely upon lead to increased student participation in that more students (quantitatively) participate while the quality of student participation is also enhanced. Even if adopting a slow approach, it would be easy to dismiss moments of silence as unwelcome or unnecessary. A pedagogy of quiet requires commitment on the part of faculty not just for changing our speed but also for disrupting the "talkative" norm. That is, slowing down creates the necessary space to implement pedagogies of quiet by opening up our time for the kinds of quiet strategies outlined shortly, which build students' comfort and creativity.

Pedagogies of quiet are a student-centered, data-driven practice that builds on while also addressing the gaps within the slow professor movement. In particular, slow scholarship is framed primarily through the lens of academics and professors. That is, theoretical arguments, such as Berg and Seeber's, make the case that this time crunch is limiting our capacity for research and publication, that we don't have enough time to teach *and* do research *and* engage with our colleagues; this framework centers the academic/teacher.

Empirical research in this vein also centers the professor. For example, Goldschmidt et al. concluded, "the more we slowed down to design learner-centered instructional practices, and the more we slowed down the pace of 'coverage' to attend more mindfully to our students' ideas and questions, the more successful our teaching became."[43] Similar to Sara Crabtree et al., the data that emerged from the implementation of a slow approach emerged from the experience of the faculty. Stephen Smith wrote that he was able to assess a "slow school in practice, and to see first-hand, students enthusiastically engaged in pursuing knowledge, skills and understanding through enquiry-based, deep learning."[44] While the benefits of slow scholarship are most often framed through successful research and teaching, pedagogies of quiet direct the attention to students' successful learning.

The students in this study commented on the ways in which the quiet practices they engaged with allowed them not just more time but the capacity to dig deeper into the material, all while respecting their personalities and needs around classroom participation. They benefit from "slowing down" not on its own but because this slowing was coupled with quiet practices that allowed them the time and space to get more comfortable with their classmates and regulate their learning in relation to their stress responses. In this way, pedagogies of quiet function not as chilly silences but as engaged silences that build wholeness and a deepening relationship to both the self and academic content. While we are incorporating the ethos of the "lazy" or "slow" approach as a component of the praxis, the engaged silence that's central to a quiet pedagogy is its own aim.

Quiet Pedagogies and Labor-Based Grading

Grading is certainly a crucial systemic component of learning, and one that hasn't escaped the impact of hegemonic discourses of power. Research highlights that teachers' grades are often inclusive of teachers' unconscious biases, from general personality assessments (for example, who is a "good" student) to the ways that ableism, racism, and heteronormativity (to name a few) shape our perceptions of our students' work.[45] As Asao Inoue writes, the white racial habitus is embedded in our grading practices, in particular when we rely on a singular standard that gets applied to all students.[46] Despite many of our best intentions to engage in antiracist pedagogy, dominant assessment practices can often limit this potential for change. Inoue argues that

> doing grading well, either at the secondary or postsecondary level, is not simply about finding the best practice, method, or mechanism. It is about understanding the various ways that the nature and function of grades might be constructed in a classroom, and the variety of consequences to learning that are possible.[47]

That is, we need to think about grading as a systemic dynamic. Grades are socially constructed and can operate in complex ways. Of course, we all want our classrooms to lead to deep and engaged learning, and as such, it's important to think about how we assess our students and how those assessment practices shape our/their learning outcomes.

The white racial habitus shapes the classroom in a multitude of ways, and as pedagogies of quiet aim to disrupt this dynamic at the level of classroom (verbal) participation, the writing assessments that are a part of pedagogies of quiet must engage in this work as well. Students' concerns—in particular, as voiced by the students in this study—around being understood when they speak are shaped by linguistic norms that privilege hearing students, white students, and those for whom English is a first language. Grading functions in the same way, so that "grading by a standard, thus, is how White [and hearing] language supremacy is perpetuated in schools."[48] We carry this understanding into our assessments of quiet pedagogical practices.

All of the practices that make up pedagogies of quiet are graded for completion and not content. I construct a clear and comprehensive set of expectations for each assignment, as well as articulating what it means to put in a good faith effort, and so long as students fulfill these expectations, they receive full credit for their work. They receive detailed conversational feedback and this, coupled with content-based assessments (such as quizzes and exams), class materials, and time in office hours functions to ensure their comprehension of the material. Utilizing the approach of labor-based grading (though without the use of grading contracts) with these quiet practices, the goal of these (participatory) assessments is to focus on the learning process and not on specific outcomes.

It is process, not outcomes, that shapes students' feelings of belongingness in the class. When asked in the survey "What made you feel cared for?" and "What made you feel connected to the class?" the conversational feedback made possible by labor-based grading emerged prominently. One student wrote that "[my teacher] give[s] great feedback. Through all three of her classes that I was in, she made me feel like I was a valued student and not just someone she needed to teach because that is her job." Another wrote that they felt cared for because the work wasn't just graded, but "she [responded] really fast and also commented back on our participation journals." As one last example, a student wrote that "for me, personally writing comments in response to something we said in our journal or study guide made me feel that [my teacher was] genuinely trying to engage with every single student." Through this pattern that emerged in the data, engaging in this kind of grading feedback was important for students, especially during the shutdown stage of the pandemic. These assessments, coupled with a labor-based grading approach, made students feel a sense of belonging, and thus were learning in the context of a culture of care.

Given the weight that students feel regarding "right" and "wrong" answers, we seek to disrupt this fear of theirs by creating a culture in which there are multiple pathways to ideas. The focus here is on critical thinking and deep thinking, not on engaging with whether or not what a student has said or done is "right" or "wrong." As Kathleen Kryger and Griffin Zimmerman write,

> While there exists a great deal of scholarship about what constitutes "good" writing, we must also be critically engaged with normative assumptions and expectations that underpin conceptions of "good" thinking. . . . We believe writing assessment must be a site of social justice intervention, and we add our voices to illuminate the challenges of the often invisible marginalized and nonnormative populations: neurodivergent students, especially for those who experience multiple marginalization.[49]

Given the impact of "traditional" assessment practices on marginalized students, the quiet classroom sees these labor-based practices as a way to engage with and value the work of all students outside of the context of the meritocratic stressors of grading. Participation grades, as evident in students' own explanations (see chapter 2), are a significant source of stress for some students. We seek instead to create a participation ecology that cultivates care and connection. The assignments take time and can be challenging, but students receive significant gains from engaging with these practices (see chapters 4 and 5).

Quiet Pedagogies, a Plethora of Practices

At the core of pedagogies of quiet is the push for an expansion of our understanding of classroom participation. Classroom engagement exercises that center on large and/or small group discussions proliferate, where the variety rests in the content of those practices. As Tomas et al. write, "a number of student centered learning theories and methods used to guide the design of in-class activities include peer-assisted learning, cooperative learning, problem-based learning, collaborative learning, and peer tutoring."[50] All of these require voice and intense peer-to-peer contact. Oyeronke Oyewumi stresses the impact of a Western worldview, arguing how the phrase—worldview—itself gives away a preference for what we can see.[51] In this case it can be argued that classroom participation is directed toward what we can hear: we feel students are successfully engaged when we hear their voices and our assessments of participation are also grounded in that which we can see. That is, teachers want to bear witness to their students' classroom participation.

The (unintended) outcome of this ideological approach to teaching is that there is a rich world of student participation that is out of our sight, out of our field of professorial vision, and thus eludes us. And yet we want them to engage deeply, we want this depth of experience and learning for our students. As Antonia Darder argues, "to achieve a liberatory practice, we have to challenge the conditions that limit our social agency and our capacity to intervene and transform our world."[52] How can we as teachers apply this to ourselves? Can we admit that we limit our own agency sometimes? Can we challenge ourselves to see how we can transform our classrooms? What would it look like to expand participation beyond the auditory and beyond what we see in class?

In these pages and in my thinking, I have reflected on the ways in which patriarchal white supremacy can shape the "conversational architecture" of my/our classrooms, producing a "chilly climate"; doing this has furthered my belief that we need to take up a more expansive understanding of our students' classroom participation. This book is as much theory as it is practice, as much sociology as pedagogy. AnaLouise Keating writes that,

> although multiculturalism has this potential to bring about change, it cannot do so unless scholars and educators define multiculturalism more expansively, incorporate a more sustained analysis of the dominant-cultural ("white" supremacist, masculinist) framework, and connect our theorizing more closely to our teaching practices.[53]

Pedagogies of quiet take up this charge by always keeping a close watch on how power shapes voice, benefiting white men in classroom conversations at the expense of those marked as "other": LGBTQ students, introverted and/or anxious students, neurodiverse students, students of color, English language learners, and female-identified students. As such, the call to a more expansive view of participation is a way to "connect our theorizing" about the social world with the classroom praxis that we incorporate into our spaces.

Some silences can be debilitating and harmful to our classes and students, especially if we respond to them with dread, or even sometimes with resentment. As stated previously, students' silences can also emerge as a result of our limited offerings for discussion. When, during lectures for example, we offer very little space between posing a question and expecting an answer, students can feel silenced by the ensuing time pressure. In this way, we take seriously what Kaufman and Schippers argue about self-compassion, understanding that pedagogies of quiet include attention to our own ideas, needs, and emotions as they play out in class. As they write,

> "We can all recall times as teachers when something went wrong" . . . and in doing so, "when we ignore challenging emotions that arise during teaching and throughout our work as educators, we become prone to bitterness, resentment, and spitefulness. As one educator remarked, 'I know too many teachers who are passive aggressive.'"[54]

I can admit to acting out some passive aggression with students: when asking students, in response to a silent room after posing a question, if anyone had "actually done the reading." My tone was certainly chilling. When we engage in this way, from a place of ego defensiveness rather than self-compassion, we reinforce the chilly classrooms that we've inherited from systemic patriarchal white supremacy.

Students are in complex ways just as impacted by classroom silences as we are. If this shared feeling of "failure" becomes embedded in the space, it can be cyclical. One student who participated in this survey wrote that "sometimes the class just feels awkward" and as a result of this feeling the student doesn't feel comfortable participating. Another wrote that they don't talk "when their comments will be met with dead silence." It is not known whether the student was referring to their peers or their professors, but either way it's telling of a culture of uncomfortable silence. It has been humbling to reflect on the extent to which I have been responsible for this awkwardness in my own classrooms. This is why it's critical for teachers to shift the dynamic from *silencing* to a kind of collective silence that cultivates an active and engaged quiet.

Thus, silence can be both problematic and useful: "Classroom silences, mine included, can be interpreted as both empowerment and disempowerment, as protective and damaging to identity, and of being an expression of compliance and attention, and of disobedience and distraction."[55] Pedagogies of quiet utilize moments of silence in the classroom, both inside and beyond the physical space of classrooms and schools, so as to deconstruct the damages of silence and instead to shine a light on the ways in which silence can be used to enhance, build, grow, and to learn. Whether students like or dislike verbal participation, we can use their insight as to what holds them back to build an approach that brings all of them in.

So how do we bring them in? If they are shy and introverted, we give them a way to share their ideas quietly; if they are loud and gregarious, we give them (and everyone else in the class) an opportunity for quiet reflection, to dig deeper than their immediate impulse responses. For all of them, we let them narrate their classroom participation, especially that which happens outside the classroom. Throughout this process, we learn more about ourselves, our students, and, in classrooms, our relationality. When freed from various social constraints, students are much more apt to share their fears, their ideas, and their life experiences.

This brings to life the goals of a multicultural education that seeks to move beyond celebrations of diversity into a space of complex knowledge of intersectional identities. We are teaching in the face of systemic inequalities, up against significant barriers.

> Since the epistemological focus is on analytical processes, other important ways of knowing are easily ignored or dismissed. As a result, student voices and other physical expressions of the body that fall outside the mainstream register are systematically silenced or shut down. It is also worth noting that this phenomenon is predicated upon a dominant notion of the individual as a psychological self, whose intelligence and "ego strength" is supposedly gauged by the ability to function, irrespective of external conditions.[56]

Pedagogies of quiet, however, allow us to incorporate contemplative silences that bring the body squarely into the nexus of learning, while recognizing that those bodies are in fact impacted by the social circumstances they operate in. At the same time, they allow us to disrupt these social circumstances to construct new classroom norms that value student wellness alongside students' engagement and critical thought.

There are many practices that emerge from a philosophy of quiet pedagogy: embodiment practices, mindfulness practices, journaling practices, silent writing prior to a verbal question and answer session, digital technology participation, close reading practices, and found poetry are all examples of the praxis that makes up pedagogies of quiet. It is incumbent upon the reader to adapt, expand upon, and create new practices of quiet, as central to this theoretical approach is an openness to new, quiet ways of engaging students. I have utilized all of these strategies and will briefly outline their utility and effectiveness. Various practices are also interspersed throughout chapters 2 through 5. While the majority of the data emerges from two such practices, many more have been successfully implemented, and many more new ideas will be thought up and tried in the future. This is a living, breathing enterprise, and as such new ideas and practices are out there to be explored. What's important is that each practice value silence, capture students' quiet inner lives, and uses these to enhance classroom engagement and connection.

Some of the practices that I have relied upon with effective results will be (briefly) outlined. Two of the practices are excluded in this chapter, as they are outlined with empirical support in chapters 4 and 5. I hope that readers see the practices that follow as sites of future research as well as locales to engage with your own sense of creativity. Creativity is something that is highly valued in the enactment quiet pedagogies, as quiet is a space, as Kevin Quashie illuminates, that is full of possibility: "Quiet is the habitat of the inner life, a selfhood not based on race or gender but on the rages of the interior, a subjectivity sobered and armed by possibility."[57] Context matters as well: journaling may be a bore for upper-level students while a boon for the introductory level students in this study. Classrooms can and should be seen as places of fun and of joy, even as no one practice will be joyful for everyone involved.

It's important to understand that while each of these practices could function well as a standalone, the philosophy behind pedagogies of quiet encourages teachers to think of the entire set of practices as working together toward a larger goal. Two of the primary concerns around silence—oppressive silences and self-censored silences—are best tackled through utilizing numerous quiet practices, as they are structured to cumulatively use silence to build toward empowerment. For those students who fear their ideas being diminished by social judgment, quiet practices help to build resilience and trust and aim to help these students work through these fears rather than perpetually avoid talking.

Further, quiet practices are a space free of the marginalizing tendencies of the white racial habitus and chilly classroom dynamics, freeing students from those pressures and allowing them to engage deeply with their own ideas without requiring verbal engagement with the collective. To reiterate: the philosophy here is to disrupt the binary logic that encourages us to value one approach (talking) more than its "opposite" (silence) and instead to allow students' inner quiet to roam free in the classroom alongside verbal conversations. It's about finding value and balance; it's about allowing students to connect deeply with themselves, the course content, and, in time, with their classmates.

In-Class Writing Portfolio

The very first quiet teaching approach I utilized in class was simple: give students a few minutes of quiet time to think about the question I asked prior to any expectation for verbal engagement. As stated previously, we know multitasking is not effective, and yet we often find ourselves expecting our students to be able to listen, take notes, read any text displayed on screens, and to answer questions immediately after posing them. As I was facing down collective silence after asking a question, rather than be frustrated by it I decided to embrace it, though it's a hard habit to break. The tactic worked and from there led to a regular in-class writing practice built into an assignment referred to as the "in-class writing portfolio."

The core of the assignment includes regular writing prompts that are intentionally scaffolded to recap concepts, clarify how questions build upon each other, and explore how understanding changes over time. Ample class time is needed for students to engage in freewriting, in silence, so as to explore their inner quiet. These writing prompts are always connected to the course content but are often also connected to reflecting on current events, their embodied reactions, and/or personal experiences. For example, a prompt could ask them to reflect on a question about content that was just presented, to illustrate their understanding of the ideas, or to write about an example, either from their personal lives or popular culture, that illustrates a concept. Another possibility is to have the students reflect on how learning this equation, or concept, or chemical reaction, or accounting strategy challenges their preconceived notions of their own abilities or about the discipline being studied. That is, no matter the content, the writing prompt gives students time to reflect on the class's ideas and also to grapple with the thought patterns and self-talk that might shape their confidence levels.

As this is a graded assignment, students keep all the in-class writing that they complete throughout the semester, and at term's end they submit this work, along with a written reflection, as a portfolio. Students are reminded, along the way, that this writing can be utilized in many ways: to study for exams, to elaborate on and incorporate into formal writing assignments, and to get a sense of their own progress throughout the semester. It is this last component that is of central focus in the end of semester reflection the students write. After reading through the entire body of freewriting from the class, they are given a reflection essay prompt that encourages them to think about what they've learned throughout the semester and how they've grown

> **QUIET PRACTICE 3D: ANALYZE YOUR DISCIPLINE**
>
> Give students an example of either (or both) harm caused by your discipline or a significant contribution to science, health, knowledge, or human wellness that your discipline is responsible for/connected to. An example that I recently used was regarding the origins of body mass index (BMI) and the gender and racial dynamics connected to both the origins and current problems with our continued reliance on BMI. Give students some context around the help or harm you have chosen to focus on, including any relevant newspaper or magazine articles about the topic, and have students read the provided materials and then write about what the provided example illuminates about science/art and critical thinking (whether your discipline is art, math, chemistry, or history). Once students have had quiet time to write and reflect, have them share something using your preferred classroom polling technology so the entire class can view the diverse perspectives in the room. Use this as a jumping off point (back) into the day's lesson.

over time. Of course, the specifics of the reflection would depend upon the nature of the writing prompts and the content matter being taught.

It is clear that rendering this work as a graded assignment adds a measure of accountability to their quiet time. There are benefits to daydreaming as well as to "controlled and focused thought," as both can enhance creativity.[58] Turning moments of freewriting into a graded assignment allows us to balance these two poles. The freewriting approach allows for some mind wandering, while the submission of this writing to the professor compels directed attention. What's important, however, to pedagogies of quiet is that students know that this work is not about being "right" but instead about engaging with their inner quiet, creativity, and critical thinking. As a result, to reiterate, labor-based grading should be utilized in conjunction with the assignment.

The in-class writing portfolio assignment can be an expansive way to engage students with multiple potential practices that can reach across disciplines. For example, students can freewrite their recollection about the previous fifteen minutes of lecture, no matter the subject. Or they can work on scientific equations in one class and write about major historical figures in another. They can be formal prompts, such as sample short-answer exam questions or questions pulled from the class study guide. At the same time, given the push toward creativity and critical thinking that is central to quiet pedagogy, the portfolio assignment sometimes strays from the formal to the "fun" and informal but still instructive practices.

Pedagogies of Play

Incorporating play into higher education pedagogy is one counter to the trends of the neoliberal university. As Norgard and Nielsen argue, a "pedagogy of playful learning in higher education [allows us] to consider the possibilities of an educational system that recognizes the importance of openness, curiosity, risk-taking and failure in learning."[59] Part of the purpose of play in the context of quiet pedagogies is to minimize some of the stressors related to the mistake making that's inevitable when students are being introduced to new ideas for the first time. Further, even as students make mistakes, they are still creating a productive outcome or final product that can engender pride and confidence.

One such practice is that of found poetry. I am not an English teacher, nor do I have any expertise in the reading or writing of poetry. The practice isn't utilized from a place of expertise but rather as a way to engage creatively with course texts and to explore new meaning-making practices. In Peter Kaufman's articulation, found poetry is a practice where you write a poem based on an important classroom text. As Kaufman writes, it's a practice "whereby you construct a poem using the words from an already existing text. By shifting around the words, changing the spacing, and making a few additions or deletions, you can craft a creative and analytical interpretation of the book, article, or excerpt that you are considering."[60] This facilitates students' capacity to find their own meaning and develop their voice, while also enhancing their ability to read and interpret key texts. The poems are recorded in their writing portfolio and can also be shared with the class, either through reading them aloud or sharing them through classroom technology (see chapter 5).

Another possibility for a pedagogy of play is the creation of a class playlist. The incorporation of music might not seem like a "quiet" pedagogy, but quiet practices need not always require complete auditory silence. That is, students can listen to music and reflect on how the song connects to the topic at hand or to the learning process in general. This, then, can be the writing that is incorporated into the portfolio. That said, students can contribute to the assignment—and an online space can be cultivated to collect the songs—by suggesting songs that the class can analyze (of course the professor should curate this to ensure the musical content is appropriate and class ground rules should be created to address inappropriate language/content). This practice engages students both inside and outside the classroom, as it facilitates deeper level thinking any time they are listening to music out in the world.

Collaging is another playful practice that I have utilized as part of my quiet pedagogical strategy. On collage day I bring the stacks of magazines that I have been storing in my office, along with some scissors and tape, and rather than having students write about a question(s), I have them construct a collage that represents their answer to the question(s). So, for example, if the question is about gender roles, they can compile images from the magazines, and then write captions for each image, so that the entire piece represents their answer to the question(s). Or, if the question is about how various biological processes show up in everyday life, they can find images that represent this question and explain their selections with brief written captions that accompany each image in the collage. Or, if your goal is to decrease test anxiety before a big midterm, you can have students create a collage full of calming and empowering images that remind them of their capacities to self-sooth their insecurities and self-inspire their confidence.

Moments of mindfulness and movement can be a part of a playful practice and incorporated into the writing portfolio; they can also be standalone practices. Embodiment practices such as the one outlined in the opening to this chapter are central to contemplative pedagogy and are crucial with pedagogies of quiet, as they allow for students to engage simultaneously with mind and body. When course content is difficult, for example, a moment of silence coupled with a few deep breaths or an opportunity to stretch can give necessary space to students' full humanity, so that they can recognize the intensity of the topic and honor their feelings. When done this way, these feelings don't disrupt continued learning as they are given room to stretch and to breath.

On that note, stretching and breathing are other central practices that have been argued for and supported by both empirical data and theoretical frameworks.[61] Other approaches include directing students to pay attention to, and then journal about, how their bodies are reacting to the course material and to their classmates (see chapter 4). A lot of students write in their participation journals that they rely on white noise, brown noise, waves, lo-fi, and jazz to help them stay both focused and calm when studying. Knowing this, having music playing in the minutes prior to the start of class, such as classical music or lo-fi beats, creates a nice transition for students as they walk into the classroom space. In online courses, reminders that include, as one example, chair yoga videos prior to exam deadlines are helpful, while in the face-to-face context, having students stretch before an in-class assessment can free up some tension and enhance focus.

One of the most wonderful aspects of the in-class writing portfolio is its flexibility; the possibilities are endless. The regular practices build a culture into the classroom that supports students' regulation of their sympathetic nervous system alongside their critical thinking. The playfulness embedded into the work cultivates a pedagogy of pleasure,[62] and the mindfulness, a pedagogy of love.[63] While they can be graded, using a labor-based grading system, grading is not required for them to be useful. Deploying a regular writing practice, whether graded or not, is of a quiet and creative benefit. As a practice of particular importance at the introductory level, it gives students the time and space to tend to their inner quiet and bear witness to their own creativity and inspiration. It also provides them with a body of work from which to speak when verbal participation opportunities arise. This is a practice of collective silence that helps to dismantle oppressive silencing.

Study Guide

One of the central goals of quiet pedagogy is to give students the time and space to focus on their own ideas, experiences, and insights. From here, students can build their confidence for verbal engagement and their resilience around making the necessary and inevitable mistakes that come from learning. As quiet pedagogy is a strategy that contributes to the slow professor movement, time is a key component of this process. That is, students need time to absorb the content and their ideas about the content to engage in verbal discussions more effectively and confidently with their classmates. One way to do this is through a graded study guide assignment that incorporates meta-cognition, personal experience, and critical thinking.

Central to the philosophy of quiet pedagogies is accepting that some classroom participation will happen outside of the instructor's view. This may be because the class is online asynchronous, because some students will never talk in class, or because students engage with their homework on their own time. No matter, we can expand our assessment practices to capture more of this participation. You know those in class discussions we fantasize about? What if we captured our students' ideas in other, quiet ways? This assignment pushes back on the teach to the test model that has students memorizing a bunch of content only to forget it all as soon as the exam is completed. It also helps students to mine the contours of their inner quiet so as to find their footing in the material and thus enhance their preparedness for classroom assessments and participation (something that students desire, as explored in chapter 2). In the study guide, for every question, topic, or key term that shows up, students are expected to answer it as the discipline—focusing on class lectures and texts—intends.

From there, however, in a separate column or bullet point, students are asked to write about each question, topic, or key term from their own perspective, such as what questions do they have, what uncertainties are lingering in their mind, what previous exposure do they have to the topic, and/or where have they seen the issue emerge in daily life? If they Google the topic, what did they learn? If they saw a movie or took another class that also mentioned the topic, how does it compare to this discipline's approach? If this is their first exposure to the topic/subject/idea, what are some follow-up questions they'd like to pose to their instructor? All of these things can/should be included in the students' study guide answers. The goal is to center critical thinking as a necessary part of the studying process, alongside the requisite content of the discipline being taught.

Through this process, students come to find themselves in the material, but not in the often feared, self-centered way that keeps students from thinking outside of their own experience. Rather, because the study guide is focused on building connections, students are coupling their experiences to the world outside themselves and, importantly, remaining open to acknowledging what they do not yet know. As a quiet practice, the work is done outside of the purview of their classmates, either on their own if done during class time or independently completed outside of class. In addition, when structured weekly—with specific questions and terms to be covered each week—this regular and quiet engagement helps students find and build the confidence in their own knowledge and thus may become more willing to take risks in (verbal) classroom participation.

Students might not always want to speak in class, but they had things to say about the study guide. The study guide and in-class writing portfolio are not practices that were explicitly addressed in the student surveys, but still they emerged in the data organically. When asked a general question about what aspects of their course helped them to be successful, 18 percent named the study guide as a key component of their success. One student elaborated:

> The aspect of the course that helped me be the most successful were the study guides. Even though they were a little tedious to complete at times, the study guides forced me to engage with the material in multiple ways. The questions forced me to listen attentively to the lectures, while the critical thinking column allowed me to connect the material with real-life experiences. The key terms section ensured that I would read the textbook.

This student highlights multiple benefits to the assignment, ranging from bringing them into interaction with the textbook, to developing critical thinking skills, to enhancing listening and focus during lectures.

Another student reiterated this capacity for focus by stating that "the lectures and the study guide helped me the most. These really allowed me to understand what we would be learning each week and having to fill out the study guide acted as taking notes which helped me stay more focused." Of course, not everyone was joyous about the assignment, such as the student who wrote that they were "draining to complete while doing an online class and during the Covid-19 era." More often, however, they wrote that "the study guides required actual thinking on my part," that "the study guide helped me in analyzing the concepts and applying [them] to daily life," and that "the study guide guided me through the course" and helped to "facilitate note taking." Here we can see how a single assignment can lead us to multiple desired outcomes, all while allowing students plenty of space to quietly explore their own minds and ideas.

Students' feelings about verbal classroom participation and the expectations around all this talk inform the aforementioned practices. As was explored in detail in chapter 2, students' discomforts around classroom participation warrants serious consideration and a set of practices that help them tend to those discomforts while building their skills and capacities. Quiet is not a way out but is instead used here as an entrance point, in particular in an introductory context, for student engagement. As we will explore further in chapter 4, these practices build students' confidence muscles. From field notes I can report that since I've implemented these assignments in face-to-face and online courses I've seen a noticeable difference in levels of student engagement. The time to think, write, and find their voice in the safety of silence leads to more students jumping into verbal discussions when they do happen.

Conclusion: Silence as Solution

Quiet can lead to more classroom dialogue, but it's up to us to push through the noise of classroom norms. The classroom is a social structure, and as such it is embedded with existing patterns, rules, and practices. Honors classes, lab classes, large classes, and small classes all have their own shape, their own feelings, and we bring our culturally inscribed habits along with us. For example, in larger classes I feel compelled to lecture, while smaller classes seem to beg me to come up with a never-ending stream of peer-based learning strategies. These macro-level forces affect us as we fulfill the social role of "teacher" and "student." It is expected that teachers talk and students listen, and yet teachers spend a significant amount of time attempting to disrupt student silence and facilitate engagement and dialogue. When students do talk it's often the same few students.

At the same time, quiet on its own is highly valuable. Further, and especially in the context of introductory classrooms, the expectation for dialogue can be overwhelming at best and silencing at worst. Introductory-level students need space and time to absorb the new ideas coming their way. Student survey data that highlights that most students know what they want and need can illuminate for educators the role that quiet could and should play in our pedagogical praxis. This chapter has explored the pedagogical theoretical context and field note and survey data, including the benefits of labor-based grading, alongside various playful but quiet practices that can cultivate classroom engagement while valuing students' desires and needs for quiet participation. In the next chapter, we will explore survey data as it pertains to one quiet practice in particular, a practice that encourages us to expand our notions of what classroom participation looks like.

NOTES

1. Michelle Page, "LGBTQ Inclusion as an Outcome of Critical Pedagogy," in *The Critical Pedagogy Reader*, third edition, ed. Antonia Darder, Marta Baltodano, and Rodolfo D. Torres (Oxfordshire, England: Routledge, 2017).

2. Page, "LGBTQ Inclusion as an Outcome of Critical Pedagogy," 355.

3. Kirsten Younghee Song and Glenn W. Muschert, "Opening the Contemplative Mind in the Sociology Classroom," *Humanity & Society* 38, no. 3 (2014).

4. Ange-Marie Hancock, *Intersectionality: An Intellectual History* (Oxford University Press, 2016).

5. Sue Nichols and Garth Stahl, "Intersectionality in Higher Education Research: A Systematic Literature Review," *Higher Education Research & Development* 38, no. 6 (2019): 1261.

6. Alison Mountz, Anne Bonds, Becky Mansfield, Jenna Loyd, Jennifer Hyndman, Margaret Walton-Roberts, and Ranu Basu, "For Slow Scholarship: A Feminist Politics of Resistance Through Collective Action in the Neoliberal University," *ACME: An International Journal for Critical Geographies* 14, no. 4 (2015): 1239.

7. Daniel P. Barbezat and Mirabai Bush, *Contemplative Practices in Higher Education: Powerful Methods to Transform Teaching and Learning* (New Jersey: John Wiley & Sons, 2013), 23.

8. Erving Goffman, *The Presentation of Self in Everyday Life* (New York: Double Day, 1959).

9. Kevin Quashie, *The Sovereignty of Quiet* (New Jersey: Rutgers University Press, 2012).

10. Jennifer Llewellyn and K. Llewellyn, "A Restorative Approach to Learning: Relational Theory as Feminist Pedagogy in Universities," in *Feminist Pedagogy in Higher Education: Critical Theory and Practice*, ed. Tracy Penny Light, Jane Nicholas, and Renée Bondy (Ontario, Canada: Wilfrid Laurier University Press, 2015).

11. "Harper Fast Facts," *Harper Fast Facts: Harper College*, accessed April 20, 2023, http://goforward.harpercollege.edu/about/news/facts.php.

12. Matt Richtel, "It's Life or Death: The Mental Health Crisis Among U.S. Teens," *New York Times*, April 23, 2022. https://www.nytimes.com/2022/04/23/health/mental-health-crisis-teens.html.

13. Sara Ashencaen Crabtree, Ann Hemingway, Sue Sudbury, Anne Quinney, Maggie Hutchings, Luciana Esteves, and Shelley Thompson, "Donning the 'Slow Professor': A Feminist Action Research Project," *Radical Teacher* 116 (2020): 57.

14. Tabitha Grier-Reed, and Anne Williams-Wengerd, "Integrating Universal Design, Culturally Sustaining Practices, and Constructivism to Advance Inclusive Pedagogy in the Undergraduate Classroom," *Education Sciences* 8, no. 4 (2018): 167.

15. Maria Isabel Ayala and Sheila Marie Contreras, "It's Capital! Understanding Latina/o Presence in Higher Education," *Sociology of Race and Ethnicity* 5, no. 2 (2019): 237.

16. Kirsten T. Behling and Thomas J. Tobin, *Reach Everyone, Teach Everyone: Universal Design for Learning in Higher Education* (West Virginia University Press, 2018), 26.

17. Behling and Tobin, *Reach Everyone, Teach Everyone*.

18. Tabitha Grier-Reed and Anne Williams-Wengerd, "Integrating Universal Design, Culturally Sustaining Practices, and Constructivism to Advance Inclusive Pedagogy in the Undergraduate Classroom," *Education Sciences* 8, no. 4 (2018): 167.

19. Peter McLaren, "Critical Pedagogy: A Look at the Major Concepts," in *The Critical Pedagogy Reader*, third edition, ed. Antonia Darder, Marta Baltodano, and Rodolfo D. Torres (Oxfordshire, England: Routledge, 2017), 57.

20. Beth Berila, *Integrating Mindfulness into Anti-Oppression Pedagogy: Social Justice in Higher Education* (Oxfordshire, England: Routledge, 2015).

21. Daniel P. Barbezat and Mirabai Bush, *Contemplative Practices in Higher Education: Powerful Methods to Transform Teaching and Learning* (New Jersey: John Wiley & Sons, 2013), xiii.

22. See the Tree of Contemplative Practices at www.contemplativemind.org.

23. Barbezat and Bush, *Contemplative Practices in Higher Education*, xii.

24. Barbezat and Bush, *Contemplative Practices in Higher Education*.

25. Agnieszka Palalas, Anastasia Mavraki, Kokkoni Drampala, Anna Krassa, and Christina Karakanta, "Mindfulness Practices in Online Learning: Supporting Learner Self-Regulation," *The Journal of Contemplative Inquiry* 7, no. 1 (2020): 248.

26. Laura M. Hill, "Contemplative Pedagogy in Times of Grief and Uncertainty: Teaching in a Global Pandemic," *The Journal of Contemplative Inquiry* 7, no. 1 (2020): 107.

27. Hill, "Contemplative Pedagogy in Times of Grief and Uncertainty," 107.

28. Ana Fonseca Conboy, "Transition in the Era of a Pandemic: An Exercise in Mindfulness," Journal of Contemplative Inquiry 9, no. 2 (2022): 17, https://journal.contemplativeinquiry.org/index.php/joci/article/view/259.

29. Amy Pucino, "Lessons from the Blurring of the Frontstage and Backstage: Community College Personnel's Experiences and Use of Contemplative Practices During the Pandemic," *Journal of Contemplative Inquiry* 9, no. 2 (2022): 7.

30. Antonia Darder, "Pedagogy of Love: Embodying Our Humanity," in *The Critical Pedagogy Reader*, third edition, ed. Antonia Darder, Marta Baltodano, and Rodolfo D. Torres (New York: Routledge, 2017), 104.

31. Yuk-Lin Renita Wong, "Knowing Through Discomfort: A Mindfulness-Based Critical Social Work Pedagogy," *Critical Social Work* 5, no. 1 (2004): 2.

32. See Beth Berila, *Integrating Mindfulness into Anti-Oppression Pedagogy: Social Justice in Higher Education* (Oxfordshire, England: Routledge, 2015); Kirsten

Younghee Song and Glenn W. Muschert, "Opening the Contemplative Mind in the Sociology Classroom," *Humanity & Society* 38, no. 3 (2014).

33. Kirsten Younghee Song and Glenn W. Muschert, "Opening the Contemplative Mind in the Sociology Classroom," *Humanity & Society* 38, no. 3 (2014): 319.

34. Barbezat and Bush, *Contemplative Practices in Higher Education: Powerful Methods to Transform Teaching and Learning* (New Jersey: John Wiley & Sons, 2013), 6.

35. Peter Kaufman and Janine Schipper, *Teaching with Compassion: An Educator's Oath to Teach from the Heart* (Maryland: Rowman & Littlefield, 2018), 2.

36. Kaufman and Schipper, *Teaching with Compassion*, 5.

37. Kaufman and Schipper, *Teaching with Compassion*, 6.

38. Maurice Holt, "It's Time to Start the Slow School Movement," *Phi Delta Kappan* 84, no. 4 (2002): 268.

39. Riyad A. Shahjahan, "Being 'Lazy' and Slowing Down: Toward Decolonizing Time, Our Body, and Pedagogy," *Educational Philosophy and Theory* 47, no. 5 (2015): 495.

40. Mary L. Goldschmidt, Jessica L. Bachman, Mary Jane K. DiMattio, and Jill A. Warker, "Exploring Slow Teaching with an Interdisciplinary Community of Practice," *Transformative Dialogues: Teaching and Learning Journal* 9, no. 1 (2016): 2.

41. Berg and Seeber, *The Slow Professor*.

42. Berg and Seeber, *The Slow Professor*.

43. Goldschmidt et al., "Exploring Slow Teaching with an Interdisciplinary Community of Practice."

44. Stephen J. Smith, "Slow Down and Smell the Eucalypts: Blue Gum Community School and the Slow Education Movement," *Journal of Global Education and Research* 1, no. 1 (2017): 31.

45. Laura J. Link and Thomas R. Guskey, "How Traditional Grading Contribute to Student Inequities and How to Fix It," *Curriculum in Context* 45, no. 1 (2019).

46. Asao B. Inoue, *Labor-Based Grading Contracts: Building Equity and Inclusion in the Compassionate Writing Classroom* (Fort Collins, CO: WAC Clearinghouse, 2019).

47. Inoue, *Labor-Based Grading Contracts*, 3.

48. Inoue, *Labor-Based Grading Contracts*, 5.

49. Kathleen Kryger and Griffin X. Zimmerman, "Neurodivergence and Intersectionality in Labor-Based Grading Contracts," *Journal of Writing Assessment* 13, no. 2 (2020), https://escholarship.org/uc/item/0934x4rm, 1.

50. Louisa Tomas et al., "Are First Year Students Ready for a Flipped Classroom? A Case for a Flipped Learning Continuum," *International Journal of Educational Technology in Higher Education* 16, no. 1 (January 2019): 2.

51. Oyèrónkẹ́ Oyěwùmí, *The Invention of Women: Making an African Sense of Western Gender Discourses* (University of Minnesota Press, 1997).

52. Antonia Darder, *Reinventing Paulo Freire: A Pedagogy of Love* (Oxfordshire, England: Routledge, 2017).

53. AnaLouise Keating, *Teaching Transformation: Transcultural Classroom Dialogues* (New York: Springer, 2007), 10.

54. Kaufman and Schipper, *Teaching with Compassion*, 30–31.

55. Merilee Hamelock and Norm Friesen, "One Student's Experience of Silence in the Classroom," *Norm Friesen*, July 2012, https://www.normfriesen.info/papers/ihsrc2012.pdf.

56. Darder, *Reinventing Paulo Freire*, 67.

57. Quashie, *The Sovereignty of Quiet*, 72.

58. Claire M. Zedelius and Jonathan W. Schooler, "The Richness of Inner Experience: Relating Styles of Daydreaming to Creative Processes," *Frontiers in Psychology* 6 (2016): 2, https://doi.org/10.3389/fpsyg.2015.02063.

59. Rikke Toft Nørgård, Claus Toft-Nielsen, and Nicola Whitton, "Playful Learning in Higher Education: Developing a Signature Pedagogy," *International Journal of Play* 6, no. 3 (2017): 273.

60. Peter Kaufman, "Poetic Sociology," *Everyday Sociology Blog*, July 8, 2013, https://www.everydaysociologyblog.com/2013/07/poetic-sociology.html.

61. Becky Thompson, *Teaching with Tenderness: Toward an Embodied Practice* (University of Illinois Press, 2017).

62. Berg and Seeber. *The Slow Professor*.

63. Darder, *Reinventing Paulo Freire*.

Chapter 4

(Quiet) Participation Leaves the Classroom

When the pandemic shut down our classrooms in March 2020, learning drastically changed for all of us. For me, one key question was about how to shift the principles of pedagogies of quiet into the context of asynchronous online learning. How do we build relationships in classes that do not structurally facilitate social interaction? My first shift was in communication. I took the approach that regular, consistent, and compassionate communication was key to establishing a connection with my students. One student wrote that "she always made sure that we were doing okay. Like actually okay and gave us time to figure stuff out. Edwards was, I think, one of my only teachers who would send out consistent emails/posts checking up on us." 31 percent of students said that the announcements, and 23 percent of students asserted that compassionate language, made them feel cared for and connected to the class.

Belonging is a crucial component of student success, and the pandemic certainly made me think through how to adapt my teaching so as to facilitate this in the context of shut downs and stay at home orders and health crises. Regular emails to students was a start, but the next step was to think through the assessment process as a whole, and participation in particular, so as to incorporate a quiet pedagogical approach during the pandemic, but in ways that would be useful beyond this context as well. Journaling, as will be explored in this chapter, became a bridge into asynchronous participation that supported the values of a quiet pedagogical praxis and that tended to the ways in which the structure of online learning could be silencing.

In earlier chapters I have explored the systemic dynamics that function to silence students—especially historically marginalized students—as well as students' explanations for their reticence toward verbal classroom participation. We have seen how pedagogies of quiet take an intersectional approach toward students' lives and learning needs—they are introverted, first year, first generation, LGBTQ, women, students with mental health diagnoses, students of color, and often hold many of these identities simultaneously—in addition to utilizing an intersectional pedagogical framework. There are many theories in existence to pull from here. We can incorporate the philosophy of slow time that emerges from the slow professor movement and the care and compassion of feminist pedagogy. We can include the labor-based grading that comes from the antiracist pedagogical framework alongside the focus on critical thinking that emerges from critical pedagogy. We can attend to all of these, along with a contemplative pedagogical approach, fusing together these theories into the overarching framework for pedagogies of quiet.

As outlined, one goal of pedagogies of quiet is to decenter "talk" as the privileged participatory approach and to both value and include quiet as a key component of our learning spaces. At the same time, we want to strike a balance, as it's important that students continue to develop their competence with verbal communication as their interpersonal and work lives depend upon these crucial skills. Thus, while we see opportunities for quiet as important in and of themselves, this pedagogical approach is a scaffolding for confidence in their inner quiet: their intellect, their ideas, their creativity, their critical thinking, and, in time, enhanced confidence with verbal conversations. This process of shifting back and forth between quiet and talk is best accomplished with a multitude of practices. While these next chapters focus on two distinct strategies, it's important to remember that pedagogies of quiet cannot be reduced to a single (or two) strategy. Given our historical inheritance, it's crucial that we continue to reflect on the philosophy of the practices, the sociological and historical reasons for bringing a quiet approach into the classroom, and the importance of multitudes.

SILENT REFLEXIVITY: PARTICIPATION JOURNAL

The first strategy that I tried in the process of developing a quiet teaching practice was the incorporation of classroom engagement technologies (see chapter 5). I had been collecting survey data for one year, asking students to reflect on how they felt about speaking in class (see chapter 2) and about the classroom technology's impact on their learning when COVID hit and campus shut down. I had also implemented the in-class writing portfolio (see chapter 3) and was contemplating how to reconfigure this to the online context. Here I was faced with a new realization: truly transformative pedagogies of quiet would require that we expand our pedagogical praxis beyond the physical classroom. Teachers construct syllabi that outline their content, policies, assessments, and grading formulas. As such, overall grades tend to emerge from individual scores on quizzes, papers, exams, group projects, and, in some cases, classroom participation. In this framework, each individual assessment is sometimes seen as a separate if even necessary piece of the whole. For example, a quiz can be seen as separate and distinct from classroom participation, even though students review their notes before the quiz, take deep breaths before taking the quiz, and put their phone on DND before taking the quiz. Pedagogies of quiet take a broad view of participation, where we can frame each and every (graded) assessment as having a participatory component. Thus, we recognize that when students prepare for and take quizzes, for example, they are also engaging in classroom participation, even if this (most often) happens outside of our field of vision, outside of the classroom.

When COVID moved everything out of the classroom it begged the question, "How do we bring more of our students' participation into view?" To answer this question I developed a journaling assignment. There are myriad ways to utilize journals in the classroom, and I am not introducing some new and shiny technique. Instead I am transforming an existing, reliable practice. As Hubbs and Brand wrote, "journaling, as a learning strategy, provides opportunities for students to mull over ideas, uncover inner secrets, and piece together life's unconnected threads, thus creating a fertile ground for the significant learning" that we hope for our students.[1] As will become clear in the following pages, this assignment sees student reflexivity as a necessity and is an important way to incorporate social justice principles (such as seeing students as knowledge producers) into the classroom. It also allows students to use their voices in myriad ways to illustrate to their teachers their participation and engagement, without having to rely solely on verbalizing in the classroom, whether on Zoom or face to face.

The goal is to use the participation journal to deconstruct our preconceived notions of what participation is and what students can do to earn a participation grade. Faculty socialization, as discussed in previous chapters, is often limited to the covert socialization of the hidden curriculum (for example, we teach the way we were taught, or in opposition) and to informal gossip. As such, students and teachers alike are enculturated into the oft-silencing practices of the neoliberal university.[2] Journaling, and including feelings into the learning space, is seen as a "feminine" endeavor and thus a counterhegemonic praxis. Engaging mind and body is a path toward new knowledge where emotions form the intellect and vice versa.

A quiet pedagogy seeks the wildness of students' inner quiet, challenging the "traditional" approach. Granting students the agency to define for themselves what participation means and to articulate their own descriptive explanation of their daily or weekly accomplishments for the class allows students and teachers alike to develop a broader and more emancipatory view of student participation. This quiet practice is a marriage of critical and contemplative pedagogical theories whereby students are given the chance to see their engaged moments of silence as participation and to experience their relationship to their teachers and to the class content relationally. Through this process students don't just answer their teacher's in-class questions; they are asking and answering their own questions and are active facilitators of their own knowledge.

The overarching premise of the participation journal is for students to keep track of everything that they do to engage with—to participate in—their class. This can include sending their teacher an email or attending office hours, as well as work they do to set homework schedules and/or read required texts prior to class. If the student sees an activity as pertinent, then they include it in their participation journal. The assignment prompt (see appendix B for the full template) asks students to reflect on/write about four categories of experience:

> (1) What you did to participate in the class and how long these tasks took. (2) The environment in which you are studying/working/quiz taking and how that environment impacts your experience. (3) Any changes you are making from day to day, week to week, in how you are approaching the class. And last, but still remarkably important: (4) How you are feeling about what you are learning—what interests you, what challenges you, what inspires you, what frustrates you, etc.

These general categories encourage students to shift beyond list making and into a reflective analysis of their experiences inside and outside of the classroom. They are encouraged to think about the course content alongside their cell phones, their nutrition, their (potential) sensitivity to noise, and their emotions, while exploring new practices in the face of struggles. Importantly, they are told to see any struggles as a place of learning.

Students are given a template to guide their experience creating both a reflective and meta-cognitive experience. The template can be scaffolded to progress throughout the semester so that the directives in the first few weeks shift as the weeks progress. The extensiveness of the journal prompt and template allows us to see how limiting it is to rely solely upon verbal classroom participation. The assumptions—such as the oft-made assumption that participation happens inside the classroom—that we bring into the classroom shape our pedagogical praxis. In this way, the Western worldview, as it is oriented around sight, impacts our desire to see our students' learning.[3] From here, we shape our participation expectations and grades around that which we bear witness to in the classroom.

I approach this with transparency: opening this up to the students, in the way that the participation journal does, begs the question of trust. How do we know that our students are doing what they are saying they are doing?

One way to approach this is by encouraging and modeling honesty and by responding to honest journal entries with compassion. In students' journals, they've written statements such as, "well, you asked us to be honest, so . . ." and then they go on to explain how they did not accomplish something that they hoped to. When I read these journal entries I respond by thanking them for their honesty and reminding them that it's hard sometimes to balance life, work, and school. I then encourage them to reach out to me for help in completing assignments and/or reminding them that there's still time to get the work done (depending on related deadlines).

As another example, we as teachers could start by opening up class with an admission of a lack of sleep, of a sick pup that had to go to the vet, or some other human experience—within the comfort of our professorial boundaries—that can pull our focus away from our studies/work. In an online context, we could post an announcement about challenging world events and include a short "meditation or yoga for stress relief" YouTube video and encourage students to take care of themselves. Thus, we are modeling humanity to our students and reiterating that the class is not the only thing that is important in our lives. We can acknowledge and balance our coursework with our lives and the weight of the world, and we can be open about how difficult it is to strike that balance, hard as we try, and keep on trying.

Further, in the years that I've been assigning the participation journal, I've found that students are very honest (without much needling) about their experiences and respond very positively to feedback comments that praise such honesty. For example, students will write in their journals that they skipped a lecture or missed a quiz, and the instructor feedback could be welcoming and encouraging by saying to the student, "some weeks are harder than others, given the complexity of life, but I'm so glad to read that you are doing your best!" Encouraging comments from the instructor beget more honesty from students, as does the labor-based grading. Rather, students who complete the journals in good faith effort are less of a concern than those who take the assignment lightly. Of course, it is a graded assignment, and as such, the instructor has the purview to assess the quantity and quality of each students' participation journal. We can encourage students to reach out when they are struggling, we can encourage them to dig deeper in their journals, we can support the larger context of their lives, all while providing the accountability of the graded assignment.

Finally, these journals address the many problems of voice that arise in the classroom—such as the white racial habitus and the chilly classroom—in that they allow students to see participation through the lens of silence. One way for teachers to disengage with faculty "moves to innocence" is to listen to what our students have to say, especially when they aren't speaking. In silence, students can focus on their quiet inner lives, seeing their list making and text highlighting (things they do without speaking) as equally important to their classroom discussions. This assignment also allows them to give voice to their experiences—nonverbally—by writing about their thoughts and feelings and practices with their instructor. Thus, we as teachers have documentation of the depth of what happens in students' quiet spaces—in their heads, in their homes, in the library—that are typically left out of our purview.

This depth is supported by the data and illuminated by the empirical themes that will be explored here, from over five semesters of student surveys (275 students opted into survey responses), where they were asked to reflect on the participation journal and its impact on their experience in their class. The data collection period overlapped with the global pandemic, and as a result, all of the students were enrolled in online courses. Given the ongoing nature of COVID and the potential for future disruptions, in addition to the neoliberal push toward asynchronous learning, online learning is here to stay for many of us, and these insights are remarkably useful for us to carry forward. At the same time, the participation journal is just as useful in the face-to-face context.

When asked to explore how the participation journal shaped their experience in the class, five themes emerged from the data: time management (44 percent), approaches to studying (29 percent), processing course content (20 percent), a mindful reflection of emotions (17 percent), and communication with the professor (8 percent). At the same time, when asked what aspects of the course made them feel cared for, many students (21 percent) elaborated on how the journal was a path to relationship building. In the pages that follow, we will see the many ways in which pedagogies of quiet can transform our students' experiences in the classes that incorporate such an approach, along with the ways in which teachers and their future students can be transformed by the knowledge we gain from this journaling assignment.

As stated, these courses were online and during the pandemic, though the practice has continued with successful results in the classroom postlockdown. Some of my preconceived notions of online teaching and learning (from prepandemic online teaching) were that it was disengaged—disingenuous even—and of lesser impact and import than in-person learning. And yet, upon the first journal that I read, I quickly realized that I learned more about my online students through these quiet assessment practices than I had gained from in-person classroom observations and conversations. I wasn't alone in seeing the benefit. When students talked about the impact of the participation journal, they used general words like helpful, good, and positive. Certainly there were some students (7 percent) who didn't find benefit in the assignment, but overwhelmingly the students who chose to participate (in the survey) framed their experiences in positive light.

Quiet Participation and Content Engagement

A reflective journal assignment, at first glance, might not feel connected to our curriculum, but students' survey responses illustrate that there is a deep tie between this broad view of participation and students' learning of their college coursework. It's important to remember that while much pedagogical theory, critical theory being prominent among them, focuses primarily on content and content delivery, the reality is that content, assessment, and classroom culture are all intertwined and interdependent. We know, too, that our nonverbal communication is just as important as our verbal communication. If we don't construct an operational definition of participation and if we aren't transparent with our students, then what will emerge is the implicit assumption that student participation means verbal participation. This hidden curriculum then constructs a normative and limiting framework, decreasing student agency and minimizing their educational capital. Instead, if we construct an emancipatory definition of participation that includes talking with friends, making connections about course content while watching television, making a weekly calendar, and listening to lectures, then we can see how the transformational educational experience cannot be confined to the walls of the classroom.

These processes are reciprocal, so that any work in addressing one area—here, assessment practices in the form of participation grades—will impact the others. For those teachers whose primary interest in curriculum development is to facilitate critical thinking, the participation journal highlights how quiet assessment practices promote students' deepening engagement with the content. So many of us come to this work with a deep passion for our students and disciplines. Teaching is an inherently political act, and our hopes for students' deep learning are connected to our hopes for our civil society. While we love to see our students' "aha" moments in class, the participation journal allows us to take this further, to become a witness to our students' learning experiences outside of the classroom.

One way this took shape for students was through shifting their learning process from a passive to an active experience. For example, students reported that the fact of the journal—of having to write down not just what they did to participate in the class but also how they felt about what they were learning—meant that they had to keep a more engaged focus when listening to lectures or reading course texts. They couldn't allow the material, as one student wrote, to "go in one ear and out the other" because they were required to journal about their experience after the fact. As a result, they were able to, in the words of another student, "be ready to absorb more material" because, as another put it, they had to "think actively while doing assignments."

Some students talked about journaling as important to their studying because it allowed them or, as some put it, "forced them" to reflect and to "recap" what they were learning each week (it is a graded assignment after all). It gave them more space to "mentally digest course content" and "helped [them] review the material." At the same time, this "second chance to review the material" was more than review: it was a way for many students to dig deeper into the content and to explore their own relational ideas. Students felt that journaling allowed them to explore not just the content but their own ideas about the content, a crucial shift for critical thinking. Through the quiet, contemplative practice of journaling, students were able to build their critical thinking skills across the sixteen weeks of the class and to "shape [their] own understanding of the material."

One student wrote about this shift from study habits and time management into a more complex relationship with the course content and the overlap with other course assessments:

> The writing journals served a few purposes for me and I think it was shown as what I was writing about changed week to week. Early on I was focusing on what my study habits were, what was distracting, and how I was adjusting to this style of class. Much more recently, I was using the journals to still talk about what I accomplished each day, but I was writing more about some of the critical thoughts I had. Examples were how I felt about the material, whether or not I was understanding the material, and if videos or parts of other lectures were helpful to me. Some of the thoughts probably should've ended up on the study guide, but I had them after I finished listening to the lecture so the journal felt a little more appropriate. The journal became an extension of the study guide in that sense. Each week, regardless of what I wrote about, the journal served a helpful purpose in me learning or digesting the material.

This student's process goes deeper than reviewing the material; the focus is on comprehension, critical thinking, and remaining mindful of how they are feeling about what they are learning. This reinforces quiet pedagogy's goal of engaging with both a universal design and a culturally inclusive praxis. These two approaches meet up in the desire for students to be centered in the learning process. Thus, "rather than relying on and reifying a normative life experience that can leave many at the margins, in the constructivist classroom instructors and students can act as co-creators of knowledge that is connected to the life experiences of those in the room as they engage in the process of making meaning of curricular material."[4]

A central component of coconstructing knowledge is relationships and centering the interactional context of learning. Like student classroom participation, however, these relationships do not just exist inside the walls of the classroom. In some cases, this was about building a relationship with their teacher, as will be discussed in more detail shortly. But for many other students, what was important about this process wasn't just that they were writing it down for themselves but that they were a part of a conversation with themselves. One student wrote,

> I think more than anything the journal encouraged a lot of self-reflection. As we talk about deep topics that are relevant to my life, I am invested and learning how I can make the world a little better place. This also helped solidify the notes I had taken and encouraged me to talk about it to others.

Many students felt encouraged that talking about course content with friends and family was seen, as outlined in the journaling assignment rubric, as a valued and important aspect of class participation. They enjoyed being able to "talk about course content with others and then write about it." The self-reflective component then allowed them to think through how these conversations shifted and developed the content they were learning.

Talking with others about what we learn—and students' ability to earn a labor-based grade for this engagement—is an important supplement to issues of curricular representation. Critical, feminist, multicultural, and contemplative pedagogical theories all share in the belief that students should be able to see themselves in the classroom. In this way, representation in the curriculum matters, and a deeper reflective engagement allows students to reveal their own life experiences and bring them into direct conversation with the course content. This could be a process of exploring their personal ideologies about a certain subject (for example, engaging with preexisting ideas about whether they "like" the subject of the class they are enrolled in) or situating themselves historically in relationship to the content being presented, among other possibilities. As one student put it,

> this class has forever changed the way that I view the world and I even have discussions with my family on an almost daily basis about what I have learned. I felt especially connected to the class . . . and I found examples of the material within my own life.

Students made it clear in their survey responses that the participation journal was a way to engage in this kind of "dialogue" without having to speak in class. This highlights the central principle of pedagogies of quiet: participation happens even when we don't hear our students talk. And, in return, we see more of them and they see more of themselves.

One student made the point that the participation journal "helped me to see the bigger connections in my life" and another said that the assignment "forced me to think about learning applications IRL [in real life]." While we could explicate the semantic differences between "helped" as compared to "forced," we can see either way that the assignment assisted—or insisted—the students in drawing a line from the course content to their daily lives, allowing them to see themselves in the material, and in the social world, in new ways. As Laura Rendón argues, "connecting knowledge to everyday life can be considered a form of wisdom," and this can be argued to be a deeper engagement than can come from textual representation alone.[5] That is, seeing oneself in the/a text is important and a crucial component of constructing an inclusive classroom. Having students reflect on how they relate to all of the course content in a weekly journal allows them to regularly make, as one student put it, "connections between the material and the real world" and their place in it, taking representation to a deeper level of learning.

The students also reflected on their level of engagement with the course content as a result of the journal. In addition to being able to "connect the readings to personal experiences" and to "look deeper into the reading[s]," they were also using the journal to "realize [their] own points of view," "deepen [their] understanding," and "share doubts" and "critical thoughts." These doubts, as outlined in chapter 2, often render them silent during class engagement opportunities, but they are encouraged and willing to express them in the participation journal. The asynchronous online learning environment and the face-to-face introductory classroom settings, especially larger classes, are both spaces that can be hard to capture students' attention. In one, there's the lack of physical connection, in the other there's an undeveloped relationship with the subject matter. In this way, the quiet practice of the participation journal allows teachers to address both of these potential concerns. The act of journaling helped online students stay connected to the course, as the assignment, in the words of one student, "deepened my engagement with the online lectures." And it is clear from all the previously mentioned quotes from student surveys that the process helped to deepen their connection to this new subject matter, making it relevant for them in a way that isn't automatically experienced in an introductory-level context.

Given macro-level concerns about achievement gaps and student success rates, this practice of quiet pedagogy is a useful teaching and learning strategy for any institution that is attentive to improving student outcomes. As Johnson and Stage write,

> Although the general population entering college rose in number, the proportion of students completing college degrees remained steady and, in some years, slightly declined (Carey, 2004; Shapiro et al., 2015). The six-year completion rate is about 50% (U.S. Department of Education, 2015), and the time taken to earn a college degree in the United States has consistently risen since the mid 1980s.

At the same time, these authors make the case that most research on student completion has focused on either the institutional or the individual level, with the latter attending to the personal characteristics of students. The study here, on the other hand, provides a framework for thinking about student engagement and persistence through classroom pedagogy, relying on quiet practices that are able to reach students where they are and to build threads that connect them to their courses.

Conversations among educational researchers about student persistence often focus on the racial and ethnic backgrounds of students, where students of color are often seen as "first-generation college students who face a number of obstacles to degree completion, particularly the absence of resources to navigate social and academic cultural practices."[6] In the face of this problematic "gaps" framework, first-generation students, through quiet journaling, were able to illuminate and become "more aware of how I use resources available to me." These students, of which 51 percent at the institution are first generation, come to us with resources; they have capital and can build more.

Quiet pedagogies shift all of us beyond normative assumptions about capital so that teachers and students alike can explore their inner quiet to strengthen the resources already present. Sociologists have argued that this individualizing "gaps" framework misses the mark, as first-generation students of color come into institutions of higher education with an abundance of cultural capital, even if it isn't recognized by the white racial habitus of their institutions.[7] Pedagogies of quiet see the need to intervene with this white racial habitus—of our classroom praxis and our assessment strategies—so as to create the space for students to utilize the capital they possess as they enter our classrooms all while developing further once inside. Through the participation journal, they can show their teacher the capital they rely upon, allowing us to eschew these assumptive, gaps-based frameworks.

Quiet Participation and Time (Management)

Time is a central component of day-to-day life, and also a feature of twenty-first-century life that is significantly impacted by capitalism. The culture that emerges from late modern capitalism is one that leaves us feeling rushed, looking for more hours in the day, and attempting to multitask our way into accomplishing all we hope to. As Judith Walker writes, "whereas the modern capitalist sought to control time, under globalization the postmodern knowledge worker attempts to outsmart time."[8] As American society transitioned into postindustrial capitalism after World War II, the hopes that capitalism would free us, producing more leisure time to enjoy our family and friends, quickly turned into a myth as we became a society of people working two to three jobs and sixty-hour work weeks.[9]

College students are living out this time pressure as they balance work (often multiple jobs), family life, and their college coursework. The wellness industry is increasingly becoming a third shift; individuals are also responsible for practicing self-care in order to cope with the demands on their time. Getting organized in the midst of all this hustle and bustle is no easy feat. Further, the shift toward more options for online learning during and since the pandemic added additional complexity, as asynchronous learning in particular requires its own relationship to time and time management. Teachers, too, feel the pressures of time. Many of us feel like we don't have enough time to get through all the content we'd like to—and in some cases have to—teach. It's clear from talking to students that the time pressures faced by faculty in the context of the neoliberal shift in higher education are impacting students' lives as well, both inside and outside of the classroom. As pedagogies of quiet urge faculty to develop a slow approach, they also facilitate students' capacities to both slow and manage their time in relation to their coursework (modeling the same for life outside class).

When thinking about time management, our goal is not to achieve greater efficiency—to increase the amount of work that can be done in a given period of time—but to think toward student success. It's true that "academic capitalism requires both the reification of time and an internalization of the importance of managing time in a demonstrably efficient manner,"[10] but we also know that student success benefits from a mindful approach to time utilization. College enrollment ebbs and flows along with historical shifts, but success rates don't always mirror enrollment: "the data shows that the successful completion rate has not kept pace with enrollment despite the increased numbers of students enrolled in colleges."[11] Thus, the approach here is to be mindful of student success while deploying an intersectional pedagogical approach toward this end.

It is true that one of the critiques of the mindfulness movement in the United States focuses on how corporations are using mindful tactics in the service of efficiency, productivity, and thus profit.[12] In this way, employees are not the ones that are most benefiting from meditation and yoga rooms in their shared office spaces. These critiques posit that mindfulness is being coopted by a predatory capitalism that is exploiting workers' desires for more relaxation and focus—itself a need shaped by capitalist working conditions—so as to access more hours of productive labor.[13] Given the neoliberal turn in higher education and the previously discussed concerns regarding the problematic consequences of academic capitalism, incorporating mindfulness into higher education is viewed with similar concerns.[14] Attention to these concerns is important.

And yet attention to time management and mindfulness can be deployed together to produce significant benefit to students. The data presented here makes it clear that students see significant benefits from quiet in general, and the participation journal in particular. Because one of the aims of mindfulness practices is focus, the potential for impact on student success rates hollows out concerns of capitalist commodification. Completion rates "are now becoming a primary concern for colleges at all levels because state and federal funding is aligning with completion rates and not just enrollment numbers, as they were in previous decades," and especially so at community colleges.[15] With increases in enrollment from first-generation students, English language learners, international students, and students of color, greater attention is being paid to the ways in which inequities in the school system shape completion rates.

Thus, when students report that the participation journal "helped them figure out the best environment for focus" or that they were able to "address procrastination" through journaling, we can see the benefits. Procrastination, for example, is strongly correlated to poor student outcomes.[16] As Hensley and Munn write, "procrastination is an ideal target for self-improvement, as college students' tendency to procrastinate often leads to academic underperformance and distress."[17] They further make the case that "researchers have found negative connections between procrastination and students' grades, use of effective learning strategies, and persistence in college."[18] As such, the participation journal is a quiet intervention. Students are able to self-assess their participation and to see everything that they do in relation to the class—from small to large—as relevant and important. Rather than relying solely on verbal participation in class—which leaves many students feeling afraid, skeptical, and doubtful—the participation journal allows them a wide berth to find their footing in the class. As a result, as they repeatedly wrote in their surveys, the assignment "kept [them] focused." In the words of another student: "I like the reflections. They help me reflect on my own tendencies and try to make adjustments to better my learning."

One aspect of twenty-first-century life that shapes students' experiences with procrastination is cell phones. Cell phones are designed to engage us, through instant gratification and the capitalist impulse to consume, connecting us to the corporations that want us to buy. It works. Especially in the context of (large) lectures, cell phones pull away students' attention and increase the likelihood of procrastination, thus impacting student outcomes.[19] As will be discussed in the next chapter, there are effective ways to incorporate cell phones into the participation environment. In addition, the participation journal is a space where students can develop the tools to bring a mindful awareness to the impact of their cell phone use. Many students wrote about the need to establish different and new relationships with their digital devices.

One student wrote about the journal, "for me it was a fun thing to do. I really enjoyed it. I think my TikTok story was the best part, and I am glad that while writing this journal I realized that I need[ed] to delete TikTok." This student's capacity to focus on the impact of social media—and to take necessary action—helped her to improve on her work and focus in the course (and arguably beyond!). The journal template guides this process for students enhancing their self-monitoring.

In reflecting on their cell phones as distractions, one student wrote in their survey response regarding their experience with the journal,

> Time management was the biggest thing! I had no clue how much time I was wasting on my phone until I started writing the weekly journals. That definitely impacted me in a positive way because I became more conscious of it and I started putting my phone on do-not-disturb or just stashing it elsewhere while I worked on my assignments.

The quiet aspect of the journal gives students, such as this student quoted here, the space to develop mindful awareness and to reflect on the conditions in which they are learning and how to deal with distractions. It also respects the attention they are giving to their experience in the course as part of a wider participatory experience, earning them a labor-based grade for the journal assignment. When we view participation through the lens of talking, or as only what happens in the classroom or Zoom room, we miss these small but crucial moments of student engagement. Instead of participation being what teachers see, student agency is enhanced through their ability to self-define their participation experience.

These actions—from turning the phone's ringer on silent to journaling about how distracting their cell phones are—all shape the participation ecology of our students. They also accumulate. Each tiny moment, like using DND, accumulates toward content engagement and introductory "mastery." The journaling experience allows students to manage their time in the midst of such distractions, so as to, in their words, "more effectively establish goals" or "stay accountable to the class." One student wrote that the journaling experience "kept me grounded in reality," while another wrote that "the weekly journal helped keep me present in the course." From this space of goal setting and attentiveness to the course, students were able to then move on to other key features of time management, and further, as established previously, into a deeper relationship with the course learning outcomes.

The students surveyed for this project were both full-time and part-time students, many of whom were also employed in one or more paid jobs. As such, they reported that the journals helped them with time management in their life overall, in addition to the origin course of the assignment. Students reported that journaling was crucial to, in the words of one student, "managing my workload," while another reported that it "helped with balancing my time with my other classes." One student, a full time employee and parent, wrote,

> I think writing the weekly journals helped me to stay focused on the work that I need to get done each week. Writing the journals held me accountable, and almost forced me to do the assignments even when I really did not feel like it. Writing about time management truly helped me the most. At the beginning of the semester, I struggled a little to keep up with the large workload because I also work full time, have two kids, and take other classes. Actually writing out everything I did in a week helped me plan out my time better and made me realize that I needed to plan in order to get everything done. Once I saw that time management was my issue, I decided to change the way that I completed my assignments, and I no longer was doing homework late at night. I found a way to balance everything in my life, and towards the end of the semester, I had a routine developed and knew when to get everything done.

This balancing is about more than managing time as an "illness" of academic capitalism, where the goal is to "outsmart time."[20]

Rather, the focus on finding balance illuminates a crucial wellness component. This student—and the many others who expressed similar sentiments—used journaling about time management not just to get work done but to find a space of calm amid all the work. For this student, journaling helped the student to balance all of their responsibilities while determining the best way to complete the course material. Other common responses included gratitude for the journaling's impact on assignment deadlines, where they were able to "ensure that I didn't miss assignments" and more generally manage all of the material and assignments. Developing this awareness—of time, workloads, working conditions—is a key outcome of this quiet practice. It is only from a place of awareness that key changes, whether micro or macro, can be made.

Finding more balance in the midst of a busy life and course load can come from taking a macro look toward scheduling as well. It's one thing to use a syllabus to look at the work for the day. The students surveyed for this project, however, also commented on how the participation journal allowed them to look at the big picture. They were able to "envision how big my workload was" and to make necessary adjustments so as to be "more aware of how I use my time." Ultimately, this led them to a greater understanding of "when to get work done" all while keeping students "from falling behind." One student elaborated on their process:

> The journal impacted my learning in this course in a positive manner because it helped me stay on track based on when to complete my assignments and

quizzes. Initially I wanted to get my assignments done by the first three days of the week but either due to a busy schedule or events, I couldn't be able to do so; thus I started journaling each week on the days I completed my assignments and noticed a pattern on the days I was getting most of my stuff done, therefore, I made that my weekly schedule based on that and was able to turn my assignments on time. Not only that but it also helped me keep a track with my quiz scores and have a goal for myself for the next time I was finishing an assignment. Therefore, the weekly journal was really beneficial for me.

This student, in essence, saw their journals as data regarding their time schedule and was able to build the most effective schedule so as to complete assignments and establish goals. We can see that the utility of this assignment isn't about getting more done or fitting more work into an already busy day but about meeting assignment deadlines and, as we previously saw, about deepening students' relationship to the material. That is, time management, or rather an awareness of time in regard to both deadlines and time of day, was a crucial jumping off point into further benefits of this and other quiet teaching practices.

The students quoted earlier make it clear that they are balancing a heavy workload and regularly feel pressed for time. Time online can also feel elusive. As one student put it, "I found it harder to keep track of things because everything is online and it doesn't feel like I actually have a deadline at times, but the participation journal really helped with that." Time is a part of the white racial habitus of academic capitalism that shapes students' experiences both outside and inside the classroom. They feel rushed by deadlines and in class are often left struggling to participate verbally as a result of this lack of time. The cultural assumptions that are reinforced about time in faculty syllabi are abundant, whether they're around assignment deadlines or late-to-class penalties. The participation journal assignment allows students to engage in quiet participation and to think through and understand their own relationship to time and thus to the course material and assignments. This is one way in which pedagogies of quiet enable student agency and success.

Quiet Participation and Study Skills

Time management was the most prominent theme that emerged in student comments, with 44 percent of students commenting on time in their open-ended survey responses. At the same time, many students (29 percent) wrote about not just time management but their overarching approach to engaging with the material and studying for assessments. The two often overlapped, as exemplified by this student, who stated that "I think writing the journal helped me to really reflect on what helped me with staying on track and made working easier. It also helped me to take note of what did not help my success, and I was able to make changes until I found what worked best for me." As the data was coded, "staying on track" was interpreted to reflect time management, as the phrase was most often used in connection to assignment deadlines. On the other hand, students spoke often, as the previous student did, about how they adjusted their learning practices toward greater success. In this way, the participation journal helped students to identify—and make any changes to—their preferred learning and study habits, enabling greater success in the course. This process was exemplified by a shift away from a focus on time and deadlines and toward self-reflection around successful learning practices.

For example, in addition to being able to schedule their time and ensure assignment deadlines were met, they also found that the journal helped them to analyze their study habits, allowing them to "identify good and bad patterns" in their behavior, so as to, in the words of another student, "develop a system for learning the material better." For example, the students were encouraged to include in their journals any changes they were making on a day-to-day and/or week-to-week basis in their approach to the class. As a result of taking note of these changes, they were able to identify patterns and to, for example, "develop better methods for notetaking." Many students elaborated and stated that they were able to realize the conditions under which they were the least distracted and thus the most productive. One student put it this way: "over time I was able to see what helped and what hurt my experience, and to make changes accordingly."

Success was at the center of these comments, as illustrated by this student who wrote:

> Writing the participation journals really helped me to stay on track with the course and learn early on in the course what study habits worked for me and what ones didn't. I learned that to really take away from the lectures, I had to be in my room in silence to really focus on the concepts being discussed in the lectures. I also learned that taking handwritten notes really helped me to be able to go back and effectively answer the study guide questions in detail. All of these habits have helped me to earn and maintain an A in the class, which I am satisfied with. I think [the teacher] should continue to use this study tool for future classes. I really liked it.

This student highlights yet another benefit of engaging in learning through the perspective of silence, through settling into and paying attention to our inner experience. Though we want students to hear others' perspectives, and to share their own, some learning happens best in the midst of silence. Further, as this student articulated, tracking their experience helped them to focus on successful outcomes, including, in this case, earning an A grade and remaining focused while learning the material.

The students, through their journals, were able to think through the ideas being presented to them through the course content and, in the process, articulated that the journaling experience was shining a light on their studying practices. "Studies have consistently demonstrated that college students who engage in self-monitoring, either through instructor/practitioner prompting or as part of their regular study habits, receive higher grades and attain learning outcomes more effectively than students who do not self-monitor."[21] And, as is being argued here, this self-monitoring should be understood as classroom participation, which requires we reframe our operational definition of participation. They wrote in their survey responses that the journaling helped them to do things like organize their ideas, solidify their notes, and "discover their best learning style." They reported that they were able to "monitor their learning patterns and study habits" and to "identify good and bad patterns." That the journaling led them to analyze their study habits facilitated continued benefits.

Before delving into the impact on deeper-level thinking, such as critical thought, students reported that the journaling process led them into greater effectiveness with organizing their ideas. One student put it this way: "I was able to keep my thoughts and ideas together in a more coherent and organized way." One problematic aspect of the "banking" educational model within neoliberal capitalism is the push to teach toward the test. Quiet pedagogies allow both teachers and students to resist this impulse; the participation journal is one useful route. As a result of journaling, some students reported being able to bear witness to their own trajectory of shifting away from learning to memorize and toward learning for knowledge production.

Students used exactly this language as they wrote that they were able to "think hard about what [they] did" and "shift from memorizing to learning." One student referenced that we often get stuck in habit loops that may not be helpful. In their words, "writing the journal positively impacted my experience in the course because it encouraged me to really evaluate the methods of learning that I engage in and whether or not those are actually helping me at all, or if I keep using those same methods simply out of habit." Journaling—a method of practice that is included in the "tree of contemplative practices"[22]—(re)produces mindful students. Whether the students are reifying what they already knew about themselves or discovering new strategies and patterns, this quiet approach to their participation in class helped them to (re)develop an awareness of best practices in learning. That they do this on their own, through journaling, and are able to develop their own unique strategy (while also earning a labor-based grade), shows how pedagogies of quiet reinforces universal design principles.

When I first began my own reflexive process around talking and silence, my intuition (alongside Susan Cain's book *Quiet*) told me that this was key to inclusivity. Quiet students, my gut said once I was paying close enough attention to listen, could have ADHD, or anxiety, or they could be in the closet, or they could fear social stigma. Research documents that self-monitoring, for example, improves learning outcomes for students with ADHD.[23] Self-monitoring, however, can have a powerful impact for students with these invisible but important threads.

Quiet Participation and Processing Emotions

Quiet pedagogy is an approach that aims to disrupt the hegemonic conversational architecture of classroom participation, to the benefit of all students but with a keen eye on those who are most marginalized by hegemonic classroom norms. One path is through embodiment. Contemplative and feminist scholars make a compelling argument for incorporating the body into the classroom. Students did so without prompting, through writing regularly in their journals about eating, hydration, sleep, and stress, and the impact of this aspect of their embodiment on their learning experience. Of course, doing so opens the door to the messy realities of human existence, of which systems of power—colonial, patriarchal white supremacy—have systematically worked to deny. While patriarchy frames emotions as irrational, journaling can be easily dismissed as an unintellectual, and thus unnecessary, pursuit. We must push against this dismissal, and, as bell hooks argues, "we must return to a state of embodiment in order to deconstruct the way power has been traditionally orchestrated in the classroom, denying subjectivity to some groups and according it to others."[24] Recognizing our bodies means allowing for our own vulnerabilities. Journaling and self-reflection are a pathway to connecting the mind and the body in learning.

This is a requirement for teachers if we hope to avoid teaching in a way that centers our own egos, leading to an increased reliance on faculty "moves to innocence" and what Peter Kaufman and Janine Schipper refer to as "teachersplaining."[25] Tied to the "popular term mansplaining," a patriarchal practice that denies women voice and authority, teachersplaining refers to the idea that teachers are the experts meant to fill the brains of our students, who come to us empty of knowledge in our subject area.[26] This practice, reliant upon teachers' presumptions about what students know and what they need, produces a culture of silent students who are meant to listen only to their professors.

Faculty moves to innocence and teachersplaining are practices that emerge from the "banking model" of education where students are seen as empty receptacles to be filled by the expert knowledge of the professor. Based in the meritocratic individualism of Western culture, these frameworks see students as "lacking" either in knowledge or in the necessary capital for learning. Both practices—faculty moves to innocence and teachersplaining—allow teachers to take the center stage, even as we profess concern for our students' learning potential. Pedagogies of quiet aim to dismantle these practices and to recenter the body alongside engaging students as active learners.

Recognizing our students' embodiment means allowing their full humanity in the classroom as well as being mindful of our place and role as teachers. Kaufman and Schippers write that "teaching with compassion means finding a way to teach from a place of humility, and at times, vulnerability. It means considering the 'big picture' needs of students and prioritizing their growth, development and well-being over our own needs for validation and approval."[27] The participation journal—and the theoretical principles of pedagogies of quiet more generally—allow these processes to unfold. There is humility and vulnerability required of us to give up the ability to witness all of our students' classroom participation and trust in their articulation of their experience; doing so, however, facilitates their growth, their well-being, and recenters the body into the classroom praxis. Quiet is a path toward both feeling and embracing this vulnerability.

Any given classroom engagement activity (or assessment practice) need not be utilized simply to entertain students. For most of us, we desire them to engage from the heart, with the goal of improving their lives and their society. Many faculty are frustrated by the culture industry's entrenchment in our students' lives, in particular their social media use on digital devices; we are all astutely aware of the impacts of social media on mental health, for example. Despite this urge to resist the attention economy, an assignment that students, in retrospect, argue was an "enjoyable assignment" that "made the class fun" is a good starting point for a more meaningful and embodied experience. The participation journal was clearly an exercise in mindful reflection for students, allowing them the space to explore their relationships and their well-being, all while reflecting on their experience in the course (and in life more generally).

Learning is a relational experience, and the mindfulness that emerges from journaling illuminated this point. Critical theory's commitment to dialogue and feminist theory's commitment to a praxis of care argue this thoroughly. AnaLouise Keating's "pedagogy of invitation" includes the belief that we must develop "relational teaching tactics based on the belief in our radical interconnectedness with everything (and everyone) that exists."[28] The participation journal assignment deployed and assessed here is one way to engage students in relational learning, albeit in a quiet way. That is, for students the journaling process itself creates a relational perspective, including self-awareness. Students reported being impacted by the experience in such a way that they were able to see, for example, "how [their] feelings shape [their] actions." The journal also allowed them to feel like they were able to "express myself personally," highlighting that in-the-classroom verbal participation is only one route to student expression. Quiet is itself a space of expressiveness.[29]

When students report that what they appreciated about the journal assignment was the ability to "express my feelings about what I was learning," they understand that they are expressing themselves relationally. That is, they are expressing themselves to themselves and also *to someone else*, and that aspect of feeling heard was a key component of their appreciation for the assignment. As has been made clear, verbal classroom participation does not always result in students' feeling heard. There are many valid reasons for students' classroom silences (as outlined in chapter 2), and historically marginalized students especially may feel this weight. As bell hooks writes, "I recognize that students from marginalized groups enter classrooms within institutions where their voices have been neither heard nor welcomed, whether these students discuss facts—those which any of us might know—or personal experience."[30] Given the demographics of the students in this study—and in the community college at large—that these students feel the assignment gives them a "necessary outlet" is compelling.

At the same time, what's also important here is the space for students to *have feelings* and, as one student said, to feel "encouraged . . . to share [their] thoughts and feelings." When classrooms are constructed around the "white guy habitus,"[31] the rational mind prevails at the expense of the emotive and physiological body. The emotionality of quiet—what we find when we look inside us—has been "constructed as the domain of women."[32] We challenge this hegemony by valuing all our students' full humanity through valuing their quiet. In this way pedagogies of quiet take seriously the need to center student wellness, outside and inside the classroom. In a multitude of ways, students reported that the participation journal positively impacted their well-being in the class.

For many students, the participation journal was experienced as self-care. When asked in the survey how the participation journal impacted their experience in the course, many of them wrote about the process as a "stress reliever." One student elaborated:

> The journal definitely brought a positive experience, it was something that I did at the end of the week that was very calming. I was able to relax and reflect about my week, whether it was a difficult or great one. I tended to use my participation journals as a reflection about my time management throughout the weeks. It was also helpful to hear feedback [from my professor] and knowing that she appreciated the time and effort I put into the journals and work even with a busy schedule.

One focus of contemplative pedagogical theory is helping students develop the tools to bring awareness to the processes of their mind and body, and per the students surveyed here, this assignment fits the bill. The students used it as a "mental check-in" for themselves and as a way to "let out [their] emotions." As a result, one student wrote that the process "made me feel less overwhelmed." Given the complexity of our students' lives, especially during the pandemic and in light of global and local political shifts/rifts, this is a clear benefit and an important way for students to grapple with these forces, both public and personal. In addition, one point that begs repeating is that students engage in much of their coursework and learning outside of our classrooms. Whether it's the unspoken ideas circulating through their minds, the studying they do in the library after class, or the to-do list they create on a break at work, there's a lot of engagement we don't see. The journal, as mentioned by the previously quoted student, helps them to feel their efforts are seen, even when we don't physically bear witness to this activity. This in turn shapes their emotional experience in the classroom, drawing them in to the content of the class.

Students also used the assignment as a route to develop not just their awareness of the full range of their experience—intellectually, emotionally, and physically—but a stronger sense of agency. Students reported that the assignment made them feel more in control of their experience. They reported that journaling was a way to not just reflect on their struggles but to "feel more in control" and to "build confidence." While using the experience to "destress" and "express emotions," they also used it as a "good reminder of [their] successes." One student elaborated by writing that "the journal helped me to respond to and address the stressors in class and life" while also making them "feel proud to see and reflect on my own accomplishments."

Laura Rendón argues that it takes "a unique kind of pedagogy to take . . . students from their self-doubts to a heightened awareness about their academic abilities and future potential."[33] Pedagogies of quiet is one such approach. Another student's comment supports this sentiment: "Overall, it was a nice assignment to complete at the end of the week because it reminds you of all the things you were able to successfully complete and how you were able to make things work." Given the extent to which verbal, in-class participation (in introductory-level courses) made students feel worried, embarrassed, and too vulnerable to social judgment, quiet participation incorporates a broad range of student participation practices that functions to build students up and helps them walk into a greater feeling of confidence.

Finally, students used the journaling experience as an opportunity to engage in self-reflection, where they felt the "freedom to write openly" and to "be honest with myself." Honesty came up repeatedly in their journals, as evident in this student's reflection:

I thought the journal really helped me with being able to see how well I did the week before and to see my progress. I know I had weeks when I wasn't on top of everything as much as I should have been so the journal helped me be honest with myself and see the things I can work on so that I don't keep making the same mistake every week.

This process of developing their self-awareness was then deployed to improve their coursework and their overall experience in the course. They were able to "collect thoughts" in an organized space. Because the journal "allowed for self-reflection," students were able to be "thoughtful about [their] effort" and to "make adjustments" as necessary. Students' survey responses made it clear that they appreciated the opportunity to be mindful, that they saw this as helpful, not just so that they could "express [their] thoughts without being judged" but so that they could "reflect on weekly work" and "make improvements."

As a result, students were able to learn the material through enhanced feelings of well-being and connectedness. The participation journal gave students the opportunity to reflect on their experiences at both the micro level and macro level and thus were able to learn "a lot about [themselves] in addition to the subject matter." This proved to be "calming" and "relaxing" in addition to being able to "tell what stuck with [them] the most" and to "process, review, and prepare" for future assignments. In particular, it was the contemplative and quiet component of this assignment that facilitated these experiences, highlighting the nuanced utility of pedagogies of quiet. As Chelá Sandoval argued, "mind formed through the imperatives of culture is transformable through self-conscious reflection," and as a result, offering up spaces of quiet to students is a powerful practice.[34]

Pedagogies of quiet sees this self-reflexivity as crucial for us all. It's especially important for students to be able to engage with their own emotions as so often they can interrupt the learning process. The attentiveness that emerges from the journaling process facilitates "contemplative practices [and the] emphasis . . . on personal awareness leading to an increased sense of understanding and wisdom."[35] As teachers we have these same needs, and as such, it's important to note our own needs for self-care, in particular for teachers with multiple, intersecting identities. Following in the footsteps of Audre Lorde, bell hooks, and Gloria Anzaldúa, who "write of the necessity of women of color to practice self-care and self-love in order to deal with the daily onslaught of racism, sexism, homophobia, and class oppression,"[36] a quiet pedagogical approach demands that we take care of ourselves alongside our students.

Pedagogies of quiet rely on an intersectional framework—both theoretically and practically—and leave plenty of space for faculty to adjust the practices as needed. For some faculty, the emotional tenor of a journaling assignment can be too much, depending on our own lives and intersectional locations. As Donna Nicol and Jennifer Yee write,

> We know that we cannot sustain ourselves if we are physically exhausted, emotionally drained, and spiritually dead. Therefore, when embarking on our careers as junior tenure-track faculty—assistant professors—we made commitments to each other to resist sacrificing our health and fulfillment as holistic beings and to "not let this job kill us."[37]

As such, we urge each faculty member to consider what's best for themselves, alongside their students, and make any necessary changes to the assignment rubric.

For example, in order to maintain the ethos of a quiet participation ecology, students can journal about their participation—their daily activities, their environments, the changes they are making to their learning practices—and faculty can put more boundaries around the emotive aspects. As Catherine Berheide et al. write, "women faculty, especially BIPOC women, do not have the same shield against student demands as men faculty do,"[38] and thus we must be attentive to our capacities to engage with the emotional labor that can come with a journaling assignment. At the same time, faculty can manage self-care through a reliance on labor-based grading practices, whereby we can give students feedback without feeling the need to comment on each and every mention in their journals. No matter, it's important for us to be mindful of our own self-care needs when constructing our assessment and participation praxis.

Teaching requires significant emotional labor, and this burden most often falls on the shoulders of women faculty, in particular women of color, queer women, and women with disabilities. Not only do many of us face gendered expectations around care taking, but we also face daily microaggressions and systemic inequalities. A quiet approach to teaching—incorporating feminist, antiracist, contemplative, and slow theories—allows faculty to reclaim some time and space for themselves, alongside their students, to tend to their emotional needs. For example, after a difficult interaction with a colleague in the hallway, I walked into my classroom frazzled and with a racing heart. Rather than push through and start class by diving right into the material, I opened with a brief deep breathing exercise that gave me a moment to collect myself and calm my nervous system, while also creating a transition for students, who also came into the room carrying their own burdens from the outside world.

Valuing embodiment as central to the classroom experience clearly has many benefits. Students can develop agency, build confidence, express themselves in a trusting environment, and inhabit their vulnerability alongside building their strengths. Faculty can benefit from this as well as we carry our own embodied needs into the classroom. In this way, the participation journal, as a component of a quiet praxis, allows for self-care, but importantly it also leads us toward a more relational practice of community care.

Quiet Participation and the Student-Teacher Relationship

Antonia Darder encourages teachers to develop a "pedagogy of love" modeled after Paulo Freire, and in this way the participation journal is a pedagogy of self-love.[39] Building on Audre Lorde's oft-quoted articulation of self-care as radical, activists and social justice advocates have come to understand the importance of self-care to any social justice project and to the human experience.[40] Of course, in this articulation self-care isn't about an expensive spa day with cucumber water and ambient flute music but about a practice of positive self-talk. As students were reflecting on their experiences with journaling about their classroom participation, they noted that through engagement with their study habits and approaches to learning they were also able to become more effective cheerleaders for themselves. Importantly, it also deepens into community care through its capacity for relationship building.

Self-care is important, but it has also been coopted. In this way, the need to incorporate self-care into our lives has become another component of productivity culture and has ballooned into a billion dollar wellness industry. Radical self-care, on the other hand, especially when coupled with an ethos of community care, can be transformative. Here, relationship building becomes a crucial component of pedagogies of quiet, where the praxis is meant to lead toward silence as a means of social connection (as opposed to isolation).

Having a classroom full of students who can engage in encouraging self-talk, and who feel connected to our course, is a goal for many of us. Find me a teacher who doesn't want to hear (read: in the case of these surveys) their students say that an assignment was "helpful" because it allowed them to feel "invested" and "motivated." Many students wrote that they used the journal as a way to "look back on their accomplishments," in particular on days where they were feeling frustrated. For example, students would write that they had a general feeling that they weren't doing enough for the course, but when they went to do the journal and wrote everything down they were able to reframe that negative perception to a positive reality of accomplishment. In this way, the journal served as a "good reminder of [their] successes." As a result, the journaling process, and the agency that it imbued students with, becomes a self-directed way for students to feel empowered and motivated. In juxtaposition to students' feelings surrounding speaking up in class, which they often experience as demotivating, pedagogies of quiet are a beneficial way to connect students to themselves, the expectations of the class, and the course content.

Indeed, students found that the participation journal allowed them to come to know themselves better. They developed a deeper understanding of their relationship to time (management) and their study habits, as well as finding a space to engage with the course material and the feelings that the content and workload evoked. While all this was happening it was also clear that social relationships were developing. In the data analysis, a final pattern that emerged from student responses was appreciation for an opportunity to develop and strengthen their relationship with their instructor. 13 percent of the students surveyed wrote directly about the value of this assignment and the possibility of a more vibrant student-teacher dialogue. AnaLouise Keating argues for "a theory and praxis of intersubjective identity formation where self-development occurs in the context of other equally important individuals."[41] Quiet pedagogy is just such a theory and praxis, and the participation journal in particular invites us into such a relationship.

Further, as will be elaborated upon in the next chapter, Sherry Turkle argues that digital technologies are transforming our capacities to engage with each other, in particular in the context of in-person conversation. Students make it clear that the messy realities of in-person discussions are fear inducing, as they are vulnerable to making mistakes, being misunderstood, and upsetting others. As a result, our pedagogical approach should include the building up of our capacities for engagement and relationship development. Pedagogies of quiet doesn't call for an end to in-person dialogue; rather, it's an approach that provides alternates to, alongside pathways toward, greater (verbal) dialogue.

The participation journal is an entrance point for these conversations and relational capacities. Critical and feminist theorists, in particular, argue for a reorganization of the relationship between teachers and students, where we (as the teachers) are encouraged to reject the "banking model" of "teacher-splaining" so as to engage students with knowledge production. Doing so, however, requires developing relationships—and open lines of communication—with our students. One student wrote, "what helped me most about writing the participation journals was the line of communication with [my professor]. Many of my classes were completely on your own with many of my teachers being hands-off. Getting the feedback on the journals made me feel heard." It is through comments such as these that the students surveyed for this project made it clear that the participation journal helped to facilitate this relational process.

While some students stated that one of the benefits of the participation journal was the open invitation to talk to others about course content, even outside of class, and to incorporate those discussions into their understanding of classroom participation (where the classroom doesn't have finite walls), others focused on the assignment's capacity to strengthen their relationship to their instructor. They reflected that the journal allowed them to "talk to the professor" and to "share their concerns with the professor." They felt that it was a "non-judgmental space to voice my struggles" and that they "felt cared for [because] the teacher wanted to hear about my struggles." This assignment, in the words of one student, "created a pathway to the professor" and, in the words of another, "felt very interactive with the professor."

As one example, the participation journal template concludes with a section titled "Just Sharing," where students can share anything on their mind, ranging from videos that remind them of the class, books they are reading, study music they are listening to, anything. In this space it is common for me to read sentiments such as, "I don't have anything additional to share this week but I really appreciate you providing the space to share." In other cases, dialogues about the benefits of listening to jazz while studying have ensued, developing a space for a back and forth written dialogue between student and teacher built around sharing and common interests.

Introductory-level courses as well as larger courses (as explored in chapter 2) can sometimes increase students' feelings of disconnection. Asynchronous online learning is also a difficult context to develop personal connections. While faculty who are teaching graduate student seminars have increased capacity—due to smaller class sizes and mentoring—to develop strong personal connections with their students, those of us teaching primarily first-year and introductory students face greater structural barriers to such relationship development. We see our (on some campuses commuter) students less often, rarely have them in more than one class, and often have too many students to develop deep ties with all of them. For part-time faculty, driving to multiple campuses and a lack of dedicated office space further complicates this relationship development. When teaching a large lecture with over one hundred students it's difficult to impossible to be able to put faces to names for all of our students. Pedagogies of quiet—and the participation journal in particular—are a way to address these structural impediments some of us face to developing relationships with our students.

Students pointed this out, as well, addressing that they were able to feel connected *despite* being in an online class. As one student wrote,

> The journal helped me express my feelings about how I felt about the material for the week. It felt good some weeks to just say "I'm unsure of myself in this class" just so the instructor knows how you are feeling overall since we are not face to face at the time. To be able to say the material this week was challenging, etc. it felt like a good outlet.

While the participation journal is an excellent tool in the face-to-face classroom (especially so in larger classrooms where there is less intimacy), students made it clear that it offered something in the online context that is sometimes missing. Just as a previously quoted student commented on their "hands off" teachers, many students felt this teacher-student connection missing in the online, pandemic context. One student elaborated,

> I think the fact that I could voice what I struggled with helped me the most. I feel like professors, especially with online learning, are not as engaged with their students, which I know is not in their control, but it's easy to feel abandoned and feel like you just have to get through your classes and do whatever needs to be done in order to get good grades. But with this journal, I felt like [my teacher] really cared about students, and like [my teacher] genuinely wanted to know how we were doing so that sense of emotional validation and connection was the most helpful to me. I liked that I could speak freely and honestly with what I was struggling with, and knowing that I would not be judged was a refreshing feeling.

When students write that they felt "like the teacher [is] actually there and listening" or that "the journaling assignment makes me feel like my work means something to my professor," it makes clear that they have often *not felt this way*.

That is, the discourse of their survey responses highlights the regularity with which they do not feel connected or important to their teachers, especially in the pandemic shutdown era. Many of them addressed this through attentiveness to faculty feedback. While we've all likely overheard many "kids-these-days" arguments from colleagues that our students don't read or value our feedback (a faculty "move to innocence" that is sometimes used as a justification for opting out of doing the required labor for providing feedback), the students surveyed here directly challenge this sentiment. They reflected that "I really appreciated when [my teacher] would take the time to read through our participation journals. In previous classes I have received automated responses when I turn in work that I genuinely wanted to be recognized for. Please keep doing this! It helped me personally to feel seen as a student."

These connections in turn lead to a deeper relationship to the course content, to learning, and to student success. Students clearly appreciated this, as evidenced by their survey responses, such as one student writing that "I felt really connected by writing the journals every week." Professors must be held to account for the classroom cultures that we create. Kaufman and Schippers write that it is remarkably difficult to address those times when we inadvertently or unintentionally humiliate students. Even the most altruistic and empathetic educators have experienced situations where students come away feeling ashamed and demeaned. Perhaps our comments or actions were interpreted differently than we intended; we assumed a level of familiarity or comfort with students that wasn't there; we failed to acknowledge their contribution to a discussion; or we had a moment where we were frustrated or lost patience and reacted in a way that was uncharacteristic.[42]

I've done all of the above over the course of my career and will not pretend that my incorporation of the practices outlined in this book render me above such moments of messy humanity in the future. That said, students made it clear in their survey responses that the participation journal is one way to build a classroom culture that allows students to "ease anxiety," "feel a personal connection with [the teacher]," and to feel "heard" and "understood" all while helping them to better understand the material being taught.

One way for students to feel heard is for us, as teachers, to read through their insights with slow attention and not just zip through to a list of "how-to" practices. That is, reading these pages, this data, is also a form of relationship building. Students have deep insights into the learning experience, and it would behoove us to listen to them. What they are saying is that the participation journal—a way of journaling that deconstructs traditional notions of classroom participation—allows them to build a better relationship with themselves, the course content, their teacher, their daily lives, and the world. In this work teachers and students alike have a bigger view into the possibilities of participation and into what's made possible through transformed relationships.

CONCLUSION: CLASSROOM WALLS OF GLASS

The quiet practice of the participation journal turns our classroom walls into glass, providing for us a window into our students' experiences with learning, and life, outside of the classroom. This is a graded assignment that gives students "participation points" but doesn't mandate that participation be either verbal or in the physical classroom. As a practice of pedagogies of quiet, it illuminates students' inner worlds alongside the engagement that we bear witness to during class time. In the process, students report, overwhelmingly, that the assignment was beneficial, allowing them to reflect on their time management and study skills and make any necessary changes to help ensure their success in the course.

That they do this on their own, through self-reflection, highlights the agency and confidence they build up in the process. Further, they deepen their understanding of themselves, while also strengthening their relationship to both the course content and their teachers. From this place of connection and belonging students, as told in their own words, thrived in the context of their course and through this quiet practice. Of course the journal alone does not make the entirety of the quiet pedagogical praxis. As such, it's important to explore other areas where we can bring a philosophy of quiet into the classroom participation ecology.

NOTES

1. Delaura L. Hubbs and Charles F. Brand, "The Paper Mirror: Understanding Reflective Journaling," *Journal of Experiential Education* 28, no. 1 (2005): 60–71, https://doi.org/10.1177/105382590502800107.

2. Antonia Darder, *Reinventing Paulo Freire: A Pedagogy of Love* (Oxfordshire, England: Routledge, 2017).

3. Oyèrónkẹ́ Oyěwùmí, *The Invention of Women: Making an African Sense of Western Gender Discourses* (University of Minnesota Press, 1997).

4. Tabitha Grier-Reed and Anne Williams-Wengerd, "Integrating Universal Design, Culturally Sustaining Practices, and Constructivism to Advance Inclusive Pedagogy in the Undergraduate Classroom," *Education Sciences* 8, no. 4 (2018): 2.

5. Laura I. Rendón, *Sentipensante (Sensing/Thinking) Pedagogy: Educating for Wholeness, Social Justice and Liberation* (Sterling, VA: Stylus Publishing, LLC, 2012), 89.

6. Sarah Randall Johnson and Frances King Stage, "Academic Engagement and Student Success: Do High-Impact Practices Mean Higher Graduation Rates?," *The Journal of Higher Education* 89, no. 5 (2018): 755.

7. Maria Isabel Ayala and Sheila Marie Contreras, "It's Capital! Understanding Latina/o Presence in Higher Education," *Sociology of Race and Ethnicity* 5, no. 2 (2019).

8. Judith Walker, "Time as the Fourth Dimension in the Globalization of Higher Education," *The Journal of Higher Education* 80, no. 5 (2009): 483.

9. Juliet B. Schor, *The Overspent American: Why We Want What We Don't Need* (New York: Harper Collins, 1999).

10. Judith Walker, "Time as the Fourth Dimension in the Globalization of Higher Education," *The Journal of Higher Education* 80, no. 5 (2009): 484.

11. Kris Kimbark, Michelle L. Peters, and Tim Richardson, "Effectiveness of the Student Success Course on Persistence, Retention, Academic Achievement, and Student Engagement," *Community College Journal of Research and Practice* 41, no. 2 (2017): 124.

12. Ronald Purser, *McMindfulness: How Mindfulness Became the New Capitalist Spirituality* (London: Repeater, 2019).

13. Purser, *McMindfulness*.

14. Purser, *McMindfulness*.

15. Kris Kimbark, Michelle L. Peters, and Tim Richardson, "Effectiveness of the Student Success Course on Persistence, Retention, Academic Achievement, and Student Engagement," *Community College Journal of Research and Practice* 41, no. 2 (2017): 125.

16. Dmitri Rozgonjuk, Mari Kattago, and Karin Täht, "Social Media Use in Lectures Mediates the Relationship Between Procrastination and Problematic Smartphone Use," *Computers in Human Behavior* 89 (2018).

17. Lauren C. Hensley and Karleton J. Munn, "The Power of Writing about Procrastination: Journaling as a Tool for Change," *Journal of Further and Higher Education* 44, no. 10 (July 2020): 1450.

18. Hensley and Munn, "The Power of Writing about Procrastination," 1451.

19. Rozgonjuk, Kattago, and Täht, "Social Media Use in Lectures Mediates the Relationship Between Procrastination and Problematic Smartphone Use."

20. Judith Walker, "Time as the Fourth Dimension in the Globalization of Higher Education," *The Journal of Higher Education* 80, no. 5 (2009): 483–509.

21. Hensley and Munn, "The Power of Writing about Procrastination," 1451.

22. Duerr Maia and Carrie Bergman, "The Center for Contemplative Mind in Society," *The Center for Contemplative Mind in Society*, accessed February 10, 2022, http://www.contemplativemind.org/practices/tree.

23. Mindy C. Scheithauer and Mary L. Kelley, "Self-Monitoring by College Students with ADHD: The Impact on Academic Performance," *Journal of Attention Disorders* 21, no. 12 (2014): 1030–39.

24. bell hooks, *Teaching to Transgress* (Oxfordshire, England: Routledge, 2014), 139.

25. Peter Kaufman and Janine Schipper, *Teaching with Compassion: An Educator's Oath to Teach from the Heart* (Maryland: Rowman & Littlefield, 2018), 21.

26. Kaufman and Schipper, *Teaching with Compassion*, 22.

27. Kaufman and Schipper, *Teaching with Compassion*, 44.

28. AnaLouise Keating, *Teaching Transformation: Transcultural Classroom Dialogues* (New York: Springer, 2007), xi.

29. Kevin Quashie, *The Sovereignty of Quiet* (New Jersey: Rutgers University Press, 2012).

30. hooks, *Teaching to Transgress*.

31. Michael A. Messner, "White Guy Habitus in the Classroom: Challenging the Reproduction of Privilege," *Men and Masculinities* 2, no. 4 (2000).

32. Quashie, *The Sovereignty of Quiet*, 130.

33. Laura I. Rendón, *Sentipensante (Sensing/Thinking) Pedagogy: Educating for Wholeness, Social Justice and Liberation* (Sterling, VA: Stylus Publishing, LLC, 2012), 93.

34. Keating, *Teaching Transformation*, 15.

35. Carla Wilson, "Unsettling Women's and Gender Studies 'Settler Logics,'" in *Teaching Gloria E. Anzaldúa: Pedagogy and Practice for Our Classrooms and Communities*, ed. Margaret Cantú-Sánchez, Candace de León-Zepeda, and Norma Elia Cantú (University of Arizona Press, 2020), 279.

36. Donna J. Nicol and Jennifer A. Yee. "'Reclaiming Our Time': Women of Color Faculty and Radical Self-Care in the Academy," *Feminist Teacher* 27, no. 2–3 (2017): 134.

37. Nicol and Yee, "'Reclaiming Our Time,'" 135.

38. Catherine White Berheide, Megan A. Carpenter, and David A. Cotter, "Teaching College in the Time of COVID-19: Gender and Race Differences in Faculty Emotional Labor," *Sex Roles* 86, no. 7 (2022): 442.

39. Darder, *Reinventing Paulo Freire*.

40. Nicol and \ Yee. "'Reclaiming Our Time.'"

41. Keating, *Transformation Now!*, 71.

42. Kaufman and Schipper, *Teaching with Compassion*, 23.

Chapter 5

Quiet Technology in the Classroom

The concerns that led to the development of a praxis of quiet pedagogies are grounded in an understanding of the structural force of patriarchal white supremacy. Classrooms can sometimes be "chilly" and silencing, especially for historically marginalized groups. According to Antonia Darder, "teachers [need] to both feel the urgency of the difficult conditions [we] are facing within schools and at the same time respond with thoughtful and reflective tactics and strategies."[1] In this vein, I have conceptualized the practices outlined here as liberating: if everyone is silent, no one is silenced. Of course, the latter only becomes true if silence is used to increase students' abilities to both access their (inner, quiet) voice as well as to send that voice into the shared space of the class. Thus, the driving force behind pedagogies of quiet is to open space for all students using a UDL framework that is especially mindful of those most often impacted by silencing forces—anxious students, introverted students, neurodiverse students, LGBTQ students, female-identified students, and students of color—to enter the conversation as whole people. Pedagogues, from feminist to multicultural to critical, recognize that classrooms are most effective when filled with a multitude of voices; we learn not through domination but in relationship.

Forcing students to speak when they are not ready is not social justice education; rather, many students, especially in the introductory context, experience it as oppressive. As one student wrote in their survey response, "if I get called on too early when still learning the material I don't want to embarrass myself. If I don't know the material yet then it'll be obvious and the professor might think I didn't try to know the material." Students want to be well perceived, and they want to learn. This student's point about getting called on "too early" highlights that participation is complex. It isn't simply a matter of those who like to talk as compared to those who don't like to talk; timing and context matters.

Given the goal of quiet pedagogy to engage students, to inspire their attentiveness to their inner quiet and thus critical thought, classroom discussions are approached creatively. And while we value students' quiet and cultivate intentional and collective silences so as to focus on the inner worlds of our students, this isn't the only aim. One goal of this approach is to *increase* students' *verbal* participation, in particular those students who report that they are never or only sometimes willing to talk in class. Given the impacts and stressors of daily life and of systems of oppression on students' lives, the ethos of quiet pedagogies is to engage the introverted, the anxious, and the marginalized in ways that are empowering, to use silence as a route to disrupt rather than reinforce power in the classroom. As outlined in the previous chapter, one way to do this is through an expansive understanding of participation by way of a weekly journaling assignment, where students have the autonomy to define for themselves what encompasses their classroom participation. In this chapter we will explore another route—this one inside the classroom—using technology as a route into voice.

Previously, we've discussed many of the possible classroom practices of quiet pedagogy in brief, while in this chapter the incorporation of interactive presentation software that allows for real time feedback[2] will be explored in depth, coupled with empirical data from students' reflections on how utilizing this classroom technology shapes their classroom voice(s). Pedagogies of quiet have relied upon numerous platforms into the classroom space, most reliably including Mentimeter, Padlet, and Perusall. The technology that is referenced in this chapter—Mentimeter—was chosen for its capacities around open-ended questions and was first implemented in face-to-face classes, and it is in this context that the data comes from. The other platforms

QUICK LIST: QUIET WAYS TO USE CLASSROOM TECHNOLOGY

- Welcome practices at the beginning of class.
- Small groups sharing their work with the large group.
- As an invitation to connect with others.
- Bringing students into a deeper relationship with course texts.
- Review course content.
- Prepare for quizzes and exams.
- Share in-class writing.
- A space for asking questions.
- Explore patterns and themes that emerge from the class's responses.

are very effective, but they were not included in the study as they weren't discovered and implemented until after the surveys were distributed. All this technology comes with both benefits and concerns.

SILENCE AS A WAY OUT

Some faculty engage in moves to innocence that shift the blame—for example, regarding poor performance and participation—onto students' relationship to digital technology, cell phones, and social media. Clearly, then, the digital landscape plays a significant role in our students' lives and classroom experiences and in faculty judgments of both. We, their teachers, carry perceptions into our syllabi and our classrooms about how technology shapes them. Some faculty, for example, have policies in their syllabi requiring students to have phones on silent and put away in their bags; some discourage the use of laptops and/or tablets. New AI technology, like ChatGPT, is continuing to upset the technological balance of the educational sphere.

Tobin and Behling write, "bring up the subject of student engagement and digital distraction at any faculty gathering and brace yourself for tales of woe involving laptops, cell phones, and their instruments of pedagogical subversion that seem to distance instructors from their students."[3] Indeed, when I have given presentations to faculty groups about quiet pedagogy's reliance on technology, the question and answer session has most often been driven by luddites and skeptics. Broadening our understanding of classroom participation, through quiet practices, includes reliance upon classroom technology. But this causes a dilemma for those of us who prefer that our students put their devices away during class. We are aware of, and concerned about, their ever-strengthening pull.

It is argued here, however, that the utility of this approach outweighs the costs. Relying on a universal design framework facilitates this: "it's about designing interaction in the learning experience and providing learners with choices about how they interact."[4] In this way, the technology embedded into the quiet classroom—coupled with assignments like the in-class writing portfolio discussed in chapter 3—provides multiple avenues for students to enter dialogue with the content and their classmates. In addition, concerns about digital technology can be validated, attended to, and minimized. Tobin and Behling outline the importance of relying on technology for universal design: "UDL allows us to design interactions that counter the kind of depersonalization that can accompany technological mediation . . . it encourages more, not less interaction and communication." As we will see, this pans out in the data from students.

How are you feeling today?

Figure 5.1. How are you feeling today?

QUIET PRACTICE 5A:
A HUMANIZING START TO CLASS

Using the word cloud function (see figure 5.1) of your digital engagement platform of choice, ask the students a question about their life, their feelings, or their body. Some commonly used questions include the following:

- What are you feeling grateful for today?
- What are you most looking forward to this week?
- How are you feeling right now?

Once all students have submitted their response, talk about them. Focus on patterns that emerge and engage in a brief dialogue. Asking some follow-up questions could lead into discussion around general and low-stakes themes, like favorite breakfast foods or places to nap (depending on the opening question and the answers that emerged). The benefits of this practice include creating a feeling of community, holding space for feelings, transition time, shared humanity, and moment of contemplative embodiment.

That said, we must keep these important critiques and concerns at the forefront of our minds. We've all been in social spaces where we are "alone together"[5]—at dinner tables, in meetings, leading classrooms—where everyone's eyes are glued to their cell phones. Our skills for togetherness seem to be atrophying in the face of our reliance on digital technology, and this is the context from which our students are coming to us. For many teachers, some of our students' silences seem grounded in the loss of social skills that comes from their attachment to devices. As such, one of the driving principles of a quiet pedagogical approach is to teach from an awareness of this context, using silence as a way in, strategically aiming to disrupt the pathway of students' use of silence to "check out." This means we must grapple with our devices and explore how to use them in a way that gives students multiple routes to share their ideas with their classmates and deepen their engagement with the class content.

Sherry Turkle's research is a guide here. As we become more immersed in digital worlds, our capacities for interpersonal connection wane. The ability to revise, edit, filter, and otherwise control our communications and presentation of self in the digital context makes the messiness of face-to-face conversations feel overwhelming.[6] How many of us have had students who struggle to make eye contact—let alone speak in front of a group—when asking a question, particularly in the beginning of the semester before a relationship has had time to grow? Certainly, there are multiple explanations for this pattern, but social media and digital technology clearly compete to be one of them.

In turn, digital devices—historically, from television to the internet—have shaped our students' (and our own) relationship to loneliness, boredom, and, thus, to solitude. Solitude is an integral ingredient for inspiring our creativity, whether at work or school.[7] Boredom is an opportunity to explore our thoughts, beliefs, and values, and solitude is a helpful condition to engage in this work. But in this structural context we run away from boredom. The technologies of modern life cultivate these feelings in us, as William Deresiewicz points out: "the internet is as powerful a machine for the production of loneliness as television is for the manufacture of boredom."[8] This in turn keeps us going back to the screen. Our brains become habituated to relying on these technologies—social media, television—to heal our messy human emotions (loneliness, boredom). The benefits of quiet practices, such as practice 5A, push back, starting the process of creating new neuropathways and classroom cultures.

Actual conversations, unmediated by digital devices, have moved into the realm of nostalgia (remember when we used to talk on the phone?), and many of us, in particular those generations of students raised with the internet, are less skilled with talking. As Sherry Turkle has argued in her research, "human relationships are rich; they're messy and demanding." She goes on to say that "in conversation we tend to one another. . . . We can attend to tone and nuance. In conversation, we are called upon to see things from another's point of view."[9] Turkle argues that self-reflection is crucial for engaged conversation. She points out that "our flight from conversation can mean diminished chances to learn skills of self-reflection"[10] because we aren't assessing our conversational work, nor are we focused on how to do better and be better in our conversational relationships with others.

We can use an awareness of this digitally informed context as a map for our classroom praxis. Self-reflection, which can be cultivated through metacognition and other quiet, contemplative practices, helps us to ground ourselves in the face of these social and technological barriers. Silence can be used to give students some space away from the tensions of conversation, but then also as a path toward it. Because "self-reflection in conversation requires trust,"[11] we can use planned and organized silences to help build students' capacities for trust and in turn engagement with others.

In addition to digital technologies shaping students' communication skills, it is likely this context is also impacting the extent to which students are comparing themselves to their peers. Psychologists call this "social comparison orientation," which refers to the ways in which people's sense of self emerges from a comparison to others. Some of this is healthy. Scholars also argue that this is directional: we can compare upward or downward, with different impacts on our sense of self.[12] Further, social comparison orientation is shaped by social media use. Studies have found that social comparisons by way of Facebook can have negative consequences for users,[13] and given our students' reliance on these technologies it should be no surprise that social comparison has a substantial impact on classroom participation. To be clear, this data does not directly implicate social media—students' stated fears about public responses to their comments did not also mention social media—but given what other researchers have illuminated, this is certainly the sociological backdrop from within which they are living their lives.

Students consistently expressed significant concerns about what their peers thought of them, especially those students who reported never being comfortable talking in class. They do not trust their classmates. This concern, especially in classrooms that require participation as part of a student's grade, creates significant anxiety. As neuroscientific research on the brain highlights, all information that is taken in is experienced in an embodied way.[14] It's important that educators develop a fuller understanding of how this impacts our students' learning experiences. This is the case with any classroom conversation, but especially so for social justice educators who integrate discussions of social inequality(ies): "in any real discussion about oppression, . . . embodied sensations will come up for many of our students (and ourselves as faculty and staff)."[15]

These embodied reactions—in response to social others—in turn shape their participation. Students' internal comparisons to their classmates often function as a form of conversational self-policing; even when they feel they know the right answer they won't speak, to avoid that "just in case" possibility of "looking dumb in front of" their classmates. This anxiety manifests whether they are extroverted and gregarious or introverted and shy; having human bodies means they will have a physiological response each time they even think about raising their hand. Just the thought of participation can increase the heart rate and turn on the sweat glands.

As stated, both those who see themselves as outgoing and those who are shy reported being concerned about participating in class because of the watchful eyes of their peers. And from within this pattern, we see that there are both internal and external forces shaping their perceptions and their embodied reactions to verbal participation. Further, these dynamics are both physiological and psychological, and both are grounded in the larger sociological context. That is, social conditions as shaped by the dominant forces of social media and social comparison, coupled with ethnocentrism and oppression, manifest as an internalized process that plays out in both the body (heart rate, flushed cheeks) and in the mind (negative self-talk, internalized oppression, perceptions of social judgment).

One student articulated why they sometimes don't participate in class by stating, "I chose not to sometimes because I do tend to have anxiety. I am afraid of saying something wrong or 'stupid.' I know there isn't such a thing as 'stupid' but I still get it in my head." The contemplative nature of moments of silence can be used to help students lean into their negative self-talk so that they can move through these thoughts, reconsider them, and/or let them pass rather than be seen as the "truth." We, as teachers, can help them engage with their insecurities (as we must also do ourselves to avoid teachersplaining and faculty moves to innocence) in a way that creates growth rather than stagnation.

As Turkle reports, digital technology's allowances for editing leads us toward a hope for conversational perfection. For students, another practice that limits growth and is grounded in a fear of social judgment is students' belief that they must be "right" before they speak. One student wrote, "if I don't know the answer confidently then I will be hesitant to speak." The words to highlight from these student's response (that reflects many of the students' stated concerns) are anxiety, afraid, and hesitant. Many leaders of the mindfulness movement talk about how we exercise our muscles and our intellects, but we don't incorporate emotional learning into our educational

QUIET PRACTICE 5B: META-COGNITION AND SELF-TALK

Have students write down a few fears they have around an upcoming assessment. In an open-ended question format using your preferred digital technology, asks them to share and explain one of the fears on their list. Then talk about each answer, normalizing the fears expressed, acknowledging both the individual response and the collective patterns. Once all the students have shared, the teacher can use this data to present any resources for students to help alleviate those fears. Remind students that we can hold our fears with care and continue to do our work in the face of them. With a new open-ended submission option via the digital platform, have everyone share one strategy they can think of to work with one of the fears that was shared. Remind students that they can take screenshots or download the presentation to access these strategies outside of the classroom. The benefits of this practice are to use meta-cognition to ease and manage fears, to humanize fears in the context of the group, as an opportunity to remind students about campus resources, to acknowledge humanity, to create community, and to build awareness around student success barriers.

contexts. Thus, students are not equipped to cope with their anxieties, their fears, or their hesitancies.

Echoing trailblazing scholars like bell hooks, I argue that we must open the classroom door to the emotional realm. In order to have the kinds of classroom experiences we desire as educators we need to remain open to engaging with emotional intelligence alongside our disciplines. What the students in this study have to teach us is that if we want our to content matter (whether chemistry, sociology, history, art, or physiology), to be absorbed, we should feel encouraged when appropriate—and to a level that is appropriate in light of our own bandwidth—to model behaviors that will help alleviate our students' fears and cultivate our students' confidence. Pedagogies of quiet are crucial tools in this educational work.

Students regularly spoke to concerns about being "wrong" and being "judged." This is reflected in this comment from a student: "I am a really shy person so I get uncomfortable in large settings. I get afraid that if I say the wrong thing/answer then I may get judged." Another student was direct in saying that "probably getting the answer wrong is what scares me the most." As Peter Kaufman writes, "most teacher education curriculums focus on neither love nor compassion, rather, the emphasis is on content areas, learning strategies, cognitive development, assessment, curriculum development, educational technologies, theory and methods, and practical classroom experience."[16] A compassionate approach, as called for by Kaufman and central to the praxis of quiet pedagogies, takes up these concerns with heart as we focus on the *process* of learning in addition to or beyond the content and outcomes of learning. How do we support these students amid their fears, culturally and historically grounded as they are?

A problematic binary culture of "right" and "wrong" is at play here. Directly acknowledging and challenging this in our classrooms should be seen as an application of both critical and contemplative theories. We can both help illuminate the hegemonic context that produces these expectations, these fears, and engage in practices that help students maneuver through them. Coupled with test-taking culture, we see in these students' explanations the impact these institutional and cultural dynamics have on their lived experiences in classes. Test-taking culture emerges from the K–12 context and policies such as No Child Left Behind and Race to the Top, and 100-level college students, specifically first-year students, are still significantly tied to this culture (upper-level students and graduate students might be more socialized into a discussion-oriented classroom culture). These students—those in this study—are searching for certainty: "if I'm positive that I know the answer to something, I do talk." Given the structural context they emerge from, these fears make sense; yet we don't want our students to get stuck there. Pedagogies of quiet aim to develop a comfort with uncertainty and in giving themselves over to their inner dialogue to finding trust there.

Laura Rendón wrote that "true learning results from a deep and continuous surrender to the unknown,"[17] and it is our task as educators to cultivate the space for this work. Comfort emerged from the data as an important point to explore for those of us who are interested in developing pedagogies that focus on care and compassion. That is, our task as teachers is not just to be the content expert imparting knowledge on behalf of our students (though that is one part of our job), but our role is also to create a context whereby students feel comfortable to engage not just with the material but with themselves and with each other as they move through the material. The lack of comfort and trust some of them bring with them is a clear hindrance for many students and something we'd be wise to address in our classrooms.

Learning is a vulnerable experience and should be acknowledged as such. It's easy to recall faculty members I've engaged with throughout my career who take pride in their masculine, hegemonic approach to their students by "scaring" them off on the first day of class with declarations of how "hard" the class would be, how rigorous. According to Tobin and Behling, this framework has also shaped resistance to a universal design approach. They write,

QUIET PRACTICE 5C: CULTIVATING EMBODIED LEARNING

Learning requires vulnerability, and pedagogies of quiet aim to work this into the classroom, to use our vulnerabilities to enhance our resilience. This practice continues the work of getting students familiar with how their fears shape their classroom experience. Have each student freewrite for a few minutes about their fears around speaking in class. Then, using an open-ended question prompt in the technological platform of your preference, have each student share one piece of their writing to illuminate that no one is alone, that this is a shared experience. Then share with your class a few embodied practices that can help them move through this fear so that they can engage in the class with more comfort and practice. A few options are breathing techniques, stretching (either while sitting or standing), and affirmations. Ask them to use one of these techniques later in the class when a question is asked that seeks a verbal response. Give the class a moment of silence after the question has been asked so that they can do their practice (breath, stretching, or affirmation) and to think of an answer to the question. Then repeat the question and move into the verbal discussion. The benefits of this practice are the creation of an embodied awareness that can be harnessed to increase students' comfort with verbal participation, as well as the creation of time and space for students to prepare for verbal engagement. The practice is also humanizing and can facilitate the creation of a sense of community through shared experiences, while also developing trust.

> Some colleagues perceive UDL not as a way to increase access to interactions; rather they feel that offering learners choices for access to information and demonstrating their skills dumbs down the course, reducing academic rigor. College is supposed to be hard, the argument goes, so why would we coddle students by making it easier to get access to the content.[18]

But to learn is to be open, including being open to making mistakes in a public context, and this requires vulnerability, not scare tactics. As Sherry Turkle points out, digital technology enhances the "in-real-life" component of being alive as we have acclimated to the digital world's capacity to edit and perfect before we engage.[19] The classroom (and all interactional spaces) is messy. We can't edit our comments once we've spoken them aloud. And students in this study make it clear that they aren't comfortable with this process.

No matter where it comes from, fear of judgment is a central concern that students expressed. For those students who are comfortable talking in class, 29 percent of online students and 21 percent of face-to-face students still expressed hesitancy around potential judgment. Those numbers only increase for those students who are not comfortable with verbal participation. 33 percent (online) and 43 percent (face to face) of the "sometimes" students mentioned judgment from others as a barrier. Those students who stated that "no" they do not feel comfortable participating in class expressed this at significant rates: 100 percent of the online students mentioned this concern in their feedback, while 74 percent of the face-to-face students did the same. These numbers are significant.

Some of the comments in this vein that emerged are as follows:

- "I'm worried how others will perceive me."
- "I'm afraid what my classmates will think of me and my answer."
- "I'm afraid my question is a stupid question."
- "I'm worried what others think of me."
- "I don't want my classmates to think I'm not smart."
- "I'm very paranoid when it comes to participating and potentially embarrassing myself and saying the wrong thing."

What is evident in this list of comments is that students aren't just concerned about what people will think of what they *say* but of what people think of *them*. Shame, unlike guilt, makes people feel bad about themselves rather than feeling bad about a particular action (like a comment made in a classroom discussion).[20] And shame and stigmatization alike are flourishing in (mediated) public life: "there absolutely is an online outrage machine that targets people, exploits the way internet platforms work and causes psychological terror in the process."[21] Internet culture looms large in our students' lives and is a strong culprit for shaping their fears of social judgment.

Thus, the pervasiveness of shame easily emerges, in part, from lives led on the internet, a context that has come to be organized to encourage teasing and bullying. Though "traditional bullying" is still more common than "cyberbullying," it has been reported that in 2019 "15.7% of students reported they were bullied electronically."[22] Per this reporting, "girls are just as if not more likely than boys to experience cyberbullying."[23] Further, anonymous online commenting can be a free-for-all of negativity and aggression, never mind the pervasiveness of hate and threats of violence. This in turn produces the kinds of mental health concerns and struggles with socializing that we are seeing shape students' experiences with participating in classrooms among their peers.

Our students experience this window into other people's thoughts so often it's no wonder they don't trust each other; one of those online commenters could be in the classroom. They are used to all of their online actions being judged with like buttons and emoticons and they know this judgment doesn't stop offline, in the classroom. Again, we are not arguing that there is an empirical cause and effect relationship here; however, placing students within this larger historical context helps us to understand their clearly stated concerns around classroom participation so that we can build a praxis that both respects and appropriately responds to their embodied experiences.

In some cases, as detailed in chapter 2, students refrain from verbal engagement as a result of their level of comfort with the learning content. That is, until they feel more confident in their understanding of the material, students wait to participate. That said, students also often talked about comfort in social terms. So while some students said what many teachers intuitively already know—"I'm afraid to look dumb or stupid in front of others"—others explicitly stated that they need to develop relationships with their classmates before they feel comfortable with verbal participation. One student stated that they won't participate if they "feel uncomfortable with people around me." Another student put it this way: "I have to be comfortable with my other classmates." Thus, relationship building is crucial, but so too is a turn inward; comfort and trust can be cultivated both internally and externally.

Comfort emerges from micro-, meso-, and macro-level social forces, from personal traits to classroom culture and then further outward to the historical context our schools are operating within. Thus, when reflecting on the demographics of the students surveyed—and of the community college at large—it is critical to remember that most of these students are women and people of color. In the context of higher education,

> The knowledge-bearing, rational, autonomous subject is conflated with dominant notions of masculinity. When the foundation is self-disclosure for public agency, critical theory ignores the contextual relations that position women and marginalized "others" within an abstract, illegitimate place from which to speak.[24]

In other words, students who are marginalized are at a heightened risk for stigmatization, regardless of their classroom participation. As explained in chapter 1, the survey data does not include demographic data for all students surveyed. However, we do have demographic data for each classroom and know that these are students who vary across race, class, gender, and sexuality. These dynamics are structural dynamics that are connected to systems of patriarchal white supremacy.

This is why an intersectional approach matters—nothing can ever be explained through a singular lens. Systems of inequality intersect with larger historical forces, such as the rise and prevalence of social media. These forces in turn shape our students' behaviors and experiences in class. Having taught approximately five hundred students every year for the past decade, I've observed a lot of student behavior. My classroom observational field notes highlight a plentitude of immature behavior. Observational notes illuminate eye rolls, whispers, unkind laughter, and snarky comments, usually among a small group of peers who think they aren't loud enough to be heard. These dynamics are even more likely in large lecture classes, which is a common structure for introductory-level courses (though maybe less so in the COVID era). It's clear that the perception of an atmosphere of judgment shapes students' concerns about verbal participation. In addition, this is connected to the sociological conditions of social media and students' acclimations to a culture where every comment receives a "like" or "dislike" response. It's inevitable that these moments of teasing will impact whether students are comfortable participating in class, knowing that they could be on the receiving end of such a gesture at any moment.

This survey only asked students about their own comfort level with participating. One gap in the study is a lack of attention to how these same students respond to other classmates when they participate. Given the social nature of the classroom, such moments of teasing are likely to be like an interactional game of "hot potato," as C. J. Pascoe highlights among boys in high school. Pascoe provides evidence that the insult at the center of boys' teasing—that of being a "fag"—was something boys would lob at others while simultaneously fearing it being attributed to themselves.[25] It can be speculated here—based on survey data alongside anecdotal evidence—that students' fear of judgment emerges in part from their own history of both receiving and passing such judgment.

In addition, students are communicating to us they have been thoroughly socialized into the Western educational system with its logic of objectivity and "absolute truth." "Many institutions of higher education are highly resistant to unconventional ways of learning, producing, and disseminating knowledge. Conventional ways of knowing include conformity, standardized testing, the idea that there is an absolute truth just waiting to be discovered, and the idea that objectivity exists, is more valid than subjectivity, and should be our goal."[26] Their fear of speaking is tied to a fear of not having obtained the "right" knowledge, and this fear is exacerbated in the introductory classroom, where the ideas are at their newest. The goal of a philosophy of quiet pedagogies is to disrupt this stranglehold of the "right" answer so that students can learn to embrace the mess, the unknown, and the multitudes, while also finding comfort with speaking and with themselves as knowledge producers.

SILENCE AS A WAY IN

There are certainly many valid concerns and critiques about using technology, and inviting cell phones, in college classrooms. Given the impact that social media has on distraction, procrastination, and mental health, many of us have the understandable impulse to ask our students to put their phones away for the duration of class. Further, polling technologies that rely on true/false and multiple choice answers might feel like an extension of the neoliberal, teach to the test trajectory. Again, this context leaves many professors skeptical of the utilization of cell phones and polling technology.

And yet platforms exist that allow us to bridge these concerns with students' needs. The majority of the students surveyed for this project reported that they were "sometimes" willing to speak in class; 16 percent of those surveyed said "no" they do not participate in class. Those "no" and "sometimes" respondents gave a multitude of explanations regarding their discomfort with verbal participation, ranging from multilingual students' anxieties about accent stigmatization to mental health concerns or a desire to listen to others. At the same time, Sherry Turkle's research highlights the often negative impact that digital technology has on our capacities and comfort with in-person, verbal communication.[27] That is, if our students are struggling with verbal participation, giving them a way out (in the way that texting gives us a way out of phone calls or takes us away from present moment socialization with friends) shouldn't be the option. Rather, we should construct a pedagogical approach that allows for quiet participation while building comfort levels with verbal participation.

The classroom practice that was utilized for this project, which builds on the aims to both allow for quiet engagement while also building comfort with verbal discussions, relied upon a polling platform with options for word clouds, quick forms, scales, and, most importantly, open-ended question responses. As Tobin and Behling argue, "students with mobile devices also present an opportunity to increase learner engagement, if done in an intentional way."[28] In this practice, there was a multipronged strategy for question and answer sessions that allowed first for a contemplative moment of silence, providing students a moment to listen to and ponder the question. From there, all students are asked to write down their response, where the depth of the question determines the amount of time given to this freewriting practice. (This writing practice can be incorporated into the in-class writing portfolio outlined in chapter 3.) Once the freewriting session is complete, all students are asked to input (at least part of) their answers, using their devices, into the polling software platform, which then displays all the answers on the projector screen. From there, the teacher talks through all the submitted answers, exploring patterns in the group's responses, while asking the class follow-up questions. It's this last point that includes potential verbal participation.

For example, in my first face-to-face classroom after the COVID shutdown, I could tell on the first day of class that this small group was a quiet group. For some students a small class can be just as intimidating as a large class due to the intimacy of the space. Thus, to start, I used the polling platform to ask easy questions: What excites you about the new year? How are you feeling today? What questions do you have about the syllabus? What do you think sociology is all about? Once these answers are inputted and on the screen I discuss the patterns that emerge in their responses, but still there is no pressure to speak. Once we shifted into the second week, after the first week of quiet sharing, I asked students to do a movement practice. I had them stand up, stretch, and then walk around the room and introduce themselves to a few classmates. I didn't rush this—I gave them time to talk. From there, verbal participation slowly started to increase, though the classroom space was still balanced with technology, the participation journal, and in-class writing time.

As previously stated, pedagogies of quiet incorporate the ethos of the slow professor movement not just in relation to content but in creating a slowed-down process that gives students ample time to think and explore their own ideas before being asked to engage verbally. This technologically infused process facilitates this slow, quiet practice. With quiet time students are able to studiously think, write, and type their thoughts before being asked to speak. Students in various introductory-level courses, across four disciplines, were asked how the utilization of this particular approach, and the polling software in particular, impacted their experience in the class.

The survey data made it clear that they found the program to be useful: 94 percent of survey respondents declared "yes" to the question "Was the Menti[29] program helpful for you?" Students were asked to elaborate in open-ended survey questions, and the responses can be seen through the lens of three key themes: anonymity and anxiety, increased engagement, and more voices. For those students who do not feel comfortable speaking in class, there was a 100 percent positive response rate regarding the use of polling technology. For these students, Menti significantly and positively impacted their classroom participation experience. Their silence, their thinking, and their participation can coexist in this tech-enhanced approach. For those students who are "always" or "sometimes" comfortable talking in class, only 1 percent said that Menti was not helpful. Thus we can see that 99 percent of students, regardless of their predisposition to verbal participation, thought that the inclusion of the classroom technology was a helpful addition to the learning environment.

Quiet Technology: Anxiety Reduced Through Anonymity

As outlined in chapter 2, students experience a significant amount of anxiety related to verbal classroom participation. As one student wrote, "sometimes I want to express my opinions but I don't want to speak, Menti helps ease the anxiety of answering to the class and allows me to express myself." Pedagogies of quiet include the goal of helping students learn to embody and tend to that discomfort (rather than fear it) while also building toward greater comfort and thus more engagement, whether quiet or verbal. The utilization of this particular technology in the classroom was most certainly seen as a benefit to those anxious students, whether the etiology of their anxiety was physiological, sociological, or both.

One student elaborated, highlighting their experience with embodied anxiety:

> I'm shy so sometimes even getting up in class to run to the washroom or something can be nerve wracking. I'm not exactly sure why, but my mentality has been like this for so long, so it just feels natural to be quiet. I don't think I participated as much as I would have liked in this class verbally only because I wanted to say something beneficial to the class and so many other people had good things to say so I stayed mostly quiet. [As for Menti], I like[d] this a lot. It helps with asking and participating with no pressure added. Plus you can ask without feeling you are interrupting the class.

This student's experience highlights that such anxiety is both social and physiological, ranging from concerns about interrupting the flow of the lecture/discussion to the stress of having the spotlight on you when speaking (or getting up to leave the room). And the social fuels the physiological, where all eyes on the speaker lead to flushed cheeks and shallow breathing. This is why students appreciate the technology: in the words of one student, "because I can actually say what I think without anyone knowing it was me," thus bypassing the physiological stress response.

The predominant response given in surveys reflected an appreciation for the anonymity of the program, which thus freed students to engage with the content questions without having to carry the added burden of social judgment. For those students who prefer not to speak in class, 38 percent wrote in their responses that what they appreciated about Menti was its anonymity. On the other hand, 20 percent of the students who are comfortable with verbal participation also appreciated this feature. More interesting, however, was the "sometimes" students, for whom anonymity was mentioned by 61 percent as a positive aspect of the experience. In this way, the technology helped those "sometimes" students toward the "yes" side when it comes to a willingness to engage in class. For all students, the momentary freedom from social pressure was a net positive.

One student summed this up by writing that the program is "an easy way to participate without worrying about how others see you." Ultimately, our students will have to learn how to speak in class and will need to develop the skills to do so with resilience, given that others' responses are out of our control. One student wrote that they appreciated the technology platform because "I was not afraid to answer questions I wasn't confident in." This mirrors the data on verbal participation in the previous chapter where students were more willing to engage verbally when they were more confident with the material. One student's comments were as follows: "Yes, Menti [technology] was helpful because when it's anonymous people express true feelings which can create good conversations/discussions." The philosophy behind this quiet approach, however, is that if given ample time to think through a question or to dig deeper into the content at hand, students will gain more confidence in their understanding and thus more freely step into verbal discussions.

Given that these are all introductory-level students, it's understandable that they aren't as confident as upper-level undergraduates or graduate students might be. Through this technology they are able to participate, but in their words, "with less pressure and anxiety." They understand the barriers to their own and others' participation when recognizing that the technology "allows shy students or uncomfortable students to still participate" or that "it gives students that might have a lot to say a chance to express their thoughts without speaking in front of everyone." Thus, this approach is particularly useful in giving students the time and space in their introductory classrooms to build up their self-confidence alongside their knowledge.

This is an important place to remember the role of teacher reflexivity in pedagogies of quiet. It's important for us to reflect on our learning goals for our students, especially in the context of introductory classrooms. Our syllabi include learning outcomes, but surely we have some unstated goals as well, even potentially some unconscious biases. One thing that was hidden from me for many years was the belief that I wanted my students to love my discipline, whereas now I've shifted to a more practical place of wanting them to learn my discipline. I also regularly remind myself that my job is to introduce my discipline, not make my students experts. This has significantly shaped my grading and assessment practices, including the shift to pedagogies of quiet. While my students need to engage with the material and perform well on assessments, they do not need to prove themselves immediately, verbally, or solely inside the classroom.

One student confirmed this by saying that the program was helpful because "we can ask for help without the nerves of public speaking," while another stated that "it offers a safe space for people to participate." This is similar to some of the stated benefits of social media reported by scholars: "It also helps shy and introvert students, who find it difficult to initiate conversation, to build social capital as it reduces the level of restrictions involved in communication and offers a forum to build healthy and strong bonds and relationships."[30] Moving slowly through the content, and allowing the students to process the material in this way, offers them the opportunity to build both their social and intellectual capital.

A significant portion of the students surveyed for this project reported that their shy and/or introverted personality impacted their comfort levels with verbal participation. They are illuminating the bias inherent in verbal participation requirements; extroverted students can be assumed to be the "good" ones or the "better" ones. This was most significant for those students who reported that "no" they do not feel comfortable speaking in class: 76 percent of them said that being shy or introverted was a reason for this, while 56 percent of them said that their mental health played a role. In the open-ended follow-up question, one student wrote that Menti technology "was very helpful because I felt that my personality of being an introvert wasn't an obstacle when answering questions on Menti."

Allowing students access to both quiet and participation through this technology reduced these "obstacles" while validating their personalities and mental health. Put another way: quiet pedagogies keep students from feeling like their embodied experience is an "obstacle"; instead it creates a culture of value. It's important, then, that we construct a classroom praxis that values and supports our students' personalities and mental health in ways that still put boundaries around our jobs, as we are not mental health practitioners. Classroom technology is one way to do this, especially when using programs alongside other assignments (see chapters 3 and 4) to produce varied quiet routes for student engagement and connection between teachers and students.

In introductory-level classrooms, students often have questions about the content, but these concerns—personality and mental health—coupled with the newness of the ideas and the people (for first-year students, a new school, new teachers, and new students) often render these questions unasked. In the face of office hours that pass by without any students stopping, Vanessa Bohns wrote that

> research shows it's more effective to address the underlying anxiety of asking for help than to focus on the practical benefits of doing so. Students need to feel

like they aren't the only ones struggling. They need to believe they won't be judged negatively for getting extra support.[31]

Quiet pedagogy is a way of accomplishing this. As one student wrote, "yes, Menti is super helpful because you can ask 'dumb' (simple) questions without anyone knowing where you are struggling." Using this technology, we can normalize the asking of questions in a context that alleviates the anxiety of doing so. For example, in a class of fifty students, during the first week of the spring 2023 semester, I received seventeen additional questions that were posted via the classroom technology; these are potentially students who would not have asked the question at all given the size of the class. The posing of the questions through the technology, and students' ability to see the questions other classmates are asking, normalizes the process.

Many students, as previously stated, expressed concerns about being judged by their classmates. As a result, a common survey response for these students was an appreciation for the opportunity to engage anonymously so as to avoid the pressure of (perceived) social judgment. One student wrote why they appreciated Menti: "that it's judgement free is awesome!" This point was reiterated by many students in myriad ways, such as they liked that it allowed space to "participate without singling students out" or that "it's a way in which I feel engaged in the class however I am not judged because it's anonymous." Digital technology, and social media in particular, is a culprit in enhancing these fears of social comparison and judgment. Research points to the fact that

> individuals with low self-esteem, whose self-concepts are inconstant and uncertain, are particularly interested in making social comparisons. This tendency towards social comparison may be facilitated by modern technologies, which have transferred many social relations from the private to the public sphere, exposing people to a continual flow of information.[32]

In this way, the classroom functions as a "front-stage" space that includes all the stressors of public performance.[33] Incorporating this opportunity for quiet engagement gives students a brief respite from the pressures of the public sphere while keeping them engaged with and learning from their classmates.

Quiet Technology: Increased Student Engagement

Through comments that referenced the technology platform's anonymity, students articulated an appreciation of an anxiety-*reducing* route to participation. As a result of having access to a way of engaging without the anxiety of being "judged" or "wrong," students found that they participated more

QUIET PRACTICE 5D: DEEP LEARNING

Present and explain a thought-provoking content question. A recent example that I used in my class is "what might be some personal, physiological, or cultural barriers to developing a sociological imagination?" Give students ten minutes to write their answers using pen and paper. Tell students that they will be turning in their answers, as this creates accountability and also creates a record of their writing that's useful in the emerging context of AI tools such as ChatGPT. Once the ten minutes are up, have each student share a two- to three-sentence summary of their response into the polling technology of your choice. In this practice, the accountability helps to encourage the deep learning, while the time and the two different writing styles (open freewrite and short summary) further engage them. Finally, they get the benefit of seeing what everyone shares, not just the three to five students who are willing to share verbally.

than they otherwise would have. This leads to deep learning, a key goal of educators. When students are engaged in deep learning they "use higher-order thinking skills and personally commit to learning the material."[34] We can see this through another of the common refrains that was clear in the survey data, where they articulated an increase in student engagement (their own and their classmates).

Students felt that the opportunity to use classroom technology increased their levels of participation and facilitated deeper thinking about the questions posed in class. One survey respondent stated that "I think that Menti is a great source for students to use to share thoughts/questions that they don't want to say aloud. It's an outlet that should be available in all classes so all students can fully engage in their own learning." This sentiment is reflected by many of the community college students who were a part of this project. They commented that the program "helps review the material," it "makes you get involved," and it "helps keep me engaged." This highlights that classroom technology has multiple functions.

The classrooms that participated in this study came to using this program in response to the philosophy of pedagogies of quiet rather than continue to perpetuate the "extrovert ideal," which is grounded in "masculine talk," whereby "the collective ear for correct speech can serve as a mechanism of exclusion/inclusion in the public cultural sphere to interpret masculine and feminine talk as practices of obeying and disobeying the linguistic order."[35] In particular, instrumental language—read as masculine and idealized in the context of patriarchy—is both interpreted as "correct" and seeks the intellectual, "correct" answer, leaving liminal space for questions, uncertainty, and emotions. Clearly, the students surveyed for this project illuminate the role emotions play in shaping their classroom experience. Acknowledging these emotions in the classroom—whether in "how are you feeling" word clouds or course announcements with stress relief tactics—can help to deconstruct the patriarchal components of the idealization of instrumentalized speech. This patriarchal context is the backdrop from which our students, with increasing mental health needs, are operating and where their anxieties proliferate.

Thus, one goal of adding classroom participation technology was to allow for some moments of reprieve from social anxiety, some moments where students could participate while freed from social constraints. As one student wrote, Menti was helpful because "it gives those who are too shy to participate a chance to give their opinion and contribute to the discussion." Another student said it this way: "anyone who wanted to speak could and whoever did not feel ready to share could through Menti." The technology allows students to strike a balance between quiet participation and vocal participation, and it grants students options regarding how they'd like to engage in class discussions. Given the options available to them, overall, student engagement increased.

To compare, of the students who said that "yes" they are comfortable speaking in class, 40 percent said that being shy or introverted sometimes impacted them and 10 percent said that their mental health did. At the same time, these students appreciated the technological option. One student wrote that "it was nice how we had the option to be anonymous, or if we felt comfortable to say it out loud we were able to." This quote may sound repetitive to the reader, but this only serves to call attention to how often statements such as this one emerged from the data. This highlights that the technology is presented as an option but not a replacement for classroom dialogue. Students can access moments of quiet, allowing them both time to think and access to participation. All the while, this quiet is coupled with space for verbal engagement, creating the kinds of choices that are encouraged by UDL practitioners.

The benefits of this praxis exceeded the original intent to provide space for students to look quietly into their mind, and to subsequently share with others while remaining quiet. Instead the utilization of classroom technology created opportunities for students to connect to the course content with more depth than is sometimes found in the introductory (especially those that are lecture based) classroom. In fact, 33 percent of the students commented that Menti was helpful for its capacity to facilitate their learning of the course content. Students who were already comfortable speaking in class reported that the opportunity to review the material made the technology beneficial

(11.5 percent), while 19 percent said that it increased (their own and others') participation. For those students who are not comfortable talking in class, 41 percent said that Menti was beneficial because of its capacity to facilitate questions and answers and that it allowed for greater expression and increased engagement. 42.5 percent of the "sometimes comfortable" students said that the technology increased their engagement, while 33 percent said that it enhanced their relationship to the course content.

One practice that was a component of this technology was integrating review questions into the beginning of class, often following a contemplative practice. Combined, these allowed for students to refresh their memories regarding the material from the previous class while also bringing them into the present moment. In this way, students can transition from the world outside of the classroom and take a few minutes to bring their full focus to the topic at hand. One student wrote of the benefits of review and framed it through this capacity for a present moment experience: "it keeps me present in the class and allows us to talk more about the subjects. It's also good for review." That said, the technology wasn't only used to review the material—an opportunity that students appreciated—but also to engage at a deeper level with content-related questions. For example, one student wrote that "it is very helpful because I was able to answer more in-depth questions I otherwise wouldn't be able to answer." Another student commented that "it adds depth to concepts that may not always be easy to understand." This depth of engagement and class participation was clearly enhanced through the integration of classroom technology.

Previously, or prior to the incorporation of this digital technology, I frequently noticed that engagement was often stifled by expectations of verbal participation. Asking students to talk—especially about new (or challenging) course content—is sometimes a great way to create collective silence. As mentioned, what students most appreciated about the technology utilized was that it was anonymous, and this freed them from being overwhelmed by fears of social judgment. Thus, students' fears function to render them silent, which in turn shuts them off from engaging with their classes, in particular those who expect public speaking. We can use this technology—important to a universal design strategy—to shift from oppressive silencing into engaged silence. So it's important to see students comment that these programs are "a way in which I feel engaged in the class [without being] judged because it is anonymous." Thus, rather than staying quiet, an act of self-policing, students are left feeling like the technology "makes you get involved" in ways that they otherwise wouldn't be. In the words of one student, "honest answers show up, and it gives me less anxiety, [so it] leads to more participation."

Introductory-level classes and large lecture classes are often spaces where students struggle to connect and engage. In this way, a quiet pedagogical approach works to bring them—and all students in any context—into a deeper conversational connection. This overlaps with another instructor's experiences with contemplative practices, where "students were living a shared experience and nourishing their already familiar, safe, and reliable community" through a silent writing exercise done in the context of the group.[36] That said, the hope is to structure expectations of participation in ways that meet students where they are, allowing for quiet engagement, and giving them the space to work alongside their social anxieties. As one student in a large lecture stated, "yes, [Menti] makes me feel *involved* even in a big class like this." It was the student who emphasized the word "involved" in their comment, alluding to the fact that they weren't expected to feel this way given the size of the class. Quiet pedagogy's incorporation of both contemplative and universal design strategies links the calming impact of quiet with participatory choices and deepened student engagement.

Quiet Technology: Seeing More Voices

Students appreciate being given options for classroom participation. Rather than a participation grade that is based only on their verbal participation, whether small or large group discussions, quiet pedagogies allow students to write, to type, to collage, to draw, *and* to speak their way to a participation grade. The technological component was one of the ways that it was immediately evident that a quiet approach to classroom participation would lead to increased engagement. Immediately upon using this program, my classroom was filled with more questions and comments from my students than I had seen in my prior years of teaching. Students noticed this pattern too. When asked if they found Menti beneficial, one student wrote that "yes, it's anonymous, you don't have to participate, and you still get to hear what others

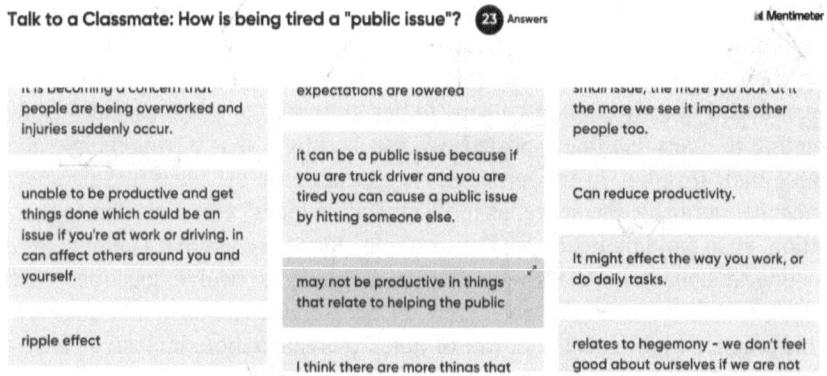

Figure 5.2. How is being tired a public issue?

in the class are thinking." This point highlights what I see in my classroom every time I use such a tool: that the technology brought more voices into the classroom space.

While polling technologies are sometimes used for content review, often with multiple choice questions, the program utilized for this study allowed for open-ended responses, thus bringing the students' words and ideas onto the screen and into the class. This component is crucial here, given that the goal isn't to reinforce a kind of teach-to-the-test learning but to develop a more thoughtful relationship to the course content, whatever the discipline. Students recognized this, as comments in the surveys made clear: the program "showed material that we could work through if necessary but also had open ended questions which I could respond to, which I would not normally respond to in class discussions." This student's response highlights that the program was used to facilitate classroom discussions, thus allowing for a quiet entrance into these dialogues.

As teachers we have all experienced classrooms where the same few students participate while the rest stay silent. Many times I have felt like I was banging my head against the wall trying to get more of my students to talk. This head banging is what led to developing pedagogies of quiet, as I pondered: How can teachers access what's happening within all that quiet? Students are impacted by these dynamics as well, as it does not evade their notice that there's often a small group of students who dominate conversations. As such, when reflecting on the benefits of classroom technology, they wrote comments such as, "it is extremely helpful. It allows for participation even through personality types that are too timid to participate and allows the teacher a generalized view of how effective their lessons are *for the class as a whole, not just the vocal few*" (emphasis added).

One of the goals of quiet pedagogies is shared by scholars who argue that we teach with compassion. Per Kaufman and Schippers, an ethos of compassion asks "for teachers at all levels to get to know students and use that knowledge to communicate to students that you are listening and valuing their contributions."[37] Utilizing classroom technology that permits for open-ended questions allows for us to get to know our students. Further, in tending to every comment posted, we can highlight that we appreciate and value their insights. In this process, we can increase the ideas and perspectives that permeate the space, as more student "voices" enter into the conversation, even amid their silence. For example, during a class that I taught while writing this chapter, a class with fifty-seven students, twelve questions were asked, and forty-seven students wrote an open-ended response to a question. This practice highlights the power of quiet to create a more inclusive participatory ecology.

Cultivating this opening in classrooms through quiet, slowed down practices challenges the "commitment to standards-led school reforms . . . [and] schools geared solely to the product" and instead focuses on "the process of creating educative experiences."[38] This technologically facilitated quiet allows students time to explore their ideas, in silence, and to share their ideas, in silence. All this quiet and silence leads to more voices entering into the conversation. This was something that students astutely noted, highlighting not just the pedagogical effectiveness of the practice but the knowledge students possess about the dynamics of the classrooms they occupy. They wrote that the technology "gives voice to people" and allows for them to "have our voices heard." They observed that "you still get to hear what others in the class are thinking." Survey data highlights that from the student perspective, this practice leads to their ability to "share ideas" and "see other perspectives," which is an important praxis for a critical pedagogy that aims to bring students in as knowledge producers, to enhance their critical thinking skills so as to live and work in a diverse and globalized world.

Students noted that relying on this tool led to "far more people participating," which was my primary goal all those days that I was banging my head against the wall, wondering why the same five students were talking in class, but not the others. Even those students who do speak up in class regularly found Menti beneficial because they too want to hear from others: "I speak in class but it is helpful to get other answers heard because not a lot of people talk out loud." Given the noted anxieties that rankle our students—from the impact of "white public space"[39] on students with noticeable accents to medical diagnoses of ADHD or social anxiety—it's important that students feel that there is always a way to "voice what [they] are really thinking" as well as to hear from their classmates who would otherwise remain on the outside of verbal class discussions.

CONCLUSION: QUIET AS AN INTERSECTIONAL PEDAGOGY

When you see the shift from four or five students who speak their minds into the classroom to upward of twenty to thirty students engaged with a question, you can explore their ideas in creative ways, finding patterns as well as nuance. This is one of the goals of intersectional theory. New understandings—of the course content, of the students themselves—emerge from this process, and quiet technology facilitates this engagement of students as knowledge producers. Pedagogies of quiet rely upon an intersectional theoretical framework in regard to understanding how power shapes classroom dynamics and individual identities and experiences. In addition, we see that classrooms—and the students inside of them—are best served through incorporating multiple, intersecting theoretical approaches to teaching and learning. As such, we are building a framework at the connecting intersections of slow, feminist, critical, and contemplative pedagogies. In light of all these intersections, it's important to see each quiet practice on its own as incomplete.

For example, there are concerns with the utilization of cell phone technology in classrooms that need to be taken seriously, and as such, reliance on such a program should not be the only practice of a quiet pedagogy. Some of the students surveyed for this project see this as well. One student wrote that they felt that the program was both helpful and not: "Yes and no. I like the Menti quizzes and find them helpful, but they seem to encourage students to not speak up." While we want quiet spaces for students to participate, there is a larger goal to pedagogies of quiet that can easily get lost. Quiet is understood as emancipatory only when it is used to enhance student voices, not keep them silenced.

The data-driven participation journal, or some of the other quiet practices mentioned throughout, should be practiced in conjunction with polling technology to encourage complex engagement. The multiplicity of practices helps to avoid the problem of silence as a means of avoidance. Core to contemplative practices and principles is learning how to hold, rather than run away from, our discomfort. As such, the goal of pedagogies of quiet isn't to produce a context where students never feel uncomfortable—to never talk in class, for example—but to learn how to engage with both the course content and their embodied feelings to work toward an experience of classroom participation that is varied rather than singular. This variability includes diving inside into their expansive inner creativity and to find routes to sharing those ideas with others.

When teachers, alongside students, are in tune with their inner experience, we might encounter the unexpected. For example, I recently left a classroom wondering, "Was that a good class? I'm not sure that went very well." My own self-talk certainly plays a role in shaping my perception of my students experience and their actions in the class. As Conboy writes, "by letting go of the frustrations brought on by not finishing a lesson plan on a given day, or by being greeted with utter silence after several of my guiding questions, or still by not guaranteeing that every student had 'air time' in a particular class, I became more aware and accepting that, 'We cannot do everything,' and there is a sense of liberation in realizing that."[40] I myself still struggle to let go of the hegemonic ideal that "good" students are talkative ones and that "good" classrooms aren't silent. But in this instance, I went back to my office after class and reviewed the data from the Menti presentation. While they didn't speak much during the class, they had plenty to say and their typed answers to the questions posed in class prove it.

Feelings aren't typically at the center of most college classrooms; they are always present, but not engaged alongside the course content. As Carla Wilson writes, "our Western educational system focuses on logic, reason and scientific inquiry and methods as dominant sources of meaning making and knowledge production that are often viewed as more legitimate per se than spiritual inquiry, feelings, intuition, imagination and contemplation."[41] The practices outlined in this book, including the use of technology to engage in embodied contemplative practices, however, engage with the subjective. Students communicate to us that they have experiences—feelings in the body—that impact their ability to speak, to listen, and to learn. Rather than dismiss our students' bodies and historical context, pedagogies of quiet aim to center them, to learn from them, and to construct a path toward embodied and engaged learning.

NOTES

1. Antonia Darder, *Reinventing Paulo Freire: A Pedagogy of Love* (Oxfordshire, England: Routledge, 2017), 51.

2. "Interactive Presentation Software," *Mentimeter Interactive Presentation Software*, accessed June 5, 2022, http://www.mentimeter.com/.

3. Kirsten T. Behling and Thomas J. Tobin, *Reach Everyone, Teach Everyone: Universal Design for Learning in Higher Education* (West Virginia University Press, 2018), 88.

4. Behling and Tobin, *Reach Everyone, Teach Everyone*, 91.

5. Sherry Turkle, *Alone Together: Why We Expect More from Technology and Less from Each Other* (New York:Basic Books, 2011).

6. Sherry Turkle, *Reclaiming Conversation: The Power of Talk in a Digital Age* (London: Penguin, 2016).

7. Susan Cain, *Quiet: The Power of Introverts in a World That Can't Stop Talking* (New York: Crown Publishing, 2013).

8. William Deresiewicz, "The End of Solitude," *The Chronicle of Higher Education* 55, no. 21 (2009): 314.

9. Sherry Turkle, "The Flight from Conversation," *New York Times*, April 21, 2012. https://www.nytimes.com/2012/04/22/opinion/sunday/the-flight-from-conversation.html, 2.

10. Turkle, "The Flight from Conversation."

11. Turkle, "The Flight from Conversation."

12. Chia-chen Yang, "Instagram Use, Loneliness, and Social Comparison Orientation: Interact and Browse on Social Media, but Don't Compare," *Cyberpsychology, Behavior, and Social Networking* 19, no. 12 (2016).

13. Erin A. Vogel, Jason P. Rose, Bradley M. Okdie, Katheryn Eckles, and Brittany Franz. "Who Compares and Despairs? The Effect of Social Comparison Orientation on Social Media Use and Its Outcomes," *Personality and Individual Differences* 86 (2015).

14. Judson Brewer, *Unwinding Anxiety: New Science Shows How to Break the Cycles of Worry and Fear to Heal Your Mind* (New York: Avery, an imprint of Penguin Random House, 2022).

15. Beth Berila, *Integrating Mindfulness into Anti-Oppression Pedagogy: Social Justice in Higher Education* (Oxfordshire, England: Routledge, 2015).

16. Peter Kaufman and Janine Schipper, *Teaching with Compassion: An Educator's Oath to Teach from the Heart* (Maryland: Rowman & Littlefield, 2018).

17. Laura I. Rendón, *Sentipensante (Sensing/Thinking) Pedagogy: Educating for Wholeness, Social Justice and Liberation* (Sterling, VA: Stylus Publishing, LLC, 2012).

18. Behling and Tobin, *Reach Everyone, Teach Everyone*, 35.

19. Turkle, *Reclaiming Conversation*.

20. Brené Brown, *The Gifts of Imperfection: Let Go of Who You Think You're Supposed to Be and Embrace Who You Are* (New York: Simon and Schuster, 2010).

21. Tressie McMillan Cottom, "What's Shame Got to Do With It," *New York Times*, April 12, 2022, https://www.nytimes.com/2022/04/12/opinion/whats-shame-got-to-do-with-it.html.

22. Cyberbullying Research Center, retrieved July 29, 2022, https://cyberbullying.org/facts.

23. Cyberbullying Research Center.

24. Jennifer Llewellyn and K. Llewellyn, "A Restorative Approach to Learning: Relational Theory as Feminist Pedagogy in Universities," in *Feminist Pedagogy in Higher Education: Critical Theory and Practice*, ed. Tracy Penny Light, Jane Nicholas, and Renée Bondy (Ontario, Canada: Wilfrid Laurier University Press, 2015), 15.

25. Cheri Jo Pascoe, "'Dude, You're a Fag': Adolescent Masculinity and the Fag Discourse," *Sexualities* 8, no. 3 (2005).

26. Carla Wilson, "Unsettling Women's and Gender Studies 'Settler Logics,'" in *Teaching Gloria E. Anzaldúa: Pedagogy and Practice for Our Classrooms and Communities*, ed. Margaret Cantú-Sánchez, Candace de León-Zepeda, and Norma Elia Cantú (University of Arizona Press, 2020).

27. Turkle, *Reclaiming Conversation*.

28. Behling and Tobin, *Reach Everyone, Teach Everyone*, 91.

29. This specific platform was selected due to its variety. Teachers are encouraged to find the platform most suited to their disciplines and their classes.

30. Muqaddas Jan, Sanobia Soomro, and Nawaz Ahmad, "Impact of Social Media on Self-Esteem," *European Scientific Journal* 13, no. 23 (2017): 331.

31. Vanessa Bohns, "The Real Reason Why Students Don't Ask Teachers for Help," *Ed Week*, October 6, 2021, https://www.edweek.org/teaching-learning/opinion-the-real-reason-why-students-dont-ask-teachers-for-help/2021/10.

32. Elisa Bergagna and Stefano Tartaglia, "Self-Esteem, Social Comparison, and Facebook Use," *Europe's Journal of Psychology* 14, no. 4 (2018): 831.

33. Erving Goffman, *The Presentation of Self in Everyday Life* (New York: Double Day, 1959).

34. Irena Burić, "The Role of Emotional Labor in Explaining Teachers' Enthusiasm and Students' Outcomes: A Multilevel Mediational Analysis," *Learning and Individual Differences* 70 (2019): 13.

35. Amalia Sa'ar, "Masculine Talk: On the Subconscious Use of Masculine Linguistic Forms among Hebrew- and Arabic-Speaking Women in Israel," *Signs: Journal of Women in Culture and Society* 32, no. 2 (2007).

36. Ana Fonseca Conboy, "Transition in the Era of a Pandemic: An Exercise in Mindfulness," Journal of Contemplative Inquiry 9, no. 2 (2022): 17, https://journal.contemplativeinquiry.org/index.php/joci/article/view /259.

37. Kaufman and Schipper, *Teaching with Compassion*.

38. Maurice Holt, "It's Time to Start the Slow School Movement," *Phi Delta Kappan* 84, no. 4 (2002): 268.

39. Jane Hill, "Language, Race, and White Public Space," *American Anthropologist* 100, no. 3 (1998): 479.

40. Conboy, "Transition in the Era of a Pandemic."

41. Wilson, "Unsettling Women's and Gender Studies 'Settler Logics,'" 278.

Conclusion
Quiet Spaces

FROM MARGINALIZATION TO CONNECTION

The pedagogical perspective outlined in this book—that of advocating for collective classroom silences that facilitate attentiveness to students' inner quiet—emerged in response to a room full of students that weren't talking. At first, I feared that not talking translates to not learning; my own expectations and discomfort drove this fear. It also emerged from a normative pedagogy that has shaped—and continues to shape—my career.

On the other hand, the students in this study allow us to see silence and quiet with more nuance. A classroom full of students who are opting into silence are communicating something to us if we are open to listening. They are telling us they don't know or feel comfortable with their classmates, or with us, or with the new ideas being presented to them. They are telling us they've experienced microaggressions, they've been misgendered, their "accent" is perceived as "difficult," they have kids, and/or they have two part-time jobs. Though they aren't giving us the specifics in the classroom (they are, after all, giving us silence), the students in this study make it clear that these are all possibilities that we could infer from student nonresponsiveness.

This is especially true in the context of the introductory classroom when students are awakened to disciplines for the first time in their lives and/or are new to the college experience. Many of my students, for example, are first-generation students in their first year of college. From within this space there is much that is new: new experiences, new school, new disciplines, new ideas, new ways of looking at the world, new perspectives to consider, new equations to practice, and new skills to develop. All these firsts can lead to participatory silences if not held with pedagogical care. In this way, what (introductory) students need is time, and quiet pedagogy is a route toward providing an enriched experience of time in the classroom.

Students—and teachers—have been socialized throughout their years in school to associate participation with verbalization. Ask any student—or teacher—to articulate what a participation grade would be based on, and they would likely report instances of speaking up in class, whether in large or small groups. As Hanesworth et al. write,

> Within its procedures, structures and systems, assessment codifies cultural, disciplinary and individual norms, values and knowledge hierarchies. Moreover, it inculcates these within the learner: to perform well in assessment, learners must adhere to these unconscious rules and value systems, continuously replicating them, and eventually, internalizing them.[1]

The authors posit that assessment practices carry normative assumptions and that our students—and us as teachers—are socialized into this hegemonic context. And importantly, those students who don't share, or cannot meet, these cultural assumptions are left out in the cold. Curriculum isn't the only educational space infused with hegemonic power dynamics. As such, it's important that we look beyond the curriculum when thinking about how to implement an equitable pedagogy. This book encourages teachers to explore their classroom participation ecology as central to social justice pedagogy and to broaden the scope of participation beyond verbalization.

Success rates highlight the promise of this quiet praxis. In the five years (2013 to 2018) before implementing pedagogies of quiet, the success rates of students in my Introduction to Sociology courses were in the upper 60s and lower 70s. In the first five years (2018 to 2022) of implementation those rates jumped up 10 percent, and in some cases higher. Hispanic students, for example, had success rates of 65 percent in the years prior to implementation of pedagogies of quiet. In the first five years of implementation, however, Hispanic students had a success rate of 79 percent in face-to-face classes and 78 percent in online sections. Female students jumped from 72 percent to 85 percent (face to face) and 88 percent (online). First-generation students shifted from 67 percent to 81 percent (face to face) and 86 percent (online). The holistic approach of pedagogies of quiet is behind these improvements.

Building Relationships with Pedagogies of Quiet

When collective silence is used as a strategy, it functions to bring students into a closer relationship with the course content and their classroom peers. On the other hand, when unattended to, feared, and/or ignored, silence can be oppressive. Unwelcome and "chilly" climates persist in classrooms, most impacting female-identified students, LGTBQ students, students with disabilities, and students of color. Faculty can unintentionally engage in silencing practices, for example, through lecturing with minimal pauses, a practice I must continually unlearn. Students reported, for example, that they didn't speak up in class because they didn't want to interrupt their professors. A cultural norm of politeness intersects here to silence students' questions and comments. Without offering collective moments of silence, this teaching practice was silencing.

Pedagogies of quiet, and specifically the participation journal and classroom technology outlined in chapters 4 and 5, offer students regular opportunities both inside and outside of the classroom to look inward and to explore learning in the context of quiet. These practices facilitate a deeper relationship with the course content, where they used the quiet and slowed down time to think critically and dig deep for personal connections and to answer questions. They also strengthened their relationships with their professors, and thus the class overall, as these practices made them feel heard and cared for.

As illuminated by a recent *Inside Higher Ed* study, undergraduate students are missing this connection. As Melissa Ezarik reported,

> Student Voice respondents are less likely to see their professors as connecting on a personal level than they are to see them as effective educators. When asked to rate their professors over all in six areas—academic rigor, communicating course expectations, choice of instructional materials, engaging lectures and assignments, use of technology, and building relationships with students—students were less likely to assess relationship-building as excellent and more likely to assess it as poor compared to all other areas.[2]

This is especially the case for students of color, with Black students reporting that their professors are "fair or poor in building relationships with students."[3] On the other hand, the students in this study reported feeling supported and cared for, illuminating the transformative power of quiet pedagogies.

The participation journal really impacted students' feelings of connection to their professors. In the words of one student,

> She gave feedback on almost every assignment I turned in—whether it be my study guide or even my participation journals. My journals were a place where I was completely honest with each word I wrote and to have her connect to what I was saying and be able to emphasize on it more made me feel connected to not only the class, but her as well.

This student reported that this journaling and feedback process facilitated a relationship to both the course and to the professor, highlighting pedagogies of quiet as an excellent resource for faculty interested in enhancing these connections.

As another student put it, "[my teacher] made me feel connected to this class by connecting with me through my journal, holding live review sessions, posting weekly updates, and constantly reminding us to allow ourselves to rest." This student's focus on rest is a key component of the quiet pedagogical approach, where care and compassion are central components of the praxis. The embodied component of quiet pedagogies allows students to listen to themselves, thus allowing them to develop their critical thinking skills while also tending to their nervous systems.

One student reported on their class, embedded with quiet pedagogies, by writing that "weekly check-ins, [journal] reflections, making sure that we take a moment to breathe and reflect if the content is too much for us to take in and learn about in the moment" were things that made them feel connected to the course. Taken together, all the outcomes that come to students through quiet pedagogical practices such as the participation journal can be seen as a linkage of embodiment practices and critical thinking formation, a crucial step in a liberatory pedagogy. While we can see a reciprocal relationship here, between body and mind, it is also clear that quiet is a useful route into bridging this connection.

In addition to this embodied component of pedagogies of quiet, the participation journal allowed students the opportunity to learn about and build on their strengths. The meta-cognitive aspect of the assignment allowed them to reflect upon and improve their time management and study skills, thus leading to deeper learning and a stronger relationship with their teachers. The in-class use of technology, a social justice strategy steeped in a universal design framework, was also a key tool of pedagogies of quiet. They appreciated that in the context of quiet practices their teacher didn't force them to speak in class; 12 percent of the students registered for face-to-face learning reported that this made them feel cared for. Another 12 percent reported that the technology's question and answer component and the teacher's persistent encouragement to ask questions made them feel cared for.

While the data here focus predominantly on two classroom practices, there's a multitude of other practices that can be successful as quiet pedagogies. Students reported (24 percent) feeling cared for because of the use of classroom technology but also because the "teacher shares personal experience as a model" and because the "teacher makes the environment feel open, comfortable and welcoming." As another example,

> The aspect of the course that helped me be the most successful were the study guides. Even though they were a little tedious to complete at times, the study guides forced me to engage with the material in multiple ways. The questions forced me to listen attentively to the lectures, while the critical thinking column

allowed me to connect the material with real-life experiences. The key terms section ensured that I would read the textbook.

In this student's (previously mentioned) response they articulate the ways in which quiet engagement allows them to develop their critical capacities, which is a crucial component of any social justice education. Further, the study guide allows them to do this on their own, while engaging with the quiet of their inner worlds in relation to the course content, helping them develop their own voice in relation to the material.

Quiet Challenges to Pedagogical Hegemony

Social justice education seeks to illuminate the hidden curriculum that reinforces hegemonic systems, including through taking an inward look, as this book suggests. Many scholars have argued that social justice education, and in particular the thread of critical pedagogy that most impacts higher education, sometimes falls short of its goals. One reason for this (lack of) outcome is a result of critical pedagogy's focus on critique more so than practice,[4] as well as a privileging of content at the expense of attentiveness to pedagogy and assessment.[5] For those of us engaged with this literature, it can often leave us hopeful ("yes, I want to change the world!") but unsure ("how, exactly, do I make this happen in my classes?"). Thus, pedagogies of quiet are deeply grounded in classroom practices that facilitate social justice goals, no matter the content being presented.

It is imperative that any pedagogical theory should be rooted in the real-world experiences of students. As Apple writes, "the development of critical theoretical resources is best done when it is dialectically and intimately connected to actual movements and struggles."[6] And the struggles tended to here—for example, physiological and sociological anxieties around classroom speaking—are those voiced by a group of students at a community college, with demographics that represent a changing society. The students enrolled at this institution are women (57 percent), students of color (49 percent), first-generation students (51 percent), Pell-eligible students (62 percent), and working students (56 percent).[7] And though we don't have demographic data on each individual student who submitted survey responses, we know from self-identification that some of them are students with (invisible) disabilities, as well as members of the LGBTQ community. The practices that are suggested in this book, and the quiet philosophy that undergirds these practices, emerge from the needs of these students and continues with their encouragement.

In addition, the practices studied here—both the journaling and the classroom technology—facilitated student success. Students' grades improved alongside their motivation and feelings of belonging, and thus no matter the content being taught—or whether that content included attentiveness to issues of social (in)justice—the students were able to both learn the material and earn the grades they desired. In the case of the journal, for example, they were able to track their success and thus to be their own cheerleader when they were feeling down; the evidence of their accomplishments countered their negative feelings, thus helping them develop strategies of self-soothing and coping and thus building their academic resiliency. In the case of the classroom technology, for example, they were able to ask questions in a space that felt "safe" and "judgment free" and thus were able to receive answers rather than struggle in silence.

Hurdles in the Path of Pedagogies of Quiet

Plenty has been mentioned throughout the pages in this book that illuminate the challenges that we find on this path toward a quiet pedagogical approach. It's been established that time is a significant classroom barrier; even if we wish to slow down, it's often difficult to step out of internal and external pushes toward always doing more. In addition, in complex ways, our own egos can be a barrier to changing our praxis or critiquing the pedagogical assumptions we carry with us in our work. Our egos and our classrooms are shaped by unconscious biases, which are themselves shaped by systemic patterns of race, class, gender, and other inequities. Moreover, the pandemic has transformed learning in ways that we do not yet fully understand. Put all of this together and it's clear that implementing pedagogies of quiet requires intention and attention to the hurdles we face when doing this work. There are three areas where specific attention is needed: ongoing expectations around talk, the youth mental health crisis, and patterns in diversity work and the emotional labor of faculty.

Hurdle #1: Hegemonic Expectations of Talk

For many years I was engaged in a battle with my students: I wanted them to talk while they were reluctant to do so. Since developing a quiet pedagogical framework, I'd like to say that the battle is over, but it is not. My students are still, quite often, quiet. In large classes it's because the number of students in the room intimidates them, while in small classes the intimacy creates a kind of pressure toward silence. In both contexts it is still hard to disrupt the hegemonic belief that it is the teacher's task to get them over this hurdle and to get them engaged. Of course, in this hegemonic framework engaged equals talking.

There have been plenty of days in the classroom in the postshutdown teaching era where I've left the room thinking, "That didn't go very well, they were so quiet!" Still, I have this knee-jerk association between "quiet students" and something having gone "wrong." This requires teacher reflexivity as well as internal reminders to push against this pattern and to reframe our understanding of quiet students. It takes practice, not just at the level of classroom engagement ideas but in our heads. I must continually remind myself that a quiet class is insufficient data for determining the efficacy of a teaching practice.

When I give professional development talks, most recently at a multidisciplinary gathering of colleagues, the suggestion to put aside our focus on getting students to talk and instead to learn how to teach through and with the quiet is often met with curious glances and questioning eyebrows. It's so ingrained in our collective praxis that it's hard to say, "Here, try this crossword puzzle!" and think that one or two new assessment practices is sufficient for developing a quiet pedagogical approach. It is not. The practices alone will not be enough for establishing pedagogies of quiet in your classroom. It takes constant internal vigilance to tend to the voices inside our heads, as teachers, telling us that there's something wrong when our students are too quiet. Of course, our students are telling us that something is wrong, but it's due time that we see the problems as residing in our hegemonic classroom participation ecology and in our society at large and resist the urge to perpetually push them toward talking.

Hurdle #2: The Youth Are in Crisis

Ask any teacher about their experiences with students who are struggling with anxiety and depression, and they will likely have plenty of stories to tell. We can see it in the way they carry and use their bodies into the classroom. We can see it in their struggles with attendance and with meeting deadlines. We can see it in their lack of eye contact and in their fears around asking for help and coming to office hours. Teachers knew their students were struggling before COVID. Research backs up what we know intuitively just from bearing witness: "In the 10 years leading up to the pandemic, feelings of persistent sadness and hopelessness—as well as suicidal thoughts and behaviors—increased by about 40% among young people, according to the Centers for Disease Control and Prevention's (CDC) Youth Risk Behavior Surveillance System."[8]

As addressed in chapter 5, social media is a huge driver of this crisis, shaping our students' mental health as well as their interactional capacities. As Jean Twenge writes, "by 2016 social media use was nearly mandatory—90% of teen girls used it every day—and hanging out in person had gone out of style."[9] Pedagogies of quiet seek to find a balance between quiet space for reflection and supporting students in developing the skills for verbal interactions. It cannot be understated the impact that social media has had on both mental health and interactional capacities, presenting a hurdle for our capacity to strike this balance. Relying on an intersectional approach grants teachers greater flexibility, but we must always remain aware of the hurdles that we face in the process.

Of course, the pandemic exacerbated these trends, along with the inequities that young people experience, such that girls, LGBTQ youth, and youth of color are disproportionately impacted by this mental health crisis.[10] While it has been clearly established that pedagogies of quiet aim to redress these dynamics as they play out in the classroom, it also must be made clear that this praxis alone will not solve the mental health crisis's impact on our students and our classrooms. A quiet praxis will only serve as a temporary solution without adequate institutional support for mental health services on our campuses and in our communities.

Further, the heightened experiences of mental health concerns among girls, young people of color, and LGBTQ youth are a result of systemic inequalities. The rise in racism, homophobia, transphobia, unrealistic beauty images, internet bullying, and the megaphone that social media provides for those who perpetuate these harms create a wildly stressful backdrop to our students' lives. As of this writing, sixteen states have enacted bans on gender-affirming care, while sixteen other states are considering such bans.[11] The week this sentence was written: a Black sixteen year old was shot because he went to the wrong address while picking his brothers up from a friend's house.[12] Just as with the mental health crisis in general, these structural problems cannot be solved in the classroom alone but must be addressed at the institutional and societal levels.

We can, however, use pedagogies of quiet as a jumping off point for pursuing policy-level supports at our schools, so that our campuses are as supportive as our classrooms. According to *The Trevor Project's 2022 National Survey on LGBTQ Youth Mental Health*, those students "who found their school to be LGBTQ-affirming reported lower rates of attempting suicide."[13] Another study reported that "having one caring adult providing connection and understanding, who is both confidante and advocate, is an invaluable resource for young LGBTQ people in their navigation of the heteronormative institutions of their early life ecology."[14] As advocates, it's incumbent upon us to recognize the hurdles that our students, especially our marginalized students, are facing and engage in policy conversations both inside and outside the classroom.

Hurdle #3: Doing Diversity Work and Emotional Labor

As teachers, we want to create classrooms—and participation ecologies—that are the most beneficial to our students. Many of us carry the values of equity into our pedagogical reflections and practices. Patterns illuminate that those of us who are most engaged with diversity, equity, and inclusion work are often those who carry on our shoulders the heaviest weight of these inequities. JoAnn Trejo refers to this as the "minority tax." She writes that "the minority tax (or cultural tax) is the burden of extra responsibilities placed on faculty of color to achieve diversity and inclusion."[15] This tax impacts women and LGTBQ faculty as well; it is taxing indeed.

This extra burden of labor is often coupled with hypervisibility within predominantly white, heterosexual, and cisgendered institutions.[16] As Sara Ahmed writes,

> Most of us with feminist commitments end up working for organizations that do not have these commitments. We often acquire commitments to do something because of what is not being done. To work as a feminist often means trying to transform the organizations that employ us.[17]

Ahmed explores how this work is most often done by women, especially women of color and LGBTQ women. When thinking through the social justice implications of pedagogies of quiet, it's important to consider this labor, so that we are doing our best to balance what's needed for our students, classrooms, institutions, and society, while also putting boundaries around our own needs.

Emotional labor is an inevitable component of teaching, and this can be heightened for those of us who are committed to social justice pedagogy. This work can lead to what scholars refer to as "identity taxation," which Berheide et al., referencing Hirschfield and Joseph, refers to as

> occurring "when faculty members shoulder any labor—physical, mental, or emotional—due to their membership in a historically marginalized group within their department or university, beyond that which is expected of other faculty members" (p. 214). They found that students and colleagues expected women faculty, for example, to take on more of the work with women students. They concluded that identity taxation created inequality in faculty workloads, particularly emotional labor.[18]

These expectations can increase as the changing historical context and demographic shifts shape our classrooms.

We are teaching students amid global pandemics, overseas wars, increases in racialized violence, and losses of and further threats to reproductive, voting, and marriage rights. We are teaching students who are Indigenous, who are English language learners, who are anxious and depressed, who are neurodiverse, and whose gender identity is nonbinary (among others). In this context, the teaching practices of past decades/centuries aren't always effectively meeting the needs of the students of this current moment. These are trying times for all of us, where prior to the pandemic, demands on our time were already heightened, in particular for faculty of color.[19] Quiet pedagogies can help us navigate these identities and contexts, giving students and teachers the time to breath, to look inward, and to find creativity and value in our full humanity.

At the same time, the strategies discussed in this book, and the praxis of quiet pedagogies, allow us to engage with our students without depleting our inner resources or adding extra labor. For example, because the practices here are also assessments, we can rely upon labor-based grading to facilitate an effective and efficient grading system that is also solidly antiracist.[20] This can limit some of the concerns that come from overengaging with students. Jayne Goode et al. write, "intrusive teaching can be defined as the ascribed supportive role that requires excessive commitment with individual students. Intrusive teaching is made up of demands on time, extensive student management, and long-term relationship maintenance."[21] For example, some of the faculty in Goode's study reported a significant time crunch, overlapping with the argument addressed by Berg and Seeber in *The Slow Professor*. Faculty reported the pressure to be available to students twenty-four hours per day, a dynamic most certainly impacted by digital communication, and the shift away from "traditional office hours." The COVID pandemic heightened this pressure, in particular for women faculty in general, and women of color in particular.[22]

These pressures are real, but they can be resisted through a practice of radical self-care. "Radical self-care involves embracing practices that keep us physically and psychologically healthy and fit, making time to reflect on what matters to us, challenging ourselves to grow, and checking ourselves to ensure that what we are doing aligns with what matters to us."[23] When thinking about adopting the practices encouraged in this book, or drumming up new quiet pedagogical strategies, it is incumbent upon faculty to construct syllabi that encourage radical self-care for students and faculty alike. The goal here isn't to add to the burden of those teachers who are already overtaxed but to teach and learn with compassion, while building crucial critical thinking skills.

Pedagogies of quiet can be utilized in such a way so as to alleviate some of these burdens and concerns. First, the journaling assignment provides a container for students' concerns and emotions, and thus faculty can engage with the reading and grading of the journal on their own terms without limiting students' ability to share and connect with their professors. Journals can be submitted weekly, biweekly, or monthly, depending on the needs of each teacher—each class, each term—thus providing teachers with flexibility and access to respite (those moments when there are no journals to read/grade). In this way we can both support students' experiences and needs and maintain our own self-care needs through establishing boundaries around our time.

The flexibility built into a quiet praxis is transformative for students and teachers alike, thus aligning this pedagogy with a social justice practice. For example, Jennifer Richardson writes that one principle of a Black feminist pedagogy is "recognizing and fostering critical awareness of a political path of resistance toward self-recovery and wholeness."[24] The contemplative components of quiet practices—from found poetry to journaling to quietly contributing to class discussions—urges both teachers and students to take this path of resistance. Again, Richardson argues, "pedagogies and praxis in the Black feminist tradition that are accountable to oppressed communities must take a serious look at healing, balance, and self-care as powerful forms of resistance to hegemonic cultures and structures."[25] Pedagogies of quiet are a practice grounded in the needs and concerns of those most often marginalized within the walls of higher education.

Gaps in Project and Future Research

The benefits that emerge from this process don't happen in isolation; journaling alone will not produce these results. This is why, throughout this book, the practice is named in the plural: pedago*gies* of quiet. Jan McArthur argues that "critical pedagogy needs to be understood as a movement that should be made up of diverse ideas, opinions, backgrounds, groups and theories."[26] Pedagogies of quiet take up this stance, making it clear that the practices here are not the only possibilities. The creativity at the heart of this approach means that there are a multitude of ideas that have yet to be thought up and utilized. There are many practices out there that *have* been implemented by others, that share the philosophy of pedagogies of quiet, but that are unknown to the author. While the assessments and classroom practices in this book are grounded in both evidence and experience, each teacher reading these pages can and should develop their own set of quiet practices to deploy. It's up to the reader to decide what quiet practices are most appropriate to the context of their students and institutions.

As outlined in the methods section (see chapter 1), this study was not designed to measure social justice outcomes. The surveys employed for this project asked students to reflect on the quiet practices that were assigned and/or provided for them in class. They were asked to articulate their feelings about participation as defined through verbalization, and they were asked to explain if and how the quiet practices they were exposed to impacted their experience in the course. At the same time, the themes that emerged from their open-ended survey question responses illuminated some patterns that have social justice implications. These practices made them feel cared for and connected to the course, they heightened their sense of human agency, and they reported feeling strong connections between themselves and the social world.

Still, it's crucial that we take some time to think about the gaps in this research as well as how this exploration points us in future directions. The quantitative success rates data make clear that the students in this study experienced high success rates. According to current data, "roughly 25% of first-year college students don't return for their second year to any school and about 35% don't return to the same school."[27] In light of this, pedagogies of quiet can function as a crucial remedy. The qualitative data illuminates that this praxis leaves students feeling both engaged and cared for, leading to a feeling of belonging that can be impactful for both success and completion rates.

At the same time there is room for more empirical data. It would be useful to engage in future research that explicitly incorporates demographic data into the qualitative experience. Without providing leading questions, future research could explore how race, class, gender, and sexuality explicitly shape students' experiences with pedagogies of quiet. As this book makes the case that race, class, gender, and sexuality function to produce oppressive silences, more data is needed to understand how students experience this at the micro level, in specific classes. In addition, longitudinal data could provide deeper insights, if future researchers were to follow students across multiple classrooms and years, comparing their experiences in classrooms that utilize pedagogies of quiet as compared to those that do not, offering some control group data.

The bulk of the data in this book come from two practices: participation journaling and in-class technologies that allow for quiet participation. The larger philosophical practice advocated here could be further supported through qualitative and quantitative data surrounding more practices, from found poetry, to the in-class writing portfolio, and deeper, into practices that have not yet been dreamed up. As has been the case throughout these pages, what has been presented to the reader here is both a philosophical, sociological exploration of why we need to develop a quiet praxis, coupled with practice suggestions, and supported through two chapters of rich empirical data supporting two prominent practices. The stepping off point, from here, is further into the realm of practice. What other quiet practices are teachers using, and why and how are they working? There is so much more to learn from our students.

Central to the assessment practices included in a quiet participation ecology is labor-based grading. At the same time, the data here didn't reflect on how, specifically, this grading practice impacted the student experience. Was labor-based grading important to them in the same way that it is sociologically important to the quiet philosophy? Are quiet practices as effective when using traditional grading methods? What about when used alongside labor-based grading contracts? These are further questions to explore as more teachers take up pedagogies of quiet for implementation in their own classrooms.

Finally, it would behoove us to explore how these practices can be implemented in different institutional contexts. The students in this study are community college students in introductory-level courses, including history, psychology, sociology, and English. What would these practices look like at four-year institutions, or in the context of graduate learning or in high schools? Certainly, each context would warrant some adjustments, but once implemented, we would benefit from research on how pedagogies of quiet are adapted to each institutional context.

Quiet Time: Care, Confidence, and Community

When thinking about time and the impact of neoliberal constructs of time on the classroom, I think of borders and boundaries. For example, when colonial powers constructed maps, they were very intentional in the borders that were constructed, and the policing of those borders has been connected to dynamics of inequities ever since. This colonial logic is also embedded in social institutions, including higher education. One pedagogical border that I learned and implemented during the early years of my career wasn't just time but also space. Yes, I gave my students homework and expected that they studied, but somehow in my mind I understood that work to be separate from class participation. I had constructed a boundary whereby classroom participation only happened in the classroom and happened verbally (if not in the large group, then at least in small groups and think-pair-share exercises). And then through assessment, grading, and my in-class praxis, I policed those boundaries to the detriment of my students.

Pedagogies of quiet encourage us to break down these boundaries and to think differently about both time and space. Classroom participation can happen anywhere and doesn't always fit our preconceived notions of the "active" student. One of my students wrote that the class "gave us space to share our own personal connections with the class material." This reference, however, isn't about verbal classroom participation. Their use of the word space highlights two key aspects of quiet pedagogies. First, space refers to the time to process, think, and make connections. Second, space refers to the opening of this participation to happen on students' own time, including outside of the classroom.

Further, through the incorporation of embodiment into pedagogies of quiet, we aim to disrupt capitalist and colonial notions of a productive and effective uses of time. Pedagogies of quiet value shared silence that is used to explore students' inner quiet and, in doing so, also value compassion and care. A moment of quiet can be, for example, a great way to structure classroom transitions, such as at the start of class, before switching to a new topic, or before an in-class assessment. Teachers can communicate compassion to their students through the adoption of quiet practices, and through quiet practices students can learn to engage in self-care alongside content engagement. Thus, the slowed down, quiet time results in deeper reflection.

In the words of the students surveyed for this project, students reported that they felt connected to the course, and cared for, because "[the teacher] always told us to take time out of our day to self-reflect and understand ourselves too." They wrote that quiet assignments allowed them to delve deeper: "yes, in the study guide we have to make personal connections with the class material. At first, it seems hard but after some time of careful thinking, we can easily make connections and I got surprised quite a [number of] times." Such surprise is a welcome addition to the learning experience, one facilitated through quiet.

Students appreciated the quiet assessment practices and their capacity to develop their critical thinking skills, a key outcome for critical pedagogues. As one student responded in the survey, "the class materials enabled me to start thinking critically on a daily basis which even provided me with opportunities to connect this to my personal experiences." Another student said, "the study guide always allowed us to connect to our personal experiences. I felt that sometimes I really had to reach to connect something, but I always came up with something after thinking for a bit." Sound repetitive? Yes, because many students shared similar insights. These assignments not only shaped the students' learning of the course content, but it also allowed them to learn more about themselves and their relationship to the world. This reaching, which can at first be experienced as a hardship, ultimately allows students to practice what most social justice educators preach, by developing a "humanizing and affirming" approach to learning that "embrace[s] what they already know by implementing it into the curriculum, while building new knowledge alongside them."[28]

Pedagogies of quiet include an understanding of time that centers student learning needs, including both setting boundaries and being flexible. As a social justice pedagogy that seeks to rethink our relationship to time in the classroom, this care and compassion is extended not just to in-class time for quiet but an appreciation of the time crunches students experience in their daily lives. Students recognized this, as time in relation to deadlines and the allowed grace were reported as key factors in shaping their connection to the course. One student wrote that they felt cared for in the course, infused with quiet pedagogy, because their teacher "gave me extended time knowing I was going through horrible hardships. I can't be thankful enough for . . . a professor who actually cared about my learning." This student is highlighting that time to focus and produce good work is more important than time regarding predetermined deadlines. Another wrote, simply, "thank you for being patient with me." This, in turn, was utilized by the students to take control over their own experience.

At the same time, being free from the strict constraints around assignment deadlines shifts the focus onto content. In the words of one student,

> I really appreciate that [my teacher] has more concern about what the student is learning and understanding rather than focusing on completion of assignments. Her motive was for us to completely learn something new for our entire life, that is not limited to the weekly assignments. This made my experience even better because this way, I enjoyed doing the learning and coursework on time.

Of course, the assignments and coursework matter, but given that the stress is placed on what students are learning (as compared with time), students feel more comfortable to shift their attention to learning and, as this student articulates, to open learning to more joy. Ironically, as the student concludes, being free from time allowed them to maintain a time structure.

One thing that is clear is that these quiet practices, the time they open and the inward gaze the implore, gave students space to develop a sense of their own agency. In line with critical and feminist pedagogy, students can bring to life both control and action over their classroom participation and, thus, their overall experience and success in the class. For example, one student reflected on the journaling process in this way:

> She had us submit weekly journals. These journals allowed us to reflect on our week and how we did regarding keeping up with class and the assignments. I also included what I did and if I was distracted or not. If I ever was [distracted or disconnected] then I could look back on the journal and determine a better solution. These were very easy and beneficial.

This student's focus on coming up with a "better solution" highlights the journal's capacity for developing agency. Another student wrote that "I believe that the weekly journal entries helped me be successful by making myself accountable to getting the work done." Whether through the participation journal's meta-cognitive components, through the classroom technology that expands participatory options, the critical thinking component of the study guide, or the quiet and reflective in-class writing, students were able to see themselves as agents of change, both at the micro and macro levels.

Social change processes depend upon an interaction between the micro and macro levels. In this way, students' ability to harness their own motivation and power to more effectively direct outcomes in the course can ultimately lead to broader impacts. A good grade on an assignment can lead to a good grade in a class, which can in turn lead to student retention from spring to fall and upward to graduation. As already noted, student success rates have jumped upward of 10 to 15 percent since implementing pedagogies of quiet in my own classrooms. Further, as outlined in chapters 4 and 5, these successes (whether small or large) enhance students' confidence, which can propel them forward.

In addition, when students see what's possible for themselves, they sometimes turn such a reflective tone outward. Some of the students addressed this in their survey responses, especially when asked if/how the course (embedded with quiet pedagogical practices) allowed them to connect their daily lives with the course content. They responded with general insights, such as, "I found that the reflection essays helped me to utilize what I was learning with what was going on in the world around me," and with some concrete changes, such as, "I planted a garden to contribute to the solutions for the climate crisis." Self-reflection can be utilized so students can think through how they choose to live and act in the world.

Many of the students reiterated in their survey responses a kind of participation they were able to develop and document in their journals, where they carried the class content into their relationships. One student wrote that

> I connected the class material to my personal experiences on a daily basis and continue to utilize the material through discussions with my family and friends. For example, I was watching the TV show, *Station 19*, with my family two nights ago and there was a part of the episode that demonstrated the challenges of interracial relationships, and I explained the complexities of "racework"[29] within interracial couples that I learned in this course to my family.

Another student mentioned that they were able to help a friend in need by talking about a concept they had learned in class. These students highlight how they bring what they are learning into their conversations with friends and family, as well as in their interactions with popular culture. Importantly, the journal—and the philosophy of contemplative quiet that undergirds the practice—allows teachers a window into a fuller picture of student participation.

Overall, these practices and outcomes create a culture of care. Quiet pedagogies help to make students feel cared for in their classrooms, in addition to developing students' relationship to their own inner quiet and, thus, their capacities for self-care. From this place, they in turn look outward, developing increased care for their social environments. One reason this happens is a result of quiet pedagogies' capacity to develop social connections and relationships. Through an expansive understanding of participation that values silence and quiet, students can gently step into new relationships: with new ideas, new peers, new teachers, new institutions, and new cultures.

This care, in turn, has social justice potential. One way is through the cultivation of a sense of connectedness and belonging that furthers student success. As O'Keefe writes,

> Retention of students is related to key factors such as feeling connected to the institution, which is established through interaction with peers, faculty, and staff (Cabrera et al., 1993; Hrabowski, 2005). A sense of belonging within the academic institutions is essential for students' academic success, "particularly for the retention of students who are considered to be at risk of non-completion" (O'Keeffe, 2013, p. 607).[30]

The intersection of critical pedagogy with both a contemplative and universal design approach helps to reach these individual and institutional goals. We can reach the students who are at the margins, bringing them all into the circle of care that a quiet classroom constructs.

One student wrote this of the instructor of their course (embedded with pedagogies of quiet):

> [My teacher] does a great job at constantly remind[ing] students that everyone matters and has importance to this life. She makes sure that students in her classroom are aware that everyone will be treated fairly regardless of their sex, race, pronouns, etc. . . . it's just nice to see a professor that cares deeply for their students and is willing to stand up for them.

As the data makes clear, students felt that they mattered in large part due to the quiet pedagogical practices on offer throughout the course. They reported feeling heard and valued because they had multiple participatory options and because they felt that the participation journal illuminated that their teacher took them seriously and cared about their experience in the class. This in turn motivated many of them to learn more, to dig deeper, to change course, and to enhance their connection to the world.

Quiet Endings

Experiencing a global pandemic is a momentous occasion for transformation. The impact on higher education—on all education—cannot be understated. How our students have changed is both evident and still unfolding. But one thing is certain in regard to pedagogies of quiet: "an orientation towards a teaching approach that explicitly emphasizes the caring for and well-being of learners may outlive the pandemic."[31] Valuing our quiet students and cultivating intentional silences to allow students access to their inner quiet—in other words, their creativity, experiences, and knowledge—is one such path to care and well-being.

There's much we can learn from our students. Constructing a classroom participation ecology that values quiet, that uses collective and intentional silences to facilitate the flourishing and expression of students' inner life, is a pathway to a deeper understanding of our students' learning needs. Pedagogies of quiet tackle this complexity and enrich the learning experience, grounding course content into a space of compassion and (self-) care. Despite the oft-repeated critiques of students as device addicted and distracted, students make it clear—if we ask and listen—that they are ready and willing to learn. Quiet practices allow them to show up—especially in introductory classrooms, on commuter campuses, and when new to the college experience—and explore new relationships and ideas. In shared quiet we can come together and learn, changing our classrooms, ourselves, and our students, all while reaching toward equity.

NOTES

1. Pauline Hanesworth, Seán Bracken, and Sam Elkington, "A Typology for a Social Justice Approach to Assessment: Learning from Universal Design and Culturally Sustaining Pedagogy," *Teaching in Higher Education* 24, no. 1 (2019): 102.

2. Melissa Ezarik, "Students Seek Stronger Connections With Professors But Rarely Take the Lead," *Inside Higher Ed*, May 20, 2022. https://www.insidehighered.com/news/2022/05/20/survey-students-want-connections-professors-may-not-initiate-them.

3. Ezarik, "Students Seek Stronger Connections With Professors But Rarely Take the Lead."

4. Jan McArthur, "Achieving Social Justice Within and Through Higher Education: The Challenge for Critical Pedagogy," *Teaching in Higher Education* 15, no. 5 (2010).

5. Hanesworth, Bracken, and Elkington, "A Typology for a Social Justice Approach to Assessment."

6. Michael W. Apple, "Paulo Freire, Critical Pedagogy and the Tasks of the Critical Scholar/Activist," *Revista E-curriculum* 7, no. 3 (2011): 15.

7. Katherine Coy and Avis Proctor, "Harper College Fact Book," *Harper College Fact Book*, 2021, https://www.harpercollege.edu/leadership/planning/pdf/fact_book_2020-2021_final_2.pdf.

8. Zara Abrams, "Kids' Mental Health Is in Crisis. Here's What Psychologists Are Doing to Help," *American Psychological Association*, January 1, 2023, http://www.apa.org/monitor/2023/01/trends-improving-youth-mental-health.

9. Jean M. Twenge, "Teen Girls Are Facing a Mental Health Epidemic," *Time*, February 14, 2023, http://www.time.com/6255448/teen-girls-mental-health-epidemic-causes.

10. Zara Abrams, "Kids' Mental Health Is in Crisis. Here's What Psychologists Are Doing to Help," *American Psychological Association*, January 1, 2023, http://www.apa.org/monitor/2023/01/trends-improving-youth-mental-health.

11. HRC Foundation, "Attacks on Gender Affirming Care by State Map," *Human Rights Campaign*, November 13, 2023, https://www.hrc.org/resources/attacks-on-gender-affirming-care-by-state-map.

12. Livia Albeck-ripka, Patrick Laforge, and Christine Hauser, "84-Year-Old Is Charged in Shooting of Black Teenager Who Went to Wrong House," *The New York Times*, April 17, 2023, https://www.nytimes.com/2023/04/17/us/ralph-yarl-kansas-city-shooting.html.

13. Amit Paley, "2022 National Survey on LGBTQ Youth Mental Health," *The Trevor Project*, 2022, http://www.thetrevorproject.org/survey-2022.

14. Clare Wilson and Laura A. Cariola, "LGBTQI+ Youth and Mental Health: A Systematic Review of Qualitative Research," *Adolescent Research Review* 5, no. 2 (2019): 187–211.

15. JoAnn Trejo, "The Burden of Service for Faculty of Color to Achieve Diversity and Inclusion: the Minority Tax," *Molecular Biology of the Cell* 31, no. 25 (2020): 2753.

16. Heidi Safia Mirza, "Transcendence Over Diversity: Black Women in the Academy," *Policy Futures in Education* 4, no. 2 (2006).

17. Sara Ahmed, *Living a Feminist Life* (North Carolina: Duke University Press, 2016), 89.

18. Catherine White Berheide, Megan A. Carpenter, and David A. Cotter, "Teaching College in the Time of COVID-19: Gender and Race Differences in Faculty Emotional Labor," *Sex Roles* 86, no. 7 (2022): 442.

19. Berheide, Carpenter, and Cotter, "Teaching College in the Time of COVID-19," 443.

20. Asao B. Inoue, *Labor-Based Grading Contracts: Building Equity and Inclusion in the Compassionate Writing Classroom* (Fort Collins, CO: WAC Clearinghouse, 2019).

21. Jayne Goode, Katherine J. Denker, Daniel Cortese, Lisa Carlson, and Kerri Morris, "Intrusive Teaching: The Strain of Care Labor, Identity, and the Emerging Majority in Higher Education," *Journal of Communication Pedagogy* 3 (2020): 56.

22. Berheide, Carpenter, and Cotter, "Teaching College in the Time of COVID-19."

23. Donna J. Nicol and Jennifer A. Yee, "'Reclaiming Our Time': Women of Color Faculty and Radical Self-Care in the Academy," *Feminist Teacher* 27, no. 2–3 (2017): 134.

24. Jennifer L. Richardson, "Healing Circles as Black Feminist Pedagogical Interventions," in *Black Women's Liberatory Pedagogies*, ed. Olivia N. Perlow, Durene

I. Wheeler, Sharon L. Bethea, and BarBara M. Scott (London: Palgrave Macmillan, 2018), 284.

25. Richardson, "Healing Circles as Black Feminist Pedagogical Interventions," 282.

26. McArthur, "Achieving Social Justice Within and Through Higher Education," 494.

27. Cole Claybourn, "Dropping Out of College: Why Students Do So and How to Avoid It," *US News and World Report*, February 9, 2023, https://www.usnews.com/education/best-colleges/articles/dropping-out-of-college-why-students-do-so-and-how-to-avoid-it.

28. Chrystal Belle, "What Is Social Justice Education Anyway," *Ed Week*, January 23, 2019. https://www.edweek.org/teaching-learning/opinion-what-is-social-justice-education-anyway/2019/01.

29. Amy C. Steinbugler, *Beyond Loving: Intimate Racework in Lesbian, Gay, and Straight Interracial Relationships* (Oxford University Press, 2012).

30. Goode et al., "Intrusive Teaching," 51.

31. Edward Maloney and Joshua Kim, "Learning and Covid-19: Inside Higher Ed," *Inside Higher Ed*, May 28, 2020, https://www.insidehighered.com/blogs/learning-innovation/learning-and-covid-19.

Appendix A
Overview of Survey Data

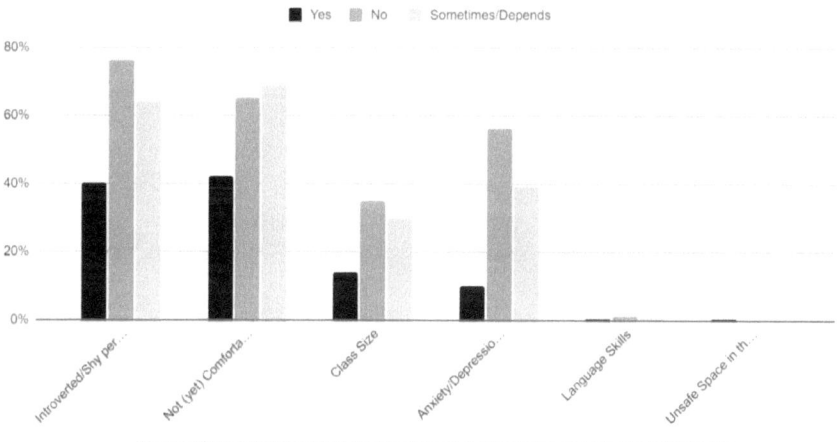

Figure A.1. Data Highlights: **When do you not feel comfortable participating and what are the reasons?**

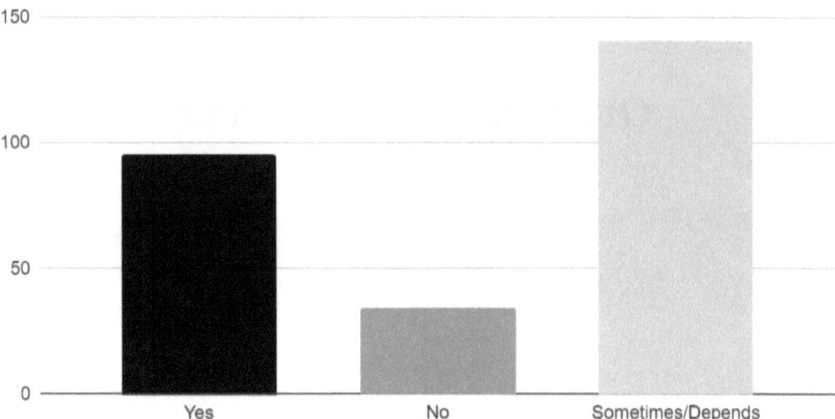

Figure A.2. In-Person Survey: Do you feel comfortable answering questions verbally during class?

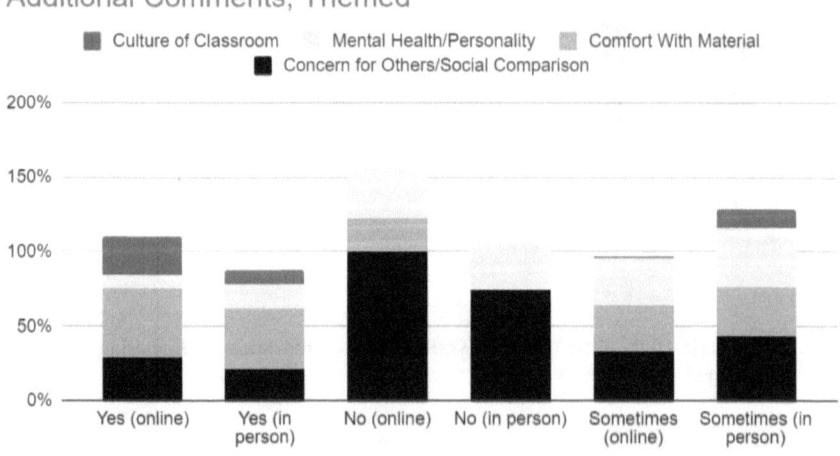

Figure A.3. Additional Comments, Themed

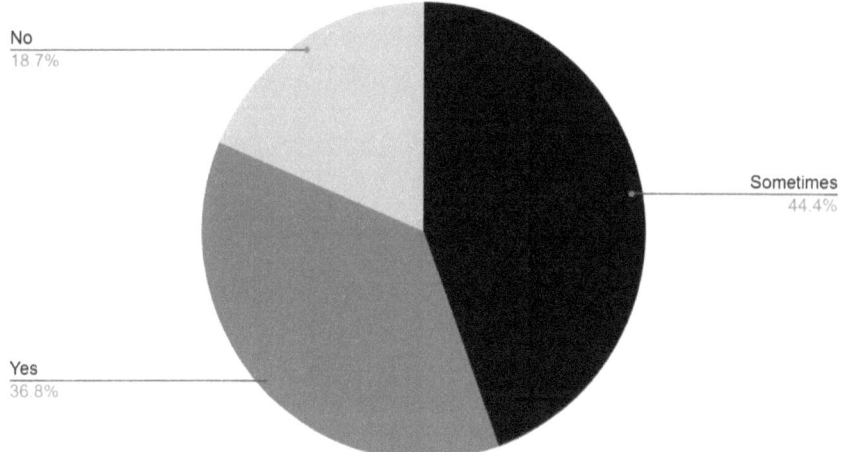

Figure A.4. In an in-person class, do you usually participate verbally?

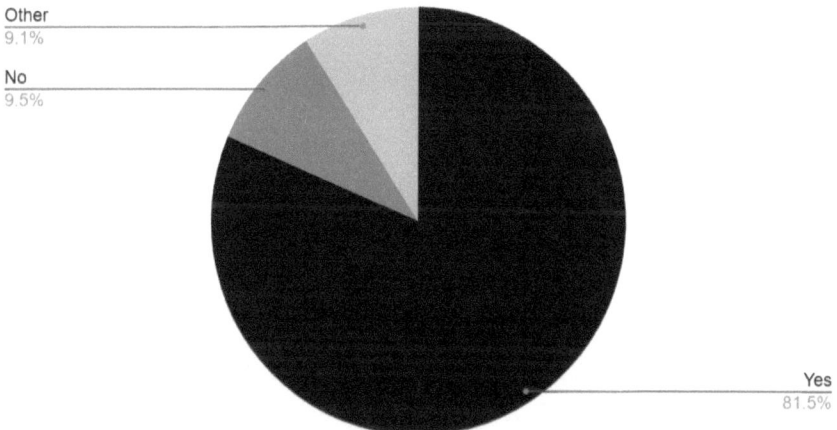

Figure A.5. Did the participation journal help you stay focused on the course?

Appendix B
Participation Journal Template

Participation Journal
Name:
Week/Date:

Participation Environment

Weekly Goals for the Class and How/If I Met Them:

To Do	Date Completed	Notes

Distractions and How I'm Managing Them:

-

What I Did Differently This Week; Or, What I Plan to Do Differently Next Week:

-

Weekly Reading Reflection (You must write in response to each bullet point for full credit)

Write about this week's reading and what stood out to you (if there is no quiz-based reading, write about the weekly reflection or textbook chapter):

-

Write about how this week's reading connects to a previous article, key term, or concept from class:

-

Personal Experience:

Pick an idea from this week and write about how it connects to your daily life; or, as Mills would say, your "personal troubles" or your "biography."

-

Critical Thinking: Emotions and Learning

What emotions did you have this week while reading and listening to the lectures? Is the material challenging you? Is it impacting how you are living your life? Are you pushing back against any of the sociological arguments? Do you have critiques or questions?

Weekly Micro-Level Sustainability Goal, Progress, and Description of Experience (You must write in response to each bullet point for full credit)

Need inspiration for a goal idea? Check out:

The Greater Good in Action, Daily Sustainability Practices, The United Nations Sustainability Goals.

Write about what change you are making this week (eating less meat, using less water, doing a gratitude practice, etc.):

-

Write about the things that make this change difficult:

-

Write about how engaging in this change makes you feel about yourself:

-

Write about how the change you are engaging in connects to the course content:

-

Write about the potential macro-level impact of your change—what if more people did the same thing, what might happen?:

-

Good News!

Share one thing each week that connects to the course content from the current or previous weeks that is an example of a small but positive social change. Go to the internet and find something that someone is doing somewhere to make some change that is grounded in the goal of collective well-being. Share here AND on the class Good News Padlet:

-

Just Sharing

Anything else on your mind that you'd like to share with Dr. Monica? Got any links to share? Stuff that you've encountered in the world that reminds you of class? Study music recommendations? Questions about the class?
-

Bibliography

Abrams, Zara. "Kids' Mental Health Is in Crisis. Here's What Psychologists Are Doing to Help." *American Psychological Association*, January 2023. https://www.apa.org/monitor/2023/01/trends-improving-youth-mental-health.

Ahmed, Sara. *Living a Feminist Life*. North Carolina: Duke University Press, 2016.

Albeck-Ripka, Livia, Patrick LaForge, and Christine Hauser. "84-Year-Old Is Charged in Shooting of Black Teenager Who Went to Wrong House." *New York Times*, April 17, 2023. https://www.nytimes.com/2023/04/17/us/ralph-yarl-kansas-city-shooting.html.

Apple, Michael W. "Paulo Freire, Critical Pedagogy and the Tasks of the Critical Scholar/Activist." *Revista E-curriculum* 7, no. 3 (2011): 1–21.

Armato, Michael. "Wolves in Sheep's Clothing: Men's Enlightened Sexism & Hegemonic Masculinity in Academia." *Women's Studies* 42, no. 5 (2013): 578–98.

Ayala, Maria Isabel, and Sheila Marie Contreras. "It's Capital! Understanding Latina/o Presence in Higher Education." *Sociology of Race and Ethnicity* 5, no. 2 (2019): 229–43.

Barbezat, Daniel P., and Mirabai Bush. *Contemplative Practices in Higher Education: Powerful Methods to Transform Teaching and Learning*. New Jersey: John Wiley & Sons, 2013.

Barrett, Kay Ulanday. "To Hold the Grief & the Growth: On Crip Ecologies." *Poetry Magazine*, January 2022. https://www.poetryfoundation.org/poetrymagazine/articles/156938/to-hold-the-grief-the-growth1-on-crip-ecologies.

Behling, Kirsten T., and Thomas J. Tobin. *Reach Everyone, Teach Everyone: Universal Design for Learning in Higher Education*. West Virginia University Press, 2018.

Belle, Chrystal. "What Is Social Justice Education Anyway." *Ed Week*, January 23, 2019. https://www.edweek.org/teaching-learning/opinion-what-is-social-justice-education-anyway/2019/01.

Berg, Maggie, and Barbara K. Seeber. *The Slow Professor*. University of Toronto Press, 2018.

Bergagna, Elisa, and Stefano Tartaglia. "Self-Esteem, Social Comparison, and Facebook Use." *Europe's Journal of Psychology* 14, no. 4 (2018): 831.

Berheide, Catherine White, Megan A. Carpenter, and David A. Cotter. "Teaching College in the Time of COVID-19: Gender and Race Differences in Faculty Emotional Labor." *Sex Roles* 86, no. 7 (2022): 441–55.

Berila, Beth. *Integrating Mindfulness into Anti-Oppression Pedagogy: Social Justice in Higher Education*. Oxfordshire, England: Routledge, 2015.

Bista, Krishna. "Silence in Teaching and Learning: Perspectives of a Nepalese Graduate Student." *College Teaching* 60, no. 2 (2012): 76–82.

Blackwell, Kelsey. "Why People of Color Need Spaces Without White People." *Arrow Journal*, August 9, 2018. https://arrow-journal.org/why-people-of-color-need-spaces-without-white-people/.

Bohns, Vanessa. "The Real Reason Why Students Don't Ask Teachers for Help." *Ed Week*, October 6, 2021. https://www.edweek.org/teaching-learning/opinion-the-real-reason-why-students-dont-ask-teachers-for-help/2021/10.

Boice, Robert. "New Faculty as Teachers." *The Journal of Higher Education* 62, no. 2 (1991): 150–73.

Brearley, Laura. "Deep Listening and Leadership: An Indigenous Model of Leadership and Community Development in Australia." In *Restoring Indigenous Leadership: Wise Practices in Community Development*, second edition, edited by C. Voyageur, L. Brearley, and B. Calliou, 91–127. Alberta, Canada: Banff Centre Press, 2015.

Brewer, Judson. *Unwinding Anxiety: New Science Shows How to Break the Cycles of Worry and Fear to Heal Your Mind*. New York: Avery, an imprint of Penguin Random House, 2022.

Brown, Brené. *The Gifts of Imperfection: Let Go of Who You Think You're Supposed to Be and Embrace Who You Are*. New York: Simon and Schuster, 2010.

Burić, Irena. "The Role of Emotional Labor in Explaining Teachers' Enthusiasm and Students' Outcomes: A Multilevel Mediational Analysis." *Learning and Individual Differences* 70 (2019): 12–20.

Cain, Susan. *Quiet: The Power of Introverts in a World That Can't Stop Talking*. New York: Crown Publishing, 2013.

Caldera, Altheria. "Toward Wholeness: Anzaldúan Theorizing Used to Imagine Culturally Accepting Educative Spaces for Black Girls." In *Teaching Gloria E. Anzaldúa: Pedagogy and Practice for Our Classrooms and Communities*, edited by Cantú-Sánchez, Margaret, Candace de León-Zepeda, and Norma Elia Cantú, 33–46. University of Arizona Press, 2020.

Carnevale, Anthony. "The Intersection of Working and Learning: Findings From Entering Students in Community College." October 21, 2020. https://cccse.org/sites/default/files/WorkingLearner.pdf.

Carr, Nicholas. "Is Google Making Us Stupid?" *Atlantic Monthly*, July 2008. https://www.theatlantic.com/magazine/archive/2008/07/is-google-making-us-stupid/306868/.

Charmaz, Kathy. *Constructing grounded theory*, 2nd ed. Thousand Oaks, CA: Sage Publications, 2014.

Claybourn, Cole. "Dropping out of College: Why Students Do So and How to Avoid It." *US News and World Report*, February 9, 2023. https://www.usnews.com/

education/best-colleges/articles/dropping-out-of-college-why-students-do-so-and-how-to-avoid-it.

Collins, Patricia Hill. *Black Feminist Thought: Knowledge, Consciousness, and the Politics of Empowerment*. Oxfordshire, England: Routledge, 1990.

Connell, Robert W., and James W. Messerschmidt. "Hegemonic Masculinity: Rethinking the Concept." *Gender & Society* 19, no. 6 (2005): 829–59.

Cottom, Tressie McMillan. "What's Shame Got to Do With It." *New York Times*, April 12, 2022. https://www.nytimes.com/2022/04/12/opinion/whats-shame-got-to-do-with-it.html.

Coy, Katherine, and Avis Proctor. "Harper College Fact Book." *Harper College Fact Book*, 2021. https://www.harpercollege.edu/leadership/planning/pdf/fact_book_2020-2021_final_2.pdf.

Crabtree, Sara Ashencaen, Ann Hemingway, Sue Sudbury, Anne Quinney, Maggie Hutchings, Luciana Esteves, and Shelley Thompson. "Donning the 'Slow Professor': A Feminist Action Research Project." *Radical Teacher* 116 (2020): 55–65.

Csikszentmihalyi, Mihaly. *Flow: The Psychology of Optimal Experience*. New York: Harper Perennial Modern Classics, 2008.

Darder, Antonia. "Pedagogy of Love: Embodying Our Humanity." In *The Critical Pedagogy Reader*, third edition, edited by Antonia Darder, Marta Baltodano, and Rodolfo D. Torres, 95–109. New York: Routledge, 2017.

———. *Reinventing Paulo Freire: A Pedagogy of Love*. Oxfordshire, England: Routledge, 2017.

Deresiewicz, William. "The End of Solitude." *The Chronicle of Higher Education* 55, no. 21 (2009): 6–9.

DeSantis, Carm, and Toni Serafina. "Classroom to Community: Reflections on Experiential Learning and Socially Just Citizenship." In *Feminist Pedagogy in Higher Education: Critical Theory and Practice*, edited by Tracy Penny Light, Jane Nicholas, and Renée Bondy, 87–112. Ontario, Canada: Wilfrid Laurier University Press, 2015.

DeVault, Marjorie L. *Liberating Method: Feminism and Social Research*. Philadelphia: Temple University Press, 1999.

Dewsbury, Bryan M. "Deep Teaching in a College STEM Classroom." *Cultural Studies of Science Education* 15, no. 1 (2020): 169–91.

DiAngelo, Robin. *Nice Racism: How Progressive White People Perpetuate Racial Harm*. Boston: Beacon Press, 2022.

———. *White Fragility: Why It's So Hard for White People to Talk About Racism*. Boston: Beacon Press, 2018.

Duquaine-Watson, Jillian M. "'Pretty Darned Cold': Single Mother Students and the Community College Climate in Post-Welfare Reform America." *Equity & Excellence in Education* 40, no. 3 (2007): 229–40.

Ellsworth, Elizabeth. "Why Doesn't This Feel Empowering? Working Through the Repressive Myths of Critical Pedagogy." *Harvard Educational Review* 59, no. 3 (1989): 297–325.

Ezarik, Melissa. "Students Seek Stronger Connections With Professors But Rarely Take the Lead." *Inside Higher Ed*, May 20, 2022. https://www.insidehighered.com/news/2022/05/20/survey-students-want-connections-professors-may-not-initiate-them.

Febos, Melissa. *Body Work: The Radical Power of Personal Narrative*. New York: Catapult, 2022.

Frambach, Janneke M., Erik W. Driessen, Philip Beh, and Cees PM Van der Vleuten. "Quiet or Questioning? Students' Discussion Behaviors in Student-Centered Education Across Cultures." *Studies in Higher Education* 39, no. 6 (2014): 1001–21.

Freire, Paulo. *Pedagogy of the Oppressed*. New York: Continuum, 2000.

Gallos, Joan V. "Gender and Silence: Implications of Women's Ways of Knowing." *College Teaching* 43, no. 3 (1995): 101–5.

Giroux, Henry A. "Public Intellectuals Against the Neoliberal University." In *Qualitative Inquiry—Past, Present, and Future*, edited by Norman K. Denzin and Michael D. Giardina, 194–220. Oxfordshire, England: Routledge, 2016.

Goffman, Erving. *The Presentation of Self in Everyday Life*. New York: Double Day, 1959.

Goldschmidt, Mary L., Jessica L. Bachman, Mary Jane K. DiMattio, and Jill A. Warker. "Exploring Slow Teaching with an Interdisciplinary Community of Practice." *Transformative Dialogues: Teaching and Learning Journal* 9, no. 1 (2016).

Goode, Jayne, Katherine J. Denker, Daniel Cortese, Lisa Carlson, and Kerri Morris. "Intrusive Teaching: The Strain of Care Labor, Identity, and the Emerging Majority in Higher Education." *Journal of Communication Pedagogy* 3 (2020): 49–64.

Greene, M. "Teaching as Possibility: A Light in Dark Times." In *Critical Pedagogy in Uncertain Times*, edited by Sheila Macrine, 137–49. New York: Palgrave Macmillan, 2009.

Grier-Reed, Tabitha, and Anne Williams-Wengerd. "Integrating Universal Design, Culturally Sustaining Practices, and Constructivism to Advance Inclusive Pedagogy in the Undergraduate Classroom." *Education Sciences* 8, no. 4 (2018): 167–80.

Grunspan, Daniel Z., Michelle Ann Kline, and Sara E. Brownell. "The Lecture Machine: A Cultural Evolutionary Model of Pedagogy in Higher Education." *CBE—Life Sciences Education* 17, no. 3 (2018): 1–11.

Hamelock, Merilee, and Norm Friesen. "One Student's Experience of Silence in the Classroom." *Norm Friesen*, July 2012. https://www.normfriesen.info/papers/ihsrc2012.pdf.

Hancock, Ange-Marie. *Intersectionality: An Intellectual History*. Oxford University Press, 2016.

Hanesworth, Pauline, Seán Bracken, and Sam Elkington. "A Typology for a Social Justice Approach to Assessment: Learning from Universal Design and Culturally Sustaining Pedagogy." *Teaching in Higher Education* 24, no. 1 (2019): 98–114.

"Harper Fast Facts." *Harper Fast Facts: Harper College*. Accessed April 20, 2023. http://goforward.harpercollege.edu/about/news/facts.php.

Harumi, Seiko. "Classroom Silence: Voices from Japanese EFL Learners." *ELT Journal* 65, no. 3 (2011): 260–69.

Hill, Jane H. "Language, Race, and White Public Space." *American Anthropologist* 100, no. 3 (1998): 680–89.

Hill, Laura M. "Contemplative Pedagogy in Times of Grief and Uncertainty: Teaching in a Global Pandemic." *The Journal of Contemplative Inquiry* 7, no. 1 (2020): 103–24.

Holmes, Ashley J. "'Being Patient Through the Quiet': Partnering in Problem-Based Learning in a Graduate Seminar." *International Journal for Students as Partners* 4, no. 1 (2020): 34–47.

Holt, Maurice. "It's Time to Start the Slow School Movement." *Phi Delta Kappan* 84, no. 4 (2002): 264–71.

hooks, bell. *Teaching to Transgress*. Oxfordshire, England: Routledge, 2014.

HRC Foundation. "Attacks on Gender Affirming Care by State Map." *Human Rights Campaign*, November 13, 2023. https://www.hrc.org/resources/attacks-on-gender-affirming-care-by-state-map.

Hu, Jing. "Toward the Role of EFL/ESL Students' Silence as a Facilitative Element in Their Success." *Frontiers in Psychology* 12 (2021). doi: 10.3389/fpsyg.2021.737123.

Human Rights Campaign. "Map: Attacks on Gender Affirming Care." May 1, 2023. https://www.hrc.org/resources/attacks-on-gender-affirming-care-by-state-map.

Hussar, B., NCES; Zhang, J.; Hein, S.; Wang, K.; Roberts, A.; Cui, J.; Smith, M., AIR; Bullock Mann, F.; Barmer, A.; and Dilig, R., RTI. "The Condition of Education 2020." May 19, 2020. https://nces.ed.gov/programs/coe/pdf/coe_ssa.pdf.

Ingraham, Chrys. "The Heterosexual Imaginary: Feminist Sociology and Theories of Gender." *Sociological Theory* (1994): 203–19.

Inoue, Asao B. *Antiracist Writing Assessment Ecologies: Teaching and Assessing Writing for a Socially Just Future*. South Carolina: Parlor Press LLC, 2015.

———. *Labor-Based Grading Contracts: Building Equity and Inclusion in the Compassionate Writing Classroom*. Fort Collins, CO: WAC Clearinghouse, 2019.

Ivory, Brian T. "Little Known, Much Needed: Addressing the Cocurricular Needs of LGBTQ Students." *Community College Journal of Research and Practice* 36, no. 7 (2012): 482–93.

Jan, Muqaddas, Sanobia Soomro, and Nawaz Ahmad. "Impact of Social Media on Self-Esteem." *European Scientific Journal* 13, no. 23 (2017): 329–41.

Jessop, Bob. "On Academic Capitalism." *Critical Policy Studies* 12, no. 1 (2018): 104–9.

Johnson, Sarah Randall, and Frances King Stage. "Academic Engagement and Student Success: Do High-Impact Practices Mean Higher Graduation Rates?" *The Journal of Higher Education* 89, no. 5 (2018): 753–81.

Kaufman, Peter. "Poetic Sociology." *Everyday Sociology Blog*, July 8, 2013. https://www.everydaysociologyblog.com/2013/07/poetic-sociology.html.

Kaufman, Peter, and Janine Schipper. *Teaching with Compassion: An Educator's Oath to Teach from the Heart*. Maryland: Rowman & Littlefield, 2018.

Keating, AnaLouise. *Teaching Transformation: Transcultural Classroom Dialogues*. New York: Springer, 2007.

———. *Transformation Now!: Toward a Post-Oppositional Politics of Change.* University of Illinois Press, 2012.

Kimbark, Kris, Michelle L. Peters, and Tim Richardson. "Effectiveness of the Student Success Course on Persistence, Retention, Academic Achievement, and Student Engagement." *Community College Journal of Research and Practice* 41, no. 2 (2017): 124–38.

King, Alison. "From Sage on the Stage to Guide on the Side." *College Teaching* 41, no. 1 (1993): 30.

Kohli, Rita. "Breaking the Cycle of Racism in the Classroom: Critical Race Reflections from Future Teachers of Color." *Teacher Education Quarterly* 35, no. 4 (2008): 177–88.

Kryger, Kathleen, and Griffin X. Zimmerman. "Neurodivergence and Intersectionality in Labor-Based Grading Contracts." *Journal of Writing Assessment* 13, no. 2 (2020). https://escholarship.org/uc/item/0934x4rm.

Lane, Jill O'Shea. "Lived Experiences of New Faculty: Nine Stages of Development Toward Learner-Centered Practice." *Journal of the Scholarship of Teaching and Learning* 18, no. 3 (2018). https://doi.org/10.14434/josotl.v18i3.23373.

Laryea, Kerri. "A Pedagogy of Deep Listening in E-Learning." *Journal of Conscious Evolution* 11, no. 11 (2018). https://digitalcommons.ciis.edu/cgi/viewcontent.cgiarticle=1078&context=cejournal.

Lee, Jennifer J., and Janice M. Mccabe. "Who Speaks and Who Listens: Revisiting the Chilly Climate in College Classrooms." *Gender & Society* 35, no. 1 (2021): 32–60.

Levitz, Eric. "Four Explanations for the Teen Mental-Health Crisis." *Intelligencer*, March 27, 2023. https://nymag.com/intelligencer/2023/03/4-explanations-for-the-teen-mental-health-crisis.html.

Link, Laura J., and Thomas R. Guskey. "How Traditional Grading Contribute to Student Inequities and How to Fix It." *Curriculum in Context* 45, no. 1 (2019).

Llewellyn, Jennifer, and K. Llewellyn. "A Restorative Approach to Learning: Relational Theory as Feminist Pedagogy in Universities." In *Feminist Pedagogy in Higher Education: Critical Theory and Practice*, edited by Tracy Penny Light, Jane Nicholas, and Renée Bondy, 11–30. Ontario, Canada: Wilfrid Laurier University Press, 2015.

López, Vivian García, and Vivian García López. "The Struggles to Eliminate the Tenacious Four-Letter 'F' Word in Education." *Counterpoints* 422 (2012): 300–324.

Lozano, Adele, Jörg Vianden, and Paige Kieler. "'No, Teach Yourself!': College Women's Expectations for White Men's Awareness of Privilege and Oppression." *JCSCORE* 7, no. 1 (2021): 13–45.

Macrine, Sheila L., ed. *Critical Pedagogy in Uncertain Times: Hope and Possibilities*. New York: Springer Nature, 2020.

Mahoney, Maureen A. "The Problem of Silence in Feminist Psychology." *Feminist Studies* 22, no. 3 (1996): 603–25.

Maia, Duerr, and Carrie Bergman. "The Center for Contemplative Mind in Society." *The Center for Contemplative Mind in Society*. Accessed February 10, 2022. http://www.contemplativemind.org/practices/tree.

Maloney, Edward, and Joshua Kim. "Learning and Covid-19: Inside Higher Ed." *Inside Higher Ed*, May 28, 2020. https://www.insidehighered.com/blogs/learning-innovation/learning-and-covid-19.

McArthur, Jan. "Achieving Social Justice Within and Through Higher Education: The Challenge for Critical Pedagogy." *Teaching in Higher Education* 15, no. 5 (2010): 493–504.

McLaren, Peter. "Critical Pedagogy: A Look at the Major Concepts." In *The Critical Pedagogy Reader*, third edition, edited by Antonia Darder, Marta Baltodano, and Rodolfo D. Torres, 56–78. Oxfordshire, England: Routledge, 2017.

———. "Critical Revolutionary Pedagogy's Relevance Today." In *Critical Pedagogy in Uncertain Times*, edited by Sheila Macrine, 209–23. London: Palgrave Macmillan, 2020.

Messner, Michael A. "White Guy Habitus in the Classroom: Challenging the Reproduction of Privilege." *Men and Masculinities* 2, no. 4 (2000): 457–69.

Motta, Sara C., and Anna Bennett. "Pedagogies of Care, Care-Full Epistemological Practice and 'Other' Caring Subjectivities in Enabling Education." *Teaching in Higher Education* 23, no. 5 (2018): 631–46.

Mountz, Alison, Anne Bonds, Becky Mansfield, Jenna Loyd, Jennifer Hyndman, Margaret Walton-Roberts, and Ranu Basu. "For Slow Scholarship: A Feminist Politics of Resistance Through Collective Action in the Neoliberal University." *ACME: An International Journal for Critical Geographies* 14, no. 4 (2015): 1235–59.

Mirza, Heidi Safia. "Transcendence Over Diversity: Black Women in the Academy." *Policy Futures in Education* 4, no. 2 (2006): 101–13.

Nicol, Donna J., and Jennifer A. Yee. "'Reclaiming Our Time': Women of Color Faculty and Radical Self-Care in the Academy." *Feminist Teacher* 27, no. 2–3 (2017): 133–56.

Nicholas, Jane, and Jamilee Baroud. "Rethinking 'Students These Days': Feminist Pedagogy and the Construction of Students." In *Feminist Pedagogy in Higher Education: Critical Theory and Practice*, edited by Tracy Penny Light, Jane Nicholas, and Renée Bondy, 245–62. Ontario, Canada: Wilfrid Laurier University Press, 2015.

Nichols, Sue, and Garth Stahl. "Intersectionality in Higher Education Research: A Systematic Literature Review." *Higher Education Research & Development* 38, no. 6 (2019): 1255–68.

Nørgård, Rikke Toft, Claus Toft-Nielsen, and Nicola Whitton. "Playful Learning in Higher Education: Developing a Signature Pedagogy." *International Journal of Play* 6, no. 3 (2017): 272–82.

Ollin, Ros. "Silent Pedagogy and Rethinking Classroom Practice: Structuring Teaching Through Silence Rather than Talk." *Cambridge Journal of Education* 38, no. 2 (2008): 265–80.

O'Reilley, Mary Rose. *Radical presence: Teaching as contemplative practice*. Portsmouth, NH: Heinemann, 1998.

Oyěwùmí, Oyèrónkẹ́. *The Invention of Women: Making an African Sense of Western Gender Discourses*. University of Minnesota Press, 1997.

Page, Michelle. "LGBTQ Inclusion as an Outcome of Critical Pedagogy." In *The Critical Pedagogy Reader*, third edition, edited by Antonia Darder, Marta Baltodano, and Rodolfo D. Torres, 346–60. Oxfordshire, England: Routledge, 2017.

Palalas, Agnieszka, Anastasia Mavraki, Kokkoni Drampala, Anna Krassa, and Christina Karakanta. "Mindfulness Practices in Online Learning: Supporting Learner Self-Regulation." *The Journal of Contemplative Inquiry* 7, no. 1 (2020): 247–77.

Paley, Amit. "2022 National Survey on LGBTQ Youth Mental Health." The Trevor Project, 2022. https://www.thetrevorproject.org/survey-2022/.

Pascoe, Cheri Jo. "'Dude, You're a Fag': Adolescent Masculinity and the Fag Discourse." *Sexualities* 8, no. 3 (2005): 329–46.

Pascoe, Michaela C., Sarah E. Hetrick, and Alexandra G. Parker. "The Impact of Stress on Students in Secondary School and Higher Education." *International Journal of Adolescence and Youth* 25, no. 1 (2019): 104–12.

Phillippi, Julia, and Jana Lauderdale, "A Guide to Field Notes for Qualitative Research: Context and Conversation." *Qualitative Health Research* 28, no. 3 (May 2017): 381.

Phillips, Carl. *My Trade Is Mystery: Seven Meditations from a Life in Writing*. New Haven, CT: Yale University Press, 2023.

Pratt, Ian S., Hunter B. Harwood, Jenel T. Cavazos, and Christopher P. Ditzfeld. "Should I Stay or Should I Go? Retention in First-Generation College Students." *Journal of College Student Retention: Research, Theory & Practice* 21, no. 1 (2019): 105–18.

Purser, Ronald. *McMindfulness: How Mindfulness Became the New Capitalist Spirituality*. London: Repeater, 2019.

Powietrzynska, Malgorzata, Linda Noble, Sharda O'Loughlin-Boncamper, and Aundrey Azeez. "Holding Space for Uncertainty and Vulnerability: Reclaiming Humanity in Teacher Education through Contemplative | Equity Pedagogy." *Cultural Studies of Science Education* 16, no. 3 (2021): 951–64.

Quashie, Kevin. *The Sovereignty of Quiet*. New Jersey: Rutgers University Press, 2012.

"Quiet Definition & Meaning." In *Merriam-Webster*. Accessed March 16, 2022. http://www.merriam-webster.com/dictionary/quiet.

Rachel C. F. Sun, and Daniel T. L. Shek. "Student Classroom Misbehavior: An Exploratory Study Based on Teachers' Perceptions." *The Scientific World Journal* (2012). https://doi.org/10.1100/2012/208907.

Reda, Mary M. *Between Speaking and Silence: A Study of Quiet Students*. New York: SUNY Press, 2009.

Rendón, Laura I. *Sentipensante (Sensing/Thinking) Pedagogy: Educating for Wholeness, Social Justice and Liberation*. Sterling, VA: Stylus Publishing, LLC, 2012.

Richardson, Jennifer L. "Healing Circles as Black Feminist Pedagogical Interventions." In *Black Women's Liberatory Pedagogies*, edited by Olivia N. Perlow, Durene I. Wheeler, Sharon L. Bethea, and BarBara M. Scott, 281–94. London: Palgrave Macmillan, 2018.

Richtel, Matt. "It's Life or Death: The Mental Health Crisis Among U.S. Teens." *New York Times*, April 23, 2022. https://www.nytimes.com/2022/04/23/health/mental-health-crisis-teens.html.

Robinson, Terrell E., and Warren C. Hope. "Teaching in Higher Education: Is There a Need for Training in Pedagogy in Graduate Degree Programs?" *Research in Higher Education Journal* 21 (2013).

Rozgonjuk, Dmitri, Mari Kattago, and Karin Täht. "Social Media Use in Lectures Mediates the Relationship Between Procrastination and Problematic Smartphone Use." *Computers in Human Behavior* 89 (2018): 191–98.

Sa'ar, Amalia. "Masculine Talk: On the Subconscious Use of Masculine Linguistic Forms among Hebrew- and Arabic-Speaking Women in Israel." *Signs: Journal of Women in Culture and Society* 32, no. 2 (2007): 405–29.

Scheithauer, Mindy C., and Mary L. Kelley. "Self-Monitoring by College Students with ADHD: The Impact on Academic Performance." *Journal of Attention Disorders* 21, no. 12 (2014): 1030–39.

Schor, Juliet B. *The Overspent American: Why We Want What We Don't Need*. New York: Harper Collins, 1999.

Sensoy, Ozlem, and Robin DiAngelo. *Is Everyone Really Equal?: An Introduction to Key Concepts in Social Justice Education*. New York: Teachers College Press, 2017.

Shahjahan, Riyad A. "Being 'Lazy' and Slowing Down: Toward Decolonizing Time, Our Body, and Pedagogy." *Educational Philosophy and Theory* 47, no. 5 (2015): 488–501.

"Silence Definition & Meaning." In *Merriam-Webster*. Accessed March 16, 2022. http://www.merriam-webster.com/dictionary/silence.

Smith, Stephen J. "Slow Down and Smell the Eucalypts: Blue Gum Community School and the Slow Education Movement." *Journal of Global Education and Research* 1, no. 1 (2017): 16–34.

Sobo, Elisa, Michael Lambert, and Valerie Lambert. "Land Acknowledgements Meant to Honor Indigenous People Too Often Do the Opposite—Erasing American Indians and Sanitizing History Instead." *The Conversation*, October 7, 2021. https://theconversation.com/land-acknowledgments-meant-to-honor-indigenous-people-too-often-do-the-opposite-erasing-american-indians-and-sanitizing-history-instead-163787.

Song, Kirsten Younghee, and Glenn W. Muschert. "Opening the Contemplative Mind in the Sociology Classroom." *Humanity & Society* 38, no. 3 (2014): 314–38.

Squire, Dian, Bianca C. Williams, and Frank Tuitt. "Plantation Politics and Neoliberal Racism in Higher Education: A Framework for Reconstructing Anti-Racist Institutions." *Teachers College Record* 120, no. 14 (2018): 1–20.

Steinbugler, Amy C. *Beyond Loving: Intimate Racework in Lesbian, Gay, and Straight Interracial Relationships*. Oxford University Press, 2012.

Sweet, Paige L. "Who Knows? Reflexivity in Feminist Standpoint Theory and Bourdieu." *Gender & Society* 34, no. 6 (2020): 922–50.

Taylor, Yvette, and Maddie Breeze. "All Imposters in the University? Striking (Out) Claims on Academic Twitter." *Women's Studies International Forum* 81 (2020). https://doi.org/10.1016/j.wsif.2020.102367.

Thompson, Becky. *Teaching with Tenderness: Toward an Embodied Practice.* University of Illinois Press, 2017.

Tomas, Louisa, Neus (Snowy) Evans, Tanya Doyle, and Keith Skamp. "Are First Year Students Ready for a Flipped Classroom? A Case for a Flipped Learning Continuum." *International Journal of Educational Technology in Higher Education* 16, no. 1 (2019).

Tovar, Esau. "The Role of Faculty, Counselors, and Support Programs on Latino/a Community College Students' Success and Intent to Persist." *Community College Review* 43, no. 1 (September 2014): 46–71.

Trejo, JoAnn. "The Burden of Service for Faculty of Color to Achieve Diversity and Inclusion: the Minority Tax." *Molecular Biology of the Cell* 31, no. 25 (2020): 2752–54.

Tuck, Eve, and K. Wayne Yang. "Decolonization Is Not a Metaphor." *Tabula Rasa* 38 (2021): 61–111.

Turkle, Sherry. *Alone Together: Why We Expect More from Technology and Less from Each Other.* New York: Basic Books, 2011.

———. *Reclaiming Conversation: The Power of Talk in a Digital Age.* London: Penguin, 2016.

———. "The Flight from Conversation." *New York Times*, April 21, 2012. https://www.nytimes.com/2012/04/22/opinion/sunday/the-flight-from-conversation.html.

Twenge, Jean. "Teen Girls Are Facing a Mental Health Epidemic. We're Doing Nothing to Stop It." *Time Magazine*, February 14, 2023. https://time.com/6255448/teen-girls-mental-health-epidemic-causes/.

Vargas, Lauren. "Complaining About Students Is Toxic. Here are 4 Ways to Stop." *Ed Week*, June 11, 2019. https://www.edweek.org/teaching-learning/opinion-complaining-about-students-is-toxic-here-are-4-ways-to-stop/2019/06.

Vogel, Erin A., Jason P. Rose, Bradley M. Okdie, Katheryn Eckles, and Brittany Franz. "Who Compares and Despairs? The Effect of Social Comparison Orientation on Social Media Use and Its Outcomes." *Personality and Individual Differences* 86 (2015): 249–56.

Walker, Judith. "Time as the Fourth Dimension in the Globalization of Higher Education." *The Journal of Higher Education* 80, no. 5 (2009): 483–509.

Whitehead, Melvin, and Needham Yancey Gulley. "LGBTQ+ Matters and the Community College: Policy and Program Considerations for Students, Faculty, and Staff." In *Rethinking LGBTQIA Students and Collegiate Contexts: Identity, Policies, and Campus Climate*, edited by Eboni M. Zamani-Gallaher, Devika Dibya Choudhuri, and Jason L. Taylor. New York: Routledge, 2019.

Whitt, E. J., M. I. Edison, E. T. Pascarella, A. Nora, and P. T. Terenzini. "Women's Perceptions of a 'Chilly Climate' and Cognitive Outcomes in College: Additional Evidence." *Journal of College Student Development* 40, no. 2 (1999): 163–77.

Wilson, Carla. "Unsettling Women's and Gender Studies 'Settler Logics.'" In *Teaching Gloria E. Anzaldúa: Pedagogy and Practice for Our Classrooms and*

Communities, edited by Margaret Cantú-Sánchez, Candace de León-Zepeda, and Norma Elia Cantú, 274–95. University of Arizona Press, 2020.

Wilson, Clare, and Laura A. Cariola. "LGBTQI+ Youth and Mental Health: A Systematic Review of Qualitative Research." *Adolescent Research Review* 5, no. 2 (2019): 187–211.

Wong, Yuk-Lin Renita. "Knowing Through Discomfort: A Mindfulness-Based Critical Social Work Pedagogy." *Critical Social Work* 5, no. 1 (2004): 1–9.

Yang, Chia-chen. "Instagram Use, Loneliness, and Social Comparison Orientation: Interact and Browse on Social Media, but Don't Compare." *Cyberpsychology, Behavior, and Social Networking* 19, no. 12 (2016): 703–8.

Zedelius, Claire M., and Jonathan W. Schooler. "The Richness of Inner Experience: Relating Styles of Daydreaming to Creative Processes." *Frontiers in Psychology* 6 (2016). https://doi.org/10.3389/fpsyg.2015.02063.

About the Author

Monica Edwards earned her master's degree in sociology from Illinois State University and her PhD in sociology from Loyola University Chicago. She has been teaching sociology for over twenty years, working at both four-year and two-year institutions. Currently, she is professor and chair of the Anthropology and Sociology Department at Willliam Rainey Harper College.

Her research focus for the past five years has been an intersectional exploration of teaching and learning, culminating in this book. Her past publications have explored the impact of LGBTQ media representation on personal identity and social relationships, the homonormativity of the same-sex marriage movement, as well as the complex dynamics at play in working with LGBTQ students in the suburban context. She is an active member of her community, volunteering for the local library as well as for the LGBTQ youth drop-in center.

www.ingramcontent.com/pod-product-compliance
Lightning Source LLC
Chambersburg PA
CBHW021848300426
44115CB00005B/71